PANTHEON
OF POLITICAL
PHILOSOPHERS

THIRD EDITION

ZVIAD KLIMENT LAZARASHVILI
CHIEKE E. IHEJIRIKA
GARI T. CHAPIDZE
GEORGE P. STASEN

Edited by Chieke E. Ihejirika

Printed in the United States of America
GEORGIAN INTERNATIONAL UNIVERSITY PRESS

General Editor: Chieke E. Ihejirika
Editor of the text, citations, quotations and annotations, and the sole responsible party
on copyright issues for the citations, quotations and paraphrases used in the book:
Chieke E. Ihejirika.

Cover Design by Demetre Dekanosidze.
Graphic Designer, Illustrator and the sole responsible party on copyright issues
for the pictures, illustrations and graphics used in the book:
Demetre Dekanosidze.

ACKNOWLEDGEMENTS

EDITORIAL COMMITTEE:

General Editor: Chieke E. Ihejirika

Cover Designer: Demetre Dekanosidze

Graphic Designer-illustrator: Demetre Dekanosidze

APPRECIATION LIST: Winford B. Johnson, Ph. D. Yale University

Janet Mathewson, Ph. D. Yale University

Guram Tavartkiladze, Ph. D.
Founder and Rector President of Tbilisi State
University of Economic Relations and Law

James J. Munnis, Esq, West Chester, PA

Prof. Robert Goodell, Strayer University

George L. Frunzi, Ph. D. Temple University

Levi Nwachuku, Ph.D. Michigan State University

Dean Judith A.W. Thomas, Lincoln University

Dean Izzeldin Bakhit, Ph. D. Strayer University

Prof. Daniel Terfassa, Strayer University

Prof. Cynthia Orth, Strayer University

Prof. Gordian Ndubizu, Drexel University

Prof. Elaine Delancey, Drexel University

Prof. Julie Mostov, Drexel University

Shota Agladze, Ph. D.
Javakhishvili Tbilisi State University

Peter Stercho, Ph.D. Drexel University

Jan Lutjes, Ph.D. Drexel University

Nugzar Tsereteli, Ph. D.
Javakhishvili Tbilisi State University

Prof. Aryeh Botwinick, Temple University

Prof. Benedict Stavis, Temple University

Giorgi Shokin, Ph. D. MAUP Universiy

Dean Besik Aladashvili,
Tbilisi State University of Economic
Relationsand and Law

Olga Metreveli, Ph. D.
Georgian Technical University

Rev. Dr. Theophilus Okere, Professor Emeritus
Whelan Research Institute Owerri

Rev. Kingsley Ihejirika, Doctoral Candidate
Pontifical Urbaniana University, Rome

Scudder G. Stevens, Esq, Kennett Square, PA

Prof. Lawrence Okere,
University of Arkansas, Pine Bluff

Prof. Ewa Unoke,
Kansas City Kansas Community College

Dr. Valeri Ramishvili
Javakhishvili Tbilisi State University

Gulkan Kmosteli, Ph. D.
Rector of Educational University Rvali

Prof. Alphonso Ogbuehi,
Park University Kansas City Missouri

Emmanuel Ihejirika, Doctoral Candidate,
Argosy University

Prof. Carol Smith-Williamson, Esq.
Lincoln University

Prof. Chris Mbah, Olive College North Carolina

Prof. Richard Deeg, Temple University

Prof. Schwartz, Temple University

TABLE OF CONTENTS

ABOUT THE AUTHORS

Dr. ZVIAD KLIMENT LAZARASHVILI
Georgian International Academy, Academician
Georgian International Academy, Ph. D.
Educational University Rvali, Doctor Emeritus
Strayer University, MBA
Educational University Rvali, Law
Tbilisi State University of Economic Relations and Law, BS

Zviad Kliment Lazarashvili is the author of several books in literature, philosophy, economics and political science. Dr. Lazarashvili is the Executive Vice President at Selective Broadcasting Corporation, the developer and manufacturer of the world's fastest and most accurate tracking technology. Dr. Lazarashvili is the Executive Vice President at RAPC National Security Division, Inc., a designer and manufacturer of highly durable high capacity computers for the defense industry. He worked as a Capital Markets analyst for Merrill Lynch on Wall Street. He served as a consultant at several universities, high-technology and financial companies, including Educational University Rvali and Mentor Special Situation Fund, L.P. He served as a professor at Tbilisi State University of Economic Relations and Law of Georgia and at Educational University Rvali of Georgia, and also as a Lecturer Emeritus in political science, economics and finance at Lincoln University of Pennsylvania. Since 2011 Dr. Lazarashvili also serves as the Vice President of Georgian International Academy – the premier postgraduate research and educational institution in Georgia. His academic researches and financial analyses were published in *Friedrich Ebert Foundation of Germany, Journal of Business Management (1998), Scholar Magazine, Washington, DC (2008)* and *Lincolnian, Lincoln University, PA (2009)*. Lazarashvili's previous literary works include *Manhope (2004)* and *Invictus-Pathos (2003)*. He also collaborated on several academic treatises and historical theses on social, political and philosophical issues with Dr. Janet Mathewson of Yale University: *Political Economy of the 19th Century New England (2000), Treatise on Christianity and Capitalism (2001)* and *American Conservatism (2001)*. In 2009-2010 Zviad Kliment Lazarashvili co-authored two academic books, *Political Philosophy: A Global Approach (2009)* and *Political Theory Made Simple (2010)*. Since fall of 2009 the books are used as undergraduate text books in Political Theory and Political Science in several universities.

Zviad Kliment Lazarashvili was the first Georgian translator of Henry David Thoreau's political essays. His pioneering translations, historical analyses and commentaries on Thoreau's works were introduced in Georgia as an academic treatise, *Hero of the American Nation (2008)*. In 2010 the second edition of the book was published in the U.S., *Henry David Thoreau: Essays (2010)*. The book is bilingual and contains 5 of Henry David Thoreau's best political essays in both, English and Georgian languages: *"Civil Disobedience", "Slavery in Massachusetts", "A Plea for Captain John Brown", "Life Without Principle"* and *"The Last Days of John Brown"*. It is the first scholarly, fully annotated edition of Thoreau's political essays in the world. It contains 700 footnotes which explain Thoreau's ideas, Slavery, Abolitionism and the 19th century American politics in broad historical context. The second edition offers an abundance of detailed annotations. It also includes an extended introduction by Dr. Lazarashvili, and the translator's biography by George P. Stasen, Ph.D. The book also contains illustrations and copies of historical documents relevant to the 19th century Abolitionism.

In 2011 Dr. Lazarashvili authored the book *American Heroes (2011)*. Besides Thoreau's five political essays, the book contains prison letters of John Brown, Brown's Speeches and his Provisional Constitution, rare biographical information obtained from archives, and extensive commentaries of John Brown's hagiographer, Franklin Benjamin Sanborn. The book also contains illustrations and copies of historical documents relevant to the 19th century Abolitionism and New England. The book is bilingual and is intended for graduate students of history of Abolitionism and political philosophy. In 2011 the book was recognized by National Academy of Sciences of Ukraine and Dr. Lazarashvili was awarded Plato Gold Medal for his *"immense contributions to the science philosophy"*.

In this particular book Dr. Lazarashvili presents broad and comprehensive descriptions of prominent political theorists and a unique approach to their concepts. Every notion is shown not only as a philosophical hypothesis, but as a corollary of diverse personal, cultural and even ethnic experiences, which all men, and especially men of keen observation, undergo throughout their lives. Dr. Lazarashvili is a polymath who easily connects political issues to economic problems and philosophical doctrines to religious concerns. Thus he creates a cross-disciplinary picture of political science, which is closely knit with other disciplines and many aspects of human existence.

Dr. CHIEKE E. IHEJIRIKA
Georgian International Academy, Academician
Temple University, Ph. D.
University of Waterloo, Ont. Canada, MA
Catholic University of Leuven, BA, MA
Alvan Ikoku College of Education, B. Ed.

Dr. Chieke E. Ihejirika is an Associate Professor of Political Science at Lincoln University, Pennsylvania. In the last fifteen years he has served as a graduate teaching fellow at Temple, Adjunct Professor at Drexel, Avila University in Kansas City and Political Science professor at Kansas City Kansas Community College. Some of his publications include*: Ndiigbo in Nigeria: A Quest for Survival and Prosperity (2010); US-Africa Relation from Nixon to Reagan (2008); African-American Elitism: A liberal and Quantitative Perspective (2008). Pan Africanism: A Survey (2006); Africa's Utopia: Economic Development without Political Development? (2002); The Communal Nature of Igbo Aesthetics (1994); Nigerian foreign policies, 1960-1983 sources and patterns, Ottawa: National Library of Canada (1988).*

Dr. Ihejirika has a unique capacity of making some of the very arcane subjects readily comprehensible to even freshmen students. He is an avid advocate of political justice. He is an idealist with infectious optimism believing that politics more than anything else can restore faith in our common humanity. Concurring with Aristotle that politics is at the same time the most nurturing and most dangerous human endeavor, he believes that with good politics human suffering could be drastically reduced. He brings the African fairness based on intrinsic spirituality to the understanding of politics. He is very committed to spreading the uniquely African humanism that is quintessential to the building of a more humane world. The need to understand the various attitudes about the acquisition, and use of power over the millennia and across the world has become imperative in this era of globalization. The holistic nature of African world view strongly suggests itself as perhaps the ultimate salvation for humanity in the post modern politico-economic era with all its fretfulness. Dr. Ihejirika conceived this book to provide a simple introductory text for political theory students at Georgian International University. The collaboration between the four co-authors of the book has tremendously enriched this work given their unique abilities and cosmopolitan worldviews. The authors share a deep sense of coalition in achieving our common destinies as members of human family and in seeking through philosophies the path to common good.

Dr. GARI T. CHAPIDZE
International Personnel Academy of Ukraine, Academician
Fazisi Academy of Sciences, Academician
Georgian National Academy of Sciences, Academician
Javakhishvili Tbilisi State University, Ph. D.
Lomonosov Moscow State University, BA, MS

Dr. Gari T. Chapidze is the world renowned academic figure in political science, pedagogy and journalism. He is an Academician and a full member of several national academies of sciences of Georgia and Ukraine. He is the author of over seventy scholarly books which have been widely accepted in scientific and academic circles of Georgia, Russia, Ukraine, Europe and now the United States. Dr. Chapidze is the author of the first and only Georgian-Ukrainian Dictionary and the first and only Georgian-Belarusian Idiomatic Dictionary.

Dr. Gari T. Chapidze has served as a Rector of Chiatura Academy of Liberal Sciences (1993-2003). Since 2003 he serves as the President of Georgian International Academy. Since 2008 he serves as the Rector of Georgia-Ukraine Institute of Social Relations. Since 1997 he serves as the Chief Editor of the academic monthly newspaper "Chiragdani". Since 2008 he serves as the Chief Representative of the International Personnel Academy of Ukraine in Georgia.

Dr. Gari Chapidze is the winner of several academic prizes and medals: Medal of Honor of Georgia (2003), Gogebashvili Medal (1993), Gogebashvili Medal (2000), Ilia Chavchavadze Prize and Medal (2003), Akaki Tsereteli Prize and Medal (2003), Tabidze Prize and Medal (2005), Plato Gold Medal of Ukraine (2010), Guramishvili Prize and Medal (2010), Georgia-Ukraine Medal of Friendship (2010), International Science Medal of Georgia (2007), International Science Medal of Georgia (2008), Gold Medal of Georgia for Accomplishments in Public Education (2008).

In this specific book Dr. Chapidze offers a global view on political science and political theory. He advocates political justice and explains its precedence throughout the world and throughout history. Chapidze conceived the book as an instrument to reintroduce global political theory, philosophy and culture in Georgian academic circles. With Dr. Chapidze's initiative the book will be used as a standard academic textbook for the disciplines of philosophy and political theory at Georgian International Academy, Georgian International University, Georgia-Ukraine Institute of Social Relations and International Personnel Academy of Ukraine.

Dr. GEORGE P. STASEN
Georgian International Academy, Ph. D.
Drexel University, LeBow College of Business, MBA
Drexel University, LeBow College of Business, BS

George P. Stasen has served as a director and/or advisor to government units, foundations, mutual funds, investment companies, private companies and public corporations as well as professor of economics and corporate finance. He has structured and provided financing and investment guidance to major corporations, investment companies, developing enterprises and municipalities.

Dr. Stasen serves as general partner of Mentor Special Situation Fund, L.P., a highly successful venture capital fund and also serves as Chairman of CoreCare Systems, a publicly held corporation; Chairman and cofounder SBC Corporation, the developer and manufacturer of the world's fastest and most accurate tracking technology; and Chairman and cofounder of RAPC Corporation, a designer and manufacturer of highly durable high capacity computers for the defense industry.

Dr. Stasen earned his BS from Drexel University with a concentration in Economics and was subsequently awarded a fellowship and earned an MBA from Drexel University. Mr. Stasen earned his Ph.D. in Economics from Georgian International Academy.

George P. Stasen would like to dedicate this labor of love to Dr. Peter Stercho, a Ukrainian Professor of Economics at the Drexel University LeBow College of Business, in Philadelphia, Pennsylvania, for his inspiration, superb scholarship and wisdom in seeing the true value of free markets, as well as Drexel University where Dr. Stasen developed his love of economics and commerce. He would also like sincerely to thank the Georgian International Academy for encouraging his continuous study of economics and education. May God Bless those hallowed halls.

George P. Stasen would also like to thank Montgomery County Community College where he spent several wonderful years teaching Economics as an adjunct faculty member.

INTRODUCTION

It goes without saying that there are numerous political philosophy books in the market today. Yet we embarked on the project of producing still another work on this subject. Obviously, we would not have undertaken this venture unless we had something new to offer to young scholars in need of both, a basic and comprehensive introduction to the subfield of political philosophy, also referred to as political theory. Any work on this subject is pertinent because political philosophy provides the necessary grounding for both, political scientists and practitioners of politics.

Consequently, the goals of this project are two-fold: first, we have made a conscious decision to provide our readers with a very lucid text in political theory by reducing the usually technical and obscure language of philosophy to everyday language that would be comprehensible to an undergraduate student for whom this book is intended. More importantly, this book is aimed at students who would normally have difficulty understanding the standard literature of philosophy, because we do not want language to constitute an obstacle to young undergraduate scholars as they try to master the basic political theories they are required to know. Hence, we decided to explain the ideas of the selected political theorists in the simplest possible language. Second, we also made a deliberate decision to eschew the pervading ethnocentrism that seems to characterize most extant texts on this subject, by attempting to introduce a text that is global in scope. It is our considered opinion that a survey of political theories must include the major peoples and regions of the world. In this era of globalism, persistent parochialism cannot but hurt our common humanity.

We have therefore provided a text that explores traditional Western ideas from Ancient Greece through contemporary European thought, much the same way as most conventional texts do. In addition, we have incorporated non-Western philosophies from Africa, Asia and the Middle East fully to inform and enrich the student in ways few texts have attempted in the past. This new and improved third edition also contains an entire section on modern American and Russian political theorists and activists.

For easy reading, we have provided brief summaries at the end of each chapter together with key terms and critical thinking questions. Hopefully, this will encourage students actually to read the text without the intimidation that often results from obscure language, as well as, the excitement to learn a few new things about African and Oriental cultures that Western scholars have traditionally ignored hitherto. Maybe the post-industrial societies of the West can learn a few things from more traditional societies to ameliorate some of the excesses of their postmodern era.

We have arranged the twenty-six philosophers and their philosophies we selected into eleven categories. For utilitarian reasons, we begin with the Greek or the Hellenist Era since this work is primarily written for Western pedagogy, not that we are not mindful that the Iberian, Chinese and African thoughts predate the Greco-Roman cradle of today's Western thought. In other words, this work progressed from the Hellenist era from whence we learned the idea of the ideal state based on natural justice as espoused by Plato to the practical understanding of the nature of the various constitutions which Aristotle afforded us.

For the Roman era we chose Cicero, an eminent Roman statesman and a passionate scholar of Hellenism, who sought to sustain Roman republicanism with the philosophical ideals he borrowed from the major Greek schools of thought. Cicero provides a model for the virtue of public life which is at the core of our conviction that public life must only be sought to make life better for one's community. We also included Marcus Aurelius for, among other things, the strong emphasis he placed on moral obligation and our social responsibility to love our fellow humans, if for nothing, but for the common kinship we share, which no one can abridge no matter how evil they become.

Theocratic philosophers have had a tremendous influence over the academic subject of political philosophy, as well as the world of politics. We have included the three prominent theocratic philosophers: St. Augustine of Hippo, Averroes and St. Thomas Aquinas. St. Augustine of Hippo preserved much of the ancient political philosophy of Cicero in his colossal book *The City of God*, and just for that reason his writings have been deemed of utmost importance for political philosophy. Averroes on the other hand has preserved Aristotle's works. St. Thomas Aquinas popularized Aristotle in Europe and reconciled Aristotelian ideas on morals and politics with Catholicism.

The section on the scientific era includes commentary on two of the most famous political works of all times: *Utopia* and *The Prince*. Thomas More's brilliant piece attempts to portray politics in a normative sense while Machiavelli's *The Prince* is the ultimate work of political realism. Although the two classics of the same period offer analysis on the conflicting ideologies of idealism and pragmatism, in the end, they showcase empiricism at its best; after all, science is nothing without careful consideration of sense experience.

Also included in this text is a set of important commentaries on the social contract theorists. Beginning with Thomas Hobbes, this section presents questions such as what is the nature of the agreement between a state and its citizens and what is the reason for a state's existence. The other two philosophers of the era, John Locke and Jean-Jacques Rousseau, put into focus the evolution of the social contract theory. By the time the reader completes the section, they will be left to conclude whether society is an absolute necessity for mankind to function or downright corrupting in its effects.

This book contains a section on political economists, which includes Adam Smith and Karl Marx. At the dawn of the 18th century the world of politics had become inseparable from economics once and for all. It was necessary and timely to speak in cross-disciplinary terms about the political and economic developments of the world. Adam Smith championed the advancement and Karl Marx climaxed the movement. Yet it is hard to find two academics with such vastly different views on the same subject. Smith was a free market proponent and a true capitalist. Marx was a supporter of government intervention and communism. They were both exceptional theorists and convincing writers, so much so that their arguments split the 20th century world into two camps and pitted countries against each other, both ideologically and militarily.

The section containing what we have called rational idealists includes two of the most outspoken philosophers for peace and liberty. No philosophical textbook would be complete without the man whom many recognize as the most important philosopher since Descartes – Immanuel Kant. Although much of Kant's work focuses heavily on metaphysical doctrines, it still has a sizable number of political ideas embedded. Equally essential to any philosophical textbook, especially one with a political focus, are the works of John Stuart Mill. Mill's treatise *On Liberty* is a must-read text for every student of political theory.

In the midst of technological advances and rapid economic growth all around the world, among the opposing camps of early capitalists and socialists arose a group of political philosophers who defended individual human liberty and argued for improvement of human life and humaneness instead of economic growth and scientific progress. The two Humanists discussed in this book could not have been more geographically removed from each other, yet their humanism, patriotism and Christian idealism could not have been any more similar. While St. Ilia Chavchavadze championed humanism in a small European country called Georgia, Henry David Thoreau advocated for humanism in the United States. While St. Ilia's patriotic writings stemmed from Russian Empire's aggression against Georgians, his fellow countrymen, Thoreau's political activism and essays branched out from the American government's aggression against its fellow citizens. Although it must be explicitly emphasized that their works and deeds did not only encompass their respectful nations, Georgia and the United States, but the entire mankind, as human liberty and rights pertain to all of humanity, not just to a privileged few.

We also included elements of oriental philosophy as represented by Confucius and Lao Tzu. With Confucius we underscored our common theme in what he described as social idealism, that is, how a man's personal good is common good. From Lao Tzu, the Old Master, we connect Socratic intellectual humility and the need for personal introspection which is an imperative for moral action, especially for those aspiring for leadership and public life.

The book contains a section on the 20th century American political theorists and activists. We feel very strongly that American theorists are often unfairly overlooked both, in academic and social circles. This country has reared some of the most brilliant political minds, who have greatly helped to advance the subject of political theory. In this book we are including Martin Luther King, Jr., Hannah Arendt and John Rawls.

We end our theoretical discussion with a section on European realists. Leo Tolstoy was the man who revolutionized not only Russian, but European and American political mindset. He abandoned cliché of romanticism and preached realism as the formula for individual, as well as national political success. Anton Makarenko's name is often overlooked in the world of political philosophy, but his theories and methodologies of pedagogy and education have transfigured the Soviet education system and moved it closer to the incentive-based Capitalism. Perhaps it was Makarenko's realism that saved the Eastern Block from the complete socialist lunacy and preserved a certain degree of common sense even in the "Evil Empire", as Ronald Reagan correctly called Russia once.

In our quest to construct a common thesis of what constitutes good governance or social contract, we also introduced some elements of traditional African political philosophy, a hitherto neglected corpus of human epistemology. Using the Igbo people of Southeast Nigeria, we highlighted the treasure in understanding and embracing African communalism and spiritual imperative even in this temporal existence as something the modern world could use as we seek to better the lot of all of humanity. Moderation had been the nature of traditional Africa interactions because every transaction, including politics, was imbued with the respect for the unknown forces of nature and the supernatural of which the living is an integral part. The Igbo represent the complex interplay of communalism and individualism in a mystical blending of moral and political aesthetics.

Perhaps, more than anything else, the juxtaposition of these philosophers and philosophies from around the world would convince the skeptic that human beings are and have always been the same, and that what is good knows no national or regional boundaries, and in deed, no timeline. Observing how similar Plato, Aristotle, Cicero, Aurelius, the Christian and Islamic theocratic philosophers, traditional Africans, Confucius and Lao Tzu are in spite of the disjuncture of time and place, it is obvious that the human consanguinity, common origin and destiny are seriously embedded in our socio cultural and political DNA, suggesting that the solution to what ails us can only be found in collective introspection to discover the primary secular purpose of human life here on earth. These authors believe there is an extricable link between here and hereafter, hence we subscribe to the relevance of political morality by those who exercise power over the human community.

To maximize resource availability for the reader of this text, the book is concluded with a large appendix consisting of four of the most significant political documents of the modern era namely: The British *Magna Carta*, the United States' *Declaration of Independence*, the *United States' Constitution*, and President Abraham Lincoln's *Gettysburg Address* of November 19, 1863, to enable the discerning student to make quick and expedient cross- references in the course of reading this text.

HELLENIST ERA

PLATO

"The unexamined life is not worth living."

PLATO

BACKGROUND

Plato's works are among the most famous of classical Greek political thought. His *Socratic dialogues* are named after his teacher Socrates. Socrates never wrote down any of his teachings, so Plato's efforts in putting his mentor's ideas in print are invaluable. It is commonly remarked that without Plato there is no Socrates and vice versa. Plato's school of thought is referred to as the *Academy*. Over the course of his life, Socrates remained a controversial figure in the city of Athens. His desire to teach his fellow citizens the truth was unyielding and ultimately led to his demise. He was put on trial and convicted of corrupting the youth and impiety. During his trial, he famously declared that: "The unexamined life isn't worth living" (Apology, 38a). Socrates rebuked the sophists for claiming absolute knowledge of things they did not know. He concluded that wisdom is in the acknowledgement of one's ignorance. While in prison and awaiting execution his friend offered the chance to escape but Socrates declined the offer stating that he would not break the laws of the state which raised him and his ancestors. Just days later they killed him by forcing him to drink hemlock. Socrates set precedence for martyrdom which to this day remains unrivalled. If only one thing is learned from Plato's dialogues it is never to sacrifice principle for anything, not even for life itself. Speaking the truth should be everyone's top priority, especially a head of state and those who aspire to lead.

THEORY OF JUSTICE

Throughout all of Plato's dialogues Socrates is well-known for his frequent use of *irony* to disprove commonly held opinions on the nature of justice. Early, in *The Republic*, Socrates begins analyzing his friends' theories of justice. First, he answers whether justice must involve returning to a man what is his property. Socrates believes this to be true to the extent that what is being given to a man is not harmful to him. He uses the example of giving a gun back to a man that is insane; this says Socrates, is unjust. Next, he discusses whether justice is the will of the strong, which is generally understood to be identical with the will of the legislator. Socrates disputes this theory by comparing statesmanship with other arts such as shoemaking. He says that justice is doing a good action within one's specific art rather than looking at how much someone intends to abide by the law. It follows, then, that a ruler who is making laws which are disadvantageous to the ruled is doing justice neither to his position nor to his people. From this arises the consensus on justice maintained throughout *The Republic*, namely, that justice means each person doing only what they are best fit to do.

THE PHILOSOPHER KING

Naturally, the question of who is best capable of ruling the state should arise. Socrates answers this by responding that the only person who should rule is the *philosopher king*. By conceptualizing the philosopher king, Socrates puts an end to the constant friction existing between those who rule and those who know. However, Socrates admits that ending the conflict is a tiresome process. Citizens must accept rule by a philosopher and philosophers must accept a life of action instead of a life of only thought. This idea fits in perfectly with his division of labor: "Until philosophers are kings, or the kings and princes of this world have the spirit and power of philosophy, and political greatness and wisdom meet in one, and those commoner natures who pursue either to the exclusion of the other are compelled to stand aside, cities will never have rest from their evils – no, nor the human race, as I believe – and then only will thus our state have a possibility of life and behold the light of day" (Republic, 5.473d-e).

In the *allegory of the cave* Socrates tactfully shows the fear of philosophers. Caring only about gaining knowledge, they do not want to have to worry about public affairs lest they should have less time to devote to wisdom.   Their utmost fear is becoming what Socrates describes as a cave dweller which is an ignorant person, who is inexperienced in thinking and becomes stubbornly attached to conventional opinions so much so that they are blinded when met by the bright light of the truth. Socrates finally summarizes the rift between philosophers and regular citizens: "The bewilderments are of two kinds, and arise from two causes, either from coming out of the light or from going into the light" (7.518a). The key to Socrates' ideal state is uniting ability with authority; giving power to a philosopher who is innately equipped with goodwill and virtue to lead a state can never be dangerous.

COMMUNISM

Many of Socrates' ideas reflect communist themes in the strictest sense of the word where communism means "of the community." Socrates vehemently believes that each person doing what they are best suited means not looking out for their own good but for the commonwealth. When people carry out their parts of the division of labor they are placed under a feeling of happiness, fulfillment and well-being or what the Greeks refer to as *eudaimonia*. As far as property is concerned Socrates says whatever a citizen owns should never be denied to the state since the purpose of the state is for society to be provided for collectively, not singly. Accordingly, he warns against excessive poverty and wealth which are both destructive to the state. He shows that when workers experience either of the two the result will be the same, namely, the deterioration of the labor. The rich man will no longer want to work any longer once excess money is acquired and the poor man will become equally indolent and careless when he sees his work is not making ends meet. Judging by advisories such as this, Socrates would surely condemn and even lament today's dominant economic system of capitalism. After all, it is largely undisputed that capitalist countries are the most unequal of all.

As mentioned earlier, Socrates had many controversial ideas, many of which are still criticized today. Among the most prominent ones are his thoughts on marriage and children. In an effort to promote unity among the citizens Socrates imagines a society in which husbands, wives and children are all held in common. This is something which brings harsh rebuke from Plato's most famous student Aristotle. He argues that the idea aims at creating one shared household rather than a state. Also, Aristotle believes that in such a society children and wives would be neglected instead of cared for excessively as Socrates thinks. Aristotle's criticism rests on the notion that people care more for things which they can call their own. The debate illustrates a fundamental difference of opinion on human nature between the Academy and Aristotle's school the Lyceum.

FORMS OF GOVERNMENT

The Republic favors an implied form of totalitarianism. Socrates makes a distinction of those who know true beauty and those who only have an opinion of it. In the end, he states that those who are not truly wise and educated in philosophy should concede power to those who do have such traits. Socrates seemingly has no preference as to whether the totalitarianism is autocratic or aristocratic; the two seem to be interchangeable.

Next, Socrates provides his account of how different types of governments decline. He says that **aristocracy** turns into **timocracy**; timocracy into **oligarchy**; oligarchy into **democracy**; and democracy into **tyranny**. Aristocracy, or the ideal state as Socrates refers to it, deteriorates into timocracy when members of the ruling class become careless in their breeding practices and create impure or mixed heirs which begin to covet the position of ruler. As timocracy begins from a love of honor, it devolves into oligarchy where honor is replaced by money. Oligarchy inevitably brings about a huge divide between the rich and the poor and the state is at odds with itself. When this is the case, the poor, being more numerous than the rich, overthrow the government and democracy ensues. To Socrates, democracy is a terrible form of government where the citizens have liberty to do whatever they please thus breeding a variety of natures and discord in the state. In a democracy liberty becomes so widespread and freedom becomes nearly anarchical. This paves the way for tyranny. The tyrant becomes so intoxicated by liberty that he loses all regard for laws and authority and is so free that the only rules followed by all are his. Again, it is important to note here that although Socrates' ideal ruler will have absolute power in all he does *The Republic's* form of government still differs from tyranny. Remember, Socrates distinguishes between the ruler who rules for private interests and the ruler that rules for the commonwealth. Since statesmanship is an art, the true ruler will rule with the purpose of self-actualizing beautiful statesmanship.

One of the most important themes of *The Republic* is that the form of government one is part of, determines what kind of person the one is. Government has a way of rubbing off on its citizens and producing a commensurate kind of people. For instance, in a democracy freedom will be most esteemed by the people and in an oligarchy wealth will be the most coveted item. Simply put, the citizens reflect their form of government.

THE TRIPARTIC SOUL

Earlier it was said that justice within a society means each citizen contributing their best work by maintaining the roles which they are most gifted for by nature. In order to facilitate the rearing of just citizens Socrates explains that each individual must first be just within themselves. This involves the three parts of the soul described by Socrates as reason, courage, desire or instinct being in a harmonious condition with one another. According to Socrates, then, each human has a **tripartic soul**. In the best educated person the soul will be ruled by reason with desire and instinct playing a supporting role. In other words, the just man's reason rules over his courage and instinct and whatever is rational will be desirable: "The just man does not permit the several elements within him to interfere with one another" (4.443d).

CONCLUSION

Plato's Republic calls for a just society in which all individuals are harmonious in relations with the state. However, this can only be achieved by providing each citizen with the proper philosophical education and demonstrating to them that happiness in a state is achieved, when every member is content with his or her station in the social division of labor. A united state is the best state because it enjoys harmony in all its parts.

The only people who should rule are the philosophers since they are the only people whose reason is able to rule within their own souls. Nevertheless, Socrates remained skeptical at the end of his life on whether a philosopher can remain just while serving the public. Ultimately, he decided that anyone with a true knowledge of justice must withdraw from society and live a private life to avoid corruption. "Anyone who really fights for what's just, if indeed he's going to survive for even a short time, must act privately, not publicly" (Apology, 32a). Therefore, according to Socrates, the realm of politics has no room for a man of conviction and moral integrity. In short, the ideal state is possible nowhere on earth, but only in the mind.

But if the ideal state is not attainable on earth, what is the practical value of *The Republic* in today's world? The answer is simple: *The Republic* sets a high standard for modern governments to strive toward. As they say, when an archer wishes to hit a target in the distance he aims higher than the target to ensure that he reaches it. The best reality, then, is only possible with a little bit of reverie.

SUMMARY

1. Plato's dialogues are considered to be the founding works of western philosophy.

2. Many of Plato's works represent actual dialogues between the people of Athens and his mentor, Socrates.

3. Socrates was ultimately convicted of corrupting the youth and impiety. At his execution, he was forced to drink a poison called hemlock.

4. Plato believed the ideal ruler should be a philosopher. This, he says, would put an end to the constant friction those who theorize and those who have authority.

5. Plato believed that a state's form of government determines what is coveted Example, in a democracy freedom, and in an oligarchy, wealth).

6. Plato believed justice means each person doing the work for which they are most fit.

7. Plato argued that for a just man to remain uncorrupted he must not enter politics.

SECTION REVIEW

KEY TERMS

Academy
Allegory of the cave
Aristocracy
Democracy
Eudaimonia
Irony
Oligarchy
Philosopher king
Socratic dialogues
Timocracy
Tripartic soul
Tyranny

CRITICAL THINKING

• Explain relationship between Socrates and Plato.

• Describe Plato's division of labor as it pertains to his theory of justice.

• What problem does Plato solve by conceptualizing a philosopher-king?

• Explain Plato's allegory of the cave.

• How might the idea of a tripartic soul result in social harmony?

HELLENIST ERA

ARISTOTLE

"A human being is by nature a political animal."

ARISTOTLE

BACKGROUND

Aristotle is widely viewed as a founding father of western intellectual culture as it is known today. He spent much of his youth studying subjects ranging from biology to metaphysics. However, his most famous achievements are in the field of political science. His interest in the area was at its peak during his long tenure as a student in Athens at Plato's Academy.

After leaving the Academy Aristotle is said to have spent a number of years tutoring the son of King Phillip of Macedonia; the child he taught was none other than Alexander, the future heir to the throne. Once Alexander died, anti-Macedonian sentiments surfaced in Athens which forced Aristotle to flee. In his own words, he saved Athens from committing a second crime against philosophy (the first was the execution of Socrates). He spent the final year of his life in exile before he died. Aristotle was a true genius of his time and made lasting contributions for which the world is forever indebted. Although it is estimated that only about one-fifth of his works survive, his thoughts on the study of politics can be clearly understood by reading *Nicomachean Ethics* and *Politics*. These works are best known for bringing Plato's Republic down from the heavens and adding a material side to it so that it may be meaningful in everyday life.

THE MASTER SCIENCE

Aristotle considers politics a practical science instead of a theoretical one. Whereas subjects like physics and mathematics have eternally fixed laws, the study of politics is concerned with the actions of human beings which are changeable. Also, the practical science aims to discover human nature by their reactions and adaptations to different things. Aristotle prefers to judge human behavior on an individual basis instead of making rash generalizations. Since humans are dynamic beings it is impossible to construct an *a priori* theoretical basis for their actions. Instead it is necessary to analyze them through observation or *empirical* data.

Aristotle states that political science is the master science since it deals with determining and attaining the highest good. "[The highest good] seems proper to the most controlling science – the highest ruling science. And this appears characteristic of political science" (N.E. 1.2.1094a28-30). Thus he believes not only that politics should be above all others but also that it encompasses all the rest. It seeks to investigate what the good life is and how it can be created. Perhaps because politics deals with the acquisition, and dispensation of power, which can make or mar human endeavors, Aristotle calls politics the master science upon which all of civilization depends. This Aristotelian assertion is validated by some of the recent egregious abuses of power such as: NAZI Germany, Stalinism in the former Soviet Union, in China during the Great Leap Forward, Idi Amin's Uganda, the Apartheid regime in South Africa, the genocide in Rwanda, Sani Abacha's Nigeria, Saddam Hussein in Iraq, Milosevic in Serbia, Robert Mugabe in Zimbabwe, and many other despots around the world who destroyed rather than advanced their countries with their abuse of power, and in some cases, crimes against humanity.

THE GOOD LIFE

Bringing about the good life in a state centers around attaining what Aristotle calls the **golden mean**. According to him, virtue consists in putting oneself between two extremes or vices: "We have said that [virtue] is a mean between two vices, one of excess and one of deficiency" (2.9.1109a20-23). For example, bravery is the point between cowardice and rashness. The terms excess and deficiency are terms used by Aristotle when comparing actions and feelings. Although the brave man finds the golden mean, he will still be viewed by a coward as rash and by a rash person as a coward. In short, Aristotle perceives virtue and vice as a relative matter which must be investigated by comparing the actions and feelings of dissimilar people.

Despite the need for virtue in a state, Aristotle addresses whether the virtuous man can also be happy at the same time. He believes happiness is the purpose of all human actions. However, this thesis should not be confused with the teachings of the **Epicureans**. Unlike the Epicureans, Aristotle distinguishes between true and false happiness. True happiness, he says, is when humans carry out a sort of duty to use reason in every activity: "We take this life to be activity and actions of the soul that involve reason; hence the function of the excellent man is to do this well and finely" (1.7.1098a10-15). Therefore, the virtuous man will always be happy. On the other hand, false happiness is that which depends on pleasure. Aristotle thinks virtue is natural to man's condition and pleasure is foreign. Nevertheless, he concedes that even a happy man needs a certain degree of **external goods**; these include elements such as wealth, political power and friends.

THEORY OF JUSTICE

One of the most famous quotes in the history of political thought is when Aristotle describes man's political nature: "A human being is by nature a **political animal**" (Politics, 1.2.1253a1-5). It is in man's best interest to seek a political community in order to live a more expedient and happy life. Accordingly, justice is a social virtue only practiced by man when he is around others and can be defined as a set of rules governing the acts of men sharing a common environment. Aristotle holds that law is the quintessential tool of justice in a state, for he defines it as "understanding without desire" (3.16.1287a33-34). Thus the law is an unbiased mediator in disputes arising between two parties; a role which a human being is simply not fit to serve as his interests will always get in the way. In summary, Aristotle believes the just man to be the one who follows the law most attentively since doing so means acting properly among other members of the same state. In the end, however, he admits law does not provide the best justice imaginable; the rule of law is only the optimum or preferred method of establishing order in a state. **Equity**, not equality, within the boundaries of law should always be the goal. "Where a universal rule has to be made, but cannot be correct, the law chooses the universal rule that is usually correct, well aware of the error being made...for the source of the error is not the law or the legislator, but the nature of the object itself" (N.E., 5.10.1137b15-20). It goes without saying, then, that the written law itself fails to consider individual circumstances. Thus according to Aristotle the proper way to adjudicate a matter is to have a well trained judge that can weigh particulars of a case and interpret the law as necessary. A good legislator and a good judge are invaluable components in Aristotle's system of government.

Aside from law-abidingness, Aristotle acknowledges other commonly held opinions on justice. The first is **distributive justice**. This involves beneficial items such as wealth and honor being distributed on the basis of merit in the form of a ration of goods to men instead of numerical equality. While this form of justice has the ability to award benefits to the most deserving citizens, it can easily become an issue of who has better political connections. Today, opponents of affirmative action often base their arguments in favor of a system of distributive justice. The overall goal of such a system is to create a **meritocracy**. The second form of justice Aristotle discusses is **corrective justice**. This idea is centered on numerical equality in transactions both voluntary (e.g. contracts) and involuntary (e.g. crime); one good is distributed to one person. Sociologists usually refer to the term as **just deserts**. Finally, he mentions **reciprocal justice**, which refers to simple addition and subtraction. It is most easily thought of as John stole ten dollars from Joe, so Joe must be repaid ten dollars by John. It is the most fundamental form of justice known to mankind and is still the most widely used today. Figuratively speaking, the scale of justice must always be made even on both sides by subtracting from one what was added unjustly to it, in order to restore the original balance.

COMMUNITY RELATIONSHIPS

According to Aristotle, the most basic form of political organization is the family. Within each family there is a set hierarchy headed by the father, followed by the mother and the children. Aristotle provides little substantial evidence to back this claim; he simply states, "The relation of male to female is that of natural superior to natural inferior, and that of ruler to ruled" (Politics, 1.5.1254b13-14). Similarly, he holds that people are either born as natural masters or slaves. He believes the master and slave relationship is beneficial to each: the master is able to pursue higher things such as politics and philosophy which he is made to do and the slave obeys commands which prevent him from becoming the prey of passion. This assertion is often at the forefront of much controversy surrounding Aristotelian political theory. It should be noted, however, that Aristotle expressly distinguishes between his mastership and the slave trade which he condemns as a form of commerce.

Aristotle is highly critical of Plato's *Republic*. First, he disputes Plato's thesis that a city-state should be as united as possible as illogical. He argues Plato's unity aims at creating what amounts to a single household rather than a state or **polis** as it was known then: "For a household is more self-sufficient than a single person, and a city-state than a household; and a city-state tends to come about as soon as a community's population is large enough to be fully self-sufficient. So since what is more self-sufficient is more choiceworthy, what is less unity is less choiceworthy than what is more so" (2.2.1261b12-15).

Next, he finds fault with Plato' idea of common children, wives and property. He says that since people naturally care more for what is their own they will no longer be able to take part in this sweet pleasure in such a radically communist community. So, he concludes that Plato's idea will have the reverse effect of what was intended, everything will be extremely neglected instead of being extremely cared for. "What is held in common by the largest number of people receives the least care" (3.1261b30). Besides, even though no one will be sure of which child, mother or father is their own they will always have suspicions from physical resemblances. As far as property is concerned,

Aristotle believes it should be held privately but the legislator should see to it that the community is able to use it. When property is held privately and not shared, the state is prevented from getting whatever it may need. Conversely, if all property is owned by the state, the pleasure a person gets from giving to the community is taken away, therefore practicing the social virtue of generosity is impossible.

FORMS OF GOVERNMENT

Without a doubt the most important contribution Aristotle made to political science is his analysis of different types of *regimes* or governments. For him it does not matter who rules but in whose interest. He opens the exploration of constitutions by recognizing three authentic constitutions and three deviant ones: "It is evident...that those constitutions that look to the common benefit turn out...to be correct, whereas those which look only to the benefit of the rulers are mistaken and are deviations" (6.1279a15-20). Kingship, aristocracy and polity are the three original forms. Kingship is characterized by one person ruling for all; aristocracy is rule by the wise for all; polity is where many rule for all. Kingship deteriorates into tyranny; aristocracy into oligarchy; polity into democracy. Tyranny means rule of one for himself; oligarchy means rule by the rich for themselves; democracy rule by the poor for themselves. Using the above criteria Aristotle classifies the 158 poleis of his time, and thus earns for himself the distinction of being the premier political scientist of the western world. In summary, each authentic constitution is ruined when its virtue is replaced by a vice and rule for common benefit is replaced by rule for a few people in power. Furthermore, Aristotle goes on to speak about what is held in highest regard in each type of government. The oligarchs speak as though they are more equal than the poor because of a higher property assessment. Similarly, the democrats believe that all who are equal in freedom should be equal in everything. In this sense Aristotle agrees with Plato in believing that a form of government makes its citizens admire whatever quality it holds most dearly.

Moreover, he sets forth four causes which comprise a strong government. The first is the *material cause* which consists of all the physical components that make up a state. These include the citizens, non-citizens, territory and other material resources available to the state. The purpose of the material cause is to provide for the protection and well-being of the people. Next, Aristotle holds that the principles that hold a nation together and the rights of the citizens must be written down in a constitution. This is known as the *formal cause*. It simply puts the ideas of a good government and how it should be run on paper. This is arguably the most important of the causes because Aristotle believes where there is no constitution there is no government. Unless the rights and rules are put into writing the citizens are subject to arbitrary rule. Aristotle solves the issue of who would create the constitution by prescribing an *efficient cause*. The efficient cause is the legislator, who will continually improve or amend the constitution. The legislators are an important part of his political theory because the constitution will in one way or another reflect the virtues of the writers. A good constitution will reflect good men and vice versa. When these three causes are carried out with the utmost precision, they will undoubtedly result in a fourth and *final cause*, that being a good government. Thus Aristotle prescribes a four step blueprint for creating a strong and lasting government.

CONCLUSION

The great Aristotle was more than simply a political philosopher, he was a scientist. Therefore he can easily be considered as the founding father of the term political science. His writings paved the way for viewing politics through the lens of the scientific method. This is demonstrated by his seminal classification of regimes into good and bad based on who benefits. Despite being a student of Plato's Academy, Aristotle went on to establish his own school called the *Lyceum*. Students of the Lyceum, who were known as Peripatetics, believed in a philosophy made of both form and matter which was contrary to the Academy that only paid attention to the former. In other words, Aristotle's followers supported a *hylomorphic* political theory.

With a perspective of human nature in mind based on observation, Aristotle set reasonable guidelines for how human beings can be governed. He gave people of the world a set of classical writings which continue to influence justice in the 21st century. He believed humans need both objective laws and judges to govern their behavior. Human beings may not be good mediators in their own affairs but are quite capable of judging the conflicts between others. By adding a *corporeal* side to Plato's spiritual philosophy, Aristotle engineered a political theory which allows man to be the political animal he truly is within the context of the complex and constantly changing society in which we live.

SUMMARY

1. Aristotle was Plato's most famous student at the Academy.

2. He founded his own school called the Lyceum.

3. Aristotle referred to the execution of Socrates as a crime against philosophy.

4. He deemed political science as the master science because it incorporates all other sciences.

5. He believed virtue consists of finding a golden mean between two vices.

6. Aristotle believed man is by nature a political animal and that he needs a community to live well.

7. He believed people are naturally born either as masters or slaves.

SECTION REVIEW

KEY TERMS

A priori
Corporeal
Corrective justice
Distributive justice
Efficient cause
Empirical
Epicureans
Equity
Final cause
Formal cause
Golden mean
Hylomorphic
Lyceum
Material cause
Peripatetics
Polis
Political animal
Reciprocal justice
Regimes

CRITICAL THINKING

• According to Aristotle, why is political science the master science?

• Explain the golden mean.

• How does Aristotle's idea of happiness differ from that of the Epicureans?

• According to Aristotle, why is it preferable for humans to abide by the law?

• List the three authentic and three deviant forms of government.

• Define the four causes of good government.

ROMAN ERA

CICERO

"To be diverted from public service...is the denial of one's duty."

CICERO

BACKGROUND

It is difficult to find anyone in the history of politics that blended philosophy and public service better than Cicero. Born into a humble family, he soon worked his way up into Rome's most aristocratic circles. To say Cicero was multi-talented would be an understatement. He was a gifted orator, politician, lawyer and philosopher. His admiration for **Hellenistic** or Greek philosophy was so great that he translated authors such as Plato and Aristotle into Latin so they could be read by his fellow Romans.

Cicero lived during both the good and bad times of the Roman Empire. Early in his life he became one of the biggest supporters of **republican government**. This sentiment would last his entire life. This obsession with republicanism was especially evident when Rome deteriorated into the dictatorship of Julius Caesar and Marcus Antony. Despite his unparalleled patriotism, he was a staunch critic of corruption within the ranks of Roman noblemen. His writings are extremely reliable from a historical standpoint because he lived through all the events of which he speaks. Such works are important since Rome is the direct ancestor for western civilization and the empire which ruled an overwhelming majority of the world. The bulk of Cicero's teachings reflect those of both a contemplative philosopher and an active statesman. Indeed he believed that striving toward moral excellence means nothing unless it is done for the purpose of serving the public. "To be diverted from public service...is the denial of one's duty. This is because praise for moral excellence accrues entirely to the active life" (On Duties, 1.19). He stands as the closest thing to Plato's philosopher king that a government has ever seen. According to Cicero, a man of action is always preferable to one that passes his days thinking in private.
On Virtue

During Cicero's time there were three dominant schools of thought: the Academics, Peripatetics, and **Stoics**. He never identified himself with any single one of them. Nevertheless, the opinions expressed throughout his various works suggest he belongs to the **academic skeptic's** tradition which stresses man is incapable true knowledge. In short, man is limited to opinions only which can be more or less true, but never absolutely true. The closest man can get to the truth is achieved when each opinion is considered among all others.

A large amount of what Cicero discusses in his works evolves around debates on the three previously mentioned schools and their ideas about virtue, so understanding each of them is vital. The Stoics, led by their founder **Zeno**, argue that virtue is the only good in the world. Things such as wealth, political power and health (what Aristotle referred to as external goods) do not matter. Cicero's favoritism of the Stoic line of thought is evident in most of his works. For instance, he cherishes the frugality of the stoics, as well as, their assertion that man only fulfills his superior and godlike nature when he acts rationally. Aristotle's Peripatetics distinguish between moral virtue and intellectual virtue. Moral virtue has the goal of controlling one's pleasures while the object of intellectual virtue is to find the truth through the use of reason. The Peripatetics also believe that there are other goods besides virtue such as pleasure, noble birth and wealth. It is interesting to note that although Cicero subscribes to many Stoic ideals he actually sent his son for philosophical training in Greece at Aristotle's Lyceum. Finally, there are the Academics which eventually evolved into skeptics. Cicero shows enduring respect towards the Academy's founder Plato and often calls him "the philosopher."

THE OBLIGATIONS OF MAN

In Cicero's *magnus opus* *On Duties* he holds that there is never a conflict between what is honorable and what is useful: "Good men do not habitually [let the honorable be confused with the useful]...It is absolutely disgraceful not merely to rate the apparently useful higher than the honorable, but even to compare the two and to hesitate between them" (3.18). With ideas such as this, it is no wonder that Cicero's work has become a cornerstone for Christian ethics. He bases his assertions on the Stoic virtues of wisdom, justice, generosity and courage.

When a philosopher searches for the truth, it should not hold him back from serving the public. Such a view on the nature and purpose of wisdom only strengthens his opinion that thinking means nothing without doing. He says there are two common errors in attaining the truth: too much faith without enough proof and wasting too much time on thinking.

In Cicero's political theory, justice has two principles: harm another only when harmed first and public property must serve the public and private property must be kept private. According to Cicero leaders must focus on the welfare of the republic res publica rather than on themselves. In his *Hortensius*, he argues that all empires are primarily destroyed by internal corruption. These thoughts on justice reflect Cicero's staunch conservatism. He lays out a series of requirements to define what justifies one's claim to private property: "Private property has been endowed not by nature, but by longstanding occupancy in the case of those who settled long ago on empty land; or by victory in the case of those who gained it in war; or by law or bargain or contract or lot" (1.21). The question as to which of the justifications is given first priority is left unanswered. In the end, justice rests on good faith alone. However, this is not the same faith which he criticizes while discussing wisdom; faith in the latter sense means simply for one to keep their promises and hold good on all contracts entered willfully. As far as injustice goes, Cicero enumerates two forms: that of a person harming another without being harmed first and that done by people who fail to protect a victim from injustice when possible. In order to give weight to the second form of injustice, he recites Plato's remark on philosophers' common dereliction because of a tendency to abandon the people around them. This idea can easily be considered as one of the first proclamations of criminal negligence, a charge frequently used in *litigation* today.

Being generous is natural to man's character and according to Cicero it means doing people favors and repaying them; thus both the benefactor and the recipient have mutual obligations to each other. Despite the importance he attaches to generosity, he admits it is a virtue which needs strict rules to govern it. First, a man looking to do a favor for someone else must not do it out of flattery so that the receiver's character is not hurt. Secondly, the benefactor should not give so much that he hurts himself. Finally, the benefactor should evaluate the recipient's merit and how close the tie is between himself and the other man. Cicero maintains that value should be assigned based on how long a person has been a friend rather than the intensity of their affection. Nevertheless, the best use of generosity is to help the person in the greatest need. The unity of a state is maintained not by people giving to those from whom they expect the largest return on investment, but by assisting those whose survival requires that which someone else can spare.

The last political virtue Cicero mentions is courage. His definition of courage means not only to find a golden mean like Aristotle speaks of but to rid the world of injustice: "We must account as courageous and high-souled not those who inflict injustice, but those who banish it" (1.65). He notes that being courageous generally requires a man to have a lofty spirit; however, the lofty spirit has the potential to make a person degenerate into someone who only cares about fame. This is detrimental to a person's character because if they enjoy fame too much it leads to unjust deeds. So, the statesman must be able to check his hunger for fame by maintaining temperance in order to rule a state justly. Also, the courageous man will feel that he can overcome any obstacles in his way. Base pleasures such as greed, wealth and glory will not entice him to commit an unjust act. All in all, Cicero's political virtues are testament to his profound respect for the Stoics who believe when a man strives towards perfection he will be completely indifferent to external goods.

CONSTITUTIONAL THEORY

Cicero puts forth some of his best opinions on different types of constitutions in *The Republic*. *The Republic* follows in the footsteps of Plato by using the Socratic dialogue. The work represents more of an exploration of various forms of government than a political treatise. Remember, since Cicero considers himself, an academic skeptic it is important for him to express ***diaphonia*** or a variety of possible viewpoints.

Not far into the dialogue, Cicero agrees with Aristotle's characterization of man as a political animal: "The primary reason for [a public] coming together is not so much weakness as a sort of innate desire on the part of human beings to form communities" (Republic, 1.39). Furthermore, he goes on to recognize three simple forms of government: monarchy, aristocracy and democracy. He holds that any of the three forms are capable of promoting a lasting bond between a community and its citizens. Before arguing the case for each type of government he acknowledges their shortcomings. In a monarchy and aristocracy the people have too small of a say in their government while in a democracy the equality which is cherished by the people represents nothing more than inequality because it effectively disregards merit.

Nevertheless, according to Cicero, democracy is the only form worthy of being called a republic. The most important concern for a democracy is that its citizens have one and the same interest; discord only comes about when multiple interests arrive. He maintains that although nothing is sweeter than liberty, it must be kept equal throughout all of society. "Since law is the bond which holds together a community of citizens, and the justice embodied in the law is the same for everyone, by what right can a community of citizens be held together when their status is unequal?" (1.49).

Aristocracy, in Cicero's political theory, takes the "middle ground between the inadequate autocrat and the reckless mob" (1.52). It is extremely beneficial for a state to have men who can think straight and who are equipped with political wisdom. In an authentic aristocracy the governing men will be the wisest and most worthy of the position. However, this form of government turns sour once people begin to mistakenly attach terms such as rich and noble birth to aristocrat. Once the people conjure up such thoughts they begin to envision not an aristocracy but an oligarchy. Thus a good form of government becomes corrupted.

The most choiceworthy form of government for Cicero is a monarchy. His reasons for this are few and rest on the Platonic division of labor. "The rule of one man is best, provided he is just" (1.61). He adds that a king should be as a father is toward his children; a state needs a moral father to guide it into peace and prosperity. Moreover, it is practically expedient for a state to have a single ruler rather than many; it is much simpler for one man to approve his own agenda instead of having to gain the approval of his peers.

This notwithstanding the limitations, monarchy is only the best of the three simple constitutions. In the end, Cicero advocates a mixed constitution, or a hybrid of all three. "A state should possess an element of regal supremacy; something else should be assigned and allotted to the aristocrats; and certain affairs should be reserved for the judgment and desires of the masses" (1.69). He believes that such a mix will invoke a widespread feeling of equality and provide long-term political stability. Not surprisingly, he cites the Roman constitution as the best example of such a government.

THEORY OF JUSTICE

Cicero is a strong proponent of *natural law* which suggests that every person is born with an innate ability to judge right and wrong. When a person commits an injustice they are cheating themselves out of using their conscience which is one of the greatest gifts given to mankind. He says, "Law in the proper sense is right reason in harmony with nature...All peoples at all times will be embraced by a single and eternal and unchangeable law" (3.33).

While denouncing legal positivism, he asserts that it makes no difference whether law is written down. It is impossible, says Cicero, to put law into writing because it leaves loopholes in the system and any man who wants only to provide for his own interest will break it as soon as he gets the opportunity. Indeed he believes that "justice is completely non-existent if it is not derived from nature" (Laws, 1.42). In short, law is only put into writing to serve someone's interest, whether it is a lobbyist, legislator or a king; just law is written not on paper but on a person's soul.

Aside from providing an account of natural law, Cicero's discussion of justice yields an insight into his just war theory. He argues that the good state will only use the option of war to defend its security or its respect: "No just war can be waged except for the sake of punishing or repelling an enemy" (Republic, 3.35). This idea reflects a typical old-fashioned Roman mindset and closely mirrors today's political reactionaries. Furthermore, he also believes in *otium cum dignitate* or that the only acceptable peace is that which does not undermine a state's dignity. An event which influenced his opinion on the matter was the way Caesar came to power. Cicero strongly believed that the Roman Senators were overly credulous and therefore were not able to recognize his secret ambitions to install himself as a dictator. The same idea draws much criticism from contemporary liberals who see it as a justification for *imperialism*. It should not be surprising that Cicero thinks in such terms because, after all, Rome was the undisputed superpower.

CONCLUSION

Cicero believed first and foremost that man's number one priority in life is to make use of the greatest gift of all, reason. As Rome's most enlightened and philosophical statesman, he considered it his duty to pass the same Greek teachings which impacted his life on to his neighbors. His strong support for a Republic led to his political fallout with the ruling dictators; he was only allowed back into Rome on the condition that he spoke in favor of the tyrants in power.

Perhaps his most influential idea is that of natural law. Undoubtedly, he believed that when a man's conscience is based on reason alone it has the capability to distinguish between just and unjust acts. A number of philosophers including St. Augustine and Henry David Thoreau later expounded on the idea. The idea of natural law still remains at the forefront of debates on the nature of justice.

The contemporary value of Cicero's writings cannot be overemphasized. Not only do his teachings stress the importance of moral virtue in public life but they also show that if a state is to survive the tests of time it must heed the advice of its most vocal critics. This means a state must not just pay respect to rights like freedom of speech but also have a willingness to have public debate and encourage a multitude of opinions. After all, the very same state which Cicero loved and patronized silenced him much like Athens did to Socrates. This proves that some of the greatest patriots a country has will criticize their homeland, not with the hope of bringing it to its knees but to save it from collapse. Rome's fall from grace and its treatment of Cicero should serve as a message for today's hegemonies that no state is exempt from a similar fate. Examination of Rome, as provided by Cicero, serves to spark more public discussion on the necessity of strong moral foundations and the study of virtue. Civil liberties such as freedom of speech, freedom of assembly and freedom of the press are essential for a democracy to prosper, but the same freedoms tend to cast a dark shadow on morality for fear that a society will fall prey to excessive entanglement with faith. The world will remain stagnant so long as a man of firm conviction and virtue like Cicero is absent. Nevertheless, the glass is still half full; if it is true that history repeats itself, then not only will some world powers fall but there will also certainly be leaders equipped with the perfect combination of virtue and public service. The world awaits another Cicero.

SUMMARY

1. Besides being one of the greatest Roman philosophers, Cicero was also a gifted orator, politician and lawyer.

2. Cicero argued that moral excellence can only be achieved in public life.

3. He did not consider himself part of any of the dominant schools of thought, but instead agreed with certain teachings of each of the schools.

4. Cicero affirmed that the good man is always happy and that anyone who says otherwise confuses short term and long term pleasure.

5. Cicero was a staunch conservative as many Romans were during his time.

6. He was one of the earliest proponents of natural law which was later supported by St. Augustine, St. Thomas Aquinas and Henry David Thoreau.

7. Cicero loved Greek philosophy so much that he undertook the task of translating many of the works into Latin so that it could be read by his fellow citizens.

8. Cicero's strong support for republican government led to many conflicts between him and tyrants of Rome.

SECTION REVIEW

KEY TERMS

Diaphonia
Hellenistic
Imperialism
Just war theory
Litigation
Magnus opus
Natural law
Otium cum dignitate
Republican government
Stoics
Zeno

CRITICAL THINKING

• Explain the importance Cicero attaches to actions.

• How does Cicero reconcile the conflict between what is honorable and what is useful?

• What are Cicero's two principles of justice?

• Describe the problems associated with written law.

• According to Cicero, what are the two reasons for justifying a war?

ROMAN ERA

PHILO

"*Ignorance brings death,
and education and instruction bring immortality.*"

PHILO

BACKGROUND

Philo, also known as Philo of Alexandria, Philo Judaeus, Yedidia or Philo the Jew was a Hellenistic Jewish philosopher born in Alexandria, Egypt. During his lifetime, from 20 BC to 50 AD, he witnessed numerous major political transformations and cataclysms. The few biographical details concerning Philo are found in his own works, especially in Legatio ad Gaium – "Embassy to Gaius", and in writings of *Josephus* – the first century Jewish historian and hagiographer. The only event in Philo's life that can be accurately determined chronologically is his participation in the embassy which the Alexandrian Jews sent to the emperor Caligula at Rome as the result of civil strife between the Alexandrian Jewish and Hellenized communities. This event occurred in the year 40 AD.

Philo used allegory to fuse and harmonize Greek philosophy and *Judaism*. His method followed the practices of both, Jewish *Exegesis* and *Stoic* philosophy. Philo's writings were not widely accepted among the Jews, Egyptians, Greeks or the Romans, because in his extensive works Philo condemned imperialism, sophistry and materialism, and, in short, everything which is ever so dear to any tyrant – a citizen of an empire. Instead Philo emphasized virtues, spiritual good and service to God, which in turn translate into an honorable public service and worthy, morally right citizenship. This being the core of his philosophy, Philo is quite similar to Socrates, Plato, Cicero, Early Christian Fathers and Orthodox Christian Theologians of *Georgia*, *Cappadocia* or Greece. On the other hand, Philo's writings are in direct and uncompromising opposition to the Sophists and to the empires which are comprised of them. Hence, it is not at all surprising that in Philo's lifetime his works were enthusiastically received only by the Early Christians, some of whom saw in him a cryptic Christian. Later his works were studied by theologians in the Orthodox Christian Church. His concept of the Logos, as God's creative principle, greatly influenced early *Christology*. To Philo Logos was God's "blueprint for the world", a governing plan.

Philo's exegetical writings encompass not only a human being's spiritual existence, but his social-political life as well. To him a man's spiritual life is inseparable from his political obligations to his native society – his fellow citizens. Philo sees an individual as a part of human mix, which is governed through political systems and comes with mutual duties and obligations. Philo's Biblical *Hermaneutics* and Exegesis focus on spiritual, as well as on secular aspects of society. Philo sees the Ten Commandments not only as a set of divine canons, but also as a legal instrument vital for a successful political government of a nation. Philo's explanations and interpretations are not only focused on Moses, as a spiritual leader of the Israelites, but they are equally attentive to Aaron, Moses' brother, as a political leader of the Jews. If, on one hand, Moses is gifted with divine silence and mysticism, Aaron, on the other hand, is endowed with eloquence and rhetorical skills necessary for political leadership. It could be said in all fairness that a reader with a keen eye, the mind's eye that is, will see right through the mysticism with which Philo has crafted his treatises and discern beyond the veil of symbolism a solid political handbook, which both, in its quality, as well as in its sheer quantity and volume, greatly surpasses Machiavelli, Marx, Rousseau and Hobbes combined.

EDUCATION

Philo's views on education are incredibly pioneering not only for his time, but for the modern era as well. Philo sees learning and instruction as vital parts of human existence, as well as the essential functions of a society and the inevitable requirements of social success, but at the same time he makes distinctions between different forms of learning. According to Philo there are three modes of learning:

1. Trade,
2. Encyclical knowledge,
3. Philosophy.

Philo asserts, and rightfully so, that trade is a necessity with which a citizen may physically sustain himself and his household, as well as contribute to the national economy. Indeed trade requires diligence and quite a bit of learning, but by no means should it be honored beyond its worth and in no way should it be called education. Trade is certainly a necessity, but it is also the basest form of learning, for its ultimate end is to sustain bodily life, which is inferior to mental or spiritual verve of a human being, whether in a single individual, or in a nation, as an ultimate aggregate of individual men.

Encyclical knowledge, such as rhetoric, grammar, geometry, engineering, astrology and many others are necessary for a political life of an individual or a state. Philo uses Biblical allegories of Abel and Cain, and of Moses' Temple to show this duality of human nature. He gives indeed a fascinating interpretation of the first slaughter in human history. According to Philo Abel was a pure-hearted and God-fearing man, who, in spite of his purity, lacked either political foresight to discern and to avoid political peril or the rhetorical skills necessary to win a political battle, if such a battle was unavoidable. Cain, on the other hand, he sees as a cunning Sophist, well skilled in grammar, rhetoric and other branches of encyclical knowledge, who drew unsuspected Abel into the battle and defeated him due to the craftiness and devious foresight which his keen, perceptive, designing, but an evil mind possessed in abundance. Such were the Sophists who plotted against Socrates; such were the Sophists who ruled the vast empires with their tyrannical deviousness in Philo's time; such were the Sophists who are in charge of the entire world order perhaps even today. And, most importantly, were not those the same Sophists, who with their learned demeanors, clever tongues and zestful rhetoric convinced both, the Jews and the Romans that the God himself, Jesus Christ was a criminal who had to be at once crucified?! Philo does not only present the problem – dominance of a learned Sophist over a pure-spirited, but naïve citizen, but also offers a solution. This solution, as well as the above-described problem is veiled in allegory and symbolism: Philo uses the design of Moses' temple and priestly attire to convey the political message, but only to the initiated. According to the Bible Moses' temple had two alters and the temple priest had two robes. The two alters symbolized two natures of a human being – physical and spiritual, which in an example of a state also translates into two natures – political and priestly, or secular and religious. Just like a single individual must attend to his physical existence, a citizen must also attend to the state's political existence and he will only accomplish this by learning the most necessary branch of education, which is encyclical knowledge, especially the rhetoric and the grammar. Now the two robes are used by the priests interchangeably. The plain robe is used to symbolize spiritual aspect of a man, which is simple, as it is closer to the perfection and the oneness, and the divine wisdom, but the embroidered robe is used to symbolize political aspect of a human being, which just like the embroidery is complicated and requires sophistication in skills. The spiritual exploration requires plainness and a priest "whenever it departs from human studies, worshipping the living God alone, it puts on the simple unvaried robe of truth". The political study requires keenness of the mind and acuteness of the outward senses: "for it is fitting that the wise man should be adorned both with the invisible excellences existing within the soul, and also with those external ones which are outwardly visible, and with prudence which is more valuable than gold."

At last Philo ascends to Philosophy – the purest and truest form of the lore available to mankind. Besides the above-described allegories of the two robes and two alters of Moses' Temple, Philo uses the allegory of Sarrah and Hagar, the former being the wife of Abraham, the latter – the handmaiden. It is most important to emphasize that Sarrah was the native, a Jew and therefore a natural match for Abraham, while Hagar was a foreigner, merely a handmaiden. Sarrah signifies Philosophy – spiritual education, which produced for Abraham the son named Isaac, which in Hebrew means "joy". Hagar signifies encyclical branches of education, which are necessary for political life of a single man, as well as of an entire nation, but represents a lesser good, for a man's spirit is superior to his body, like immortality is superior to mortal life, or true wisdom and education, which is philosophy, is superior to encyclical instructions, or like a wife, who is a native to a man is superior to a handmaiden, who is foreign to a man and serves only temporary use – philosophy is natural to a man, while rhetoric, natural sciences and other branches of encyclical knowledge are only necessary while he exists bodily, and therefore are not part of a man's true, immortal, spiritual nature. Hence, philosophy, as it is the only part of education, which has spiritual existence of a man and divine wisdom as its "subject" of study, is superior both, to encyclical knowledge and trade.

A PERFECT CITIZEN

Philo, not unlike Cicero or Orthodox Christian Theologians, is aware of a man's tendency to indulge in pleasure. Seeking pleasure for pleasure's sake leads to habitual harmful action, action – to addiction, addiction – to effeminacy and the eventual destruction of a human being, as well as of a state, as a man, instead of being the master of the world, becomes a slave of his pleasures and everything which is worldly. Such effeminate men left in charge of once successful vast countries or empires brought them to utter destruction – Egypt, Persia, Greece, Rome – they were all shattered chiefly because of the overindulgence of its own citizens. Cicero too feared that destruction of Carthage, which was Rome's greatest and the only significant enemy, would result in excessive ease in the empire and that Romans would turn to excesses and immoderate pleasures, which would eventually result in effeminacy of the entire nation and ultimately in its annihilation – Emperor Nero and the eventual downfall of the Roman empire were certainly good proofs of this theory.

Philo veils his theory in the Biblical story about Joseph: "And Joseph was brought down to Egypt, and a eunuch became his master, Pharaoh's chief cook." (Genesis 39:1). Here the Pharaoh symbolizes a worldly man made effeminate with indulgence in pleasures; the cook, who is also a eunuch, is a man who dedicates his life to fruitless labors of producing worldly pleasures, and just as eunuch is barren and unproductive, so are the results of pleasure – they bring no benefit either to a man or to his nation. Philo investigates the issue even deeper. He names three chief eunuchs who produce such harmful excesses for the mankind: "the chief baker, the cup-bearer, and the maker of delicacies". Drunkenness and overindulgence in food, as well as in sweet confections, demoralize a man and make him into a complete slave. In the best case he becomes an impotent as a citizen, in the worst – a parasite. It renders a man ineffective, who is no longer able to adhere to wisdom, and, in the result, he is also unable to benefit himself or the society: "For what advantage is there, from the hearing of the sacred scriptures, to a man who is destitute of wisdom, whose faith has been eradicated, and who is unable to preserve that deposit of doctrines most advantageous to all human life?" Such a man is dead as an individual, as well as a political member of the society.

Instead of indulgence in pleasures Philo commands men to devote their life to "leanness". He gives the explanation of the word "*Hebrew*", which interpreted means the "one who passes over and beyond" – the one who can look over and beyond pleasures. The word is also symbolized in the name of the Holiday of Passover – passing over the worldly pleasures. In short, Philo tries to convey the message that the salvation of the Jewish people, or any people for that, is only in temperance. It is temperance which makes a human being into a spiritually and politically useful and therefore successful man. Purposeful life, which can be only achieved with the denial of pleasures, eradication of the traces of effeminacy and toughening up – such is the road to personal, as well as political, national success. It must be mentioned that the similar view was shared by Plato and Socrates – both were proponents of temperance, which was entailed in the concept of Sophrosyne, ancient Spartans – the war-like and well organized Greek state, Iberians – the ancient Georgian state which, according to Greek historians, was even more organized and war-like than Spartans, as among the Iberians not only men, but women too were engaged in battles and politics, and Orthodox Christian Fathers who advocated and to this day still promote fasting and denial of worldly pleasures. Philo rightfully asserts that the true self-benefit, as well as benefiting the society, must be the primary goal of every individual citizen.

IMPERIALISM

Philo condemns empires and imperialism. He uses the archetypal microcosm of human history to show its evils – the Biblical story of Abel and Cain. Philo, not unlike St. Augustine of Hippo, asserts that an empire starts with selfishness. All it takes is one politically successful selfish man, a young tyrant, that soon first his family members, than his neighbors, his native town, his country and soon after neighboring states too are oppressed, enslaved and tyrannized in order to provide means for this man's bodily or spiritual voraciousness, which usually consists of, on one hand, excessive love of bodily pleasures, and on the other – fame and power.

Philo noticed that tyrants are proud of their sins – they boast of their injustices and evil accomplishments, for which, truth be told, they should feel shame: "And it is well for them to boast over and pride themselves, upon seeking for reputation from actions which it would be more seemly to hide and to be ashamed of." Certainly pomp and circumstance of today's vast empires or their loyal subjects who belong to exclusive, but decadent societies, serve as proofs of Philo's theory. After all, is not shame virtually extinct in today's culture? Was it not shamelessness that Friedrich Nietzsche advocated in his "Thus Spoke Zarathustra"? Was not shamelessness the staple character of his Superman, which later on ever so "benevolently" permeated the entire world culture via comic books and films?

Industry and growth, both, economic and political, are honorable goals, which should be desired, but achieving this objective by oppressing and enslaving others is morally wrong. And the tyrant is precisely that man, who can take up with violence such goals and by use of brutality achieve the perverted form of industry and growth – *Totalitarian Advantage*. It is difficult for moral, freedom-loving citizens to war against such immoral and sinister forces – tyrants, as it is difficult for peaceful, freedom-loving countries to war against such immoral and sinister aggregates – empires. Etymology of Hebrew names clearly shows the character of Cain and Abel: Cain was the selfish man who attributed everything to himself, while God-fearing Abel praised the Lord for all his gifts. Cain killed Abel. Such killing continued in Philo's time, and it continues still: freedom-loving men are enslaved by tyrants, free countries are terrorized and crushed by vast and evil empires.

Totalitarian Advantage has nothing in common with Competitive Advantage, even though both to an extent result in economic growth – the former is achieved by dishonesty and total disregard for morality, as well as legality, the latter – with honesty and adherence to moral principles. The result of Totalitarian Advantage is the narrow economic and political growth, growth of a tyrannical individual or the tyrannical special interest groups or the states, while the result of the Competitive Advantage is common good, as a person with such an advantage keeps contributing to common economic welfare of the society or the state.

CONCLUSION

It is impossible to comprehend Philo's political theories without having elementary knowledge of Exegesis, symbolism, mysticism and allegory, just like it is not possible to understand Jonathan Swift's "Gulliver's Travels" without the ability to discern political issues in sarcasm and, in a way, naïve fairy telling. Clearly Philo's political views are not for the beginners, but this should not deter students from trying to discern his pioneering theories, many of which are advanced even for our era.

SUMMARY

1. Philo was a Hellenistic Jewish philosopher born in Alexandria, Egypt. Biographical details about Philo are found in the historical writings of Josephus – the first century Jewish historian and hagiographer.

2. Philo used allegory to fuse and harmonize Greek philosophy and *Judaism*. His method followed the practices of both, Jewish *Exegesis* and *Stoic* philosophy.

3. Philo's writings were not widely accepted among the Jews, Egyptians, Greeks or the Romans, because in his extensive works Philo condemned imperialism, sophistry and materialism, and, in short, everything which is ever so dear to any tyrant – a citizen of an empire.

4. Philo's Biblical *Hermaneutics* and Exegesis focus on spiritual, as well as on secular aspects of society. Philo sees the Ten Commandments not only as a set of divine canons, but also as a legal instrument vital for a successful political government of a nation.

5. According to Philo there are three modes of learning: Trade, Encyclical knowledge and Philosophy.

6. Philo, not unlike Cicero or Orthodox Christian Theologians, is aware of a man's tendency to indulge in pleasure. Seeking pleasure for pleasure's sake leads to habitual harmful action, action – to addiction, addiction – to effeminacy and the eventual destruction of a human being, as well as of a state, as a man, instead of being the master of the world, becomes a slave of his pleasures and everything which is worldly.

7. According to Philo effeminate men left in charge of once successful vast countries or empires brought them to utter destruction – Egypt, Persia, Greece, Rome – they were all shattered chiefly because of the overindulgence of its own citizens.

8. Instead of indulgence in pleasures Philo commands men to devote their life to "leanness". He gives the explanation of the word "*Hebrew*", which interpreted means the "one who passes over and beyond" – the one who can look over and beyond pleasures.

9. Philo tries to convey the message that the salvation of the Jewish people, or any people for that, is only in temperance. It is temperance which makes a human being into a spiritually and politically useful and therefore successful man.

10. Philo condemns empires and imperialism. He uses the archetypal microcosm of human history to show its evils – the Biblical story of Abel and Cain.

11. Philo, not unlike St. Augustine of Hippo, asserts that an empire starts with selfishness. All it takes is one politically successful selfish man, a young tyrant, that soon first his family members, than his neighbors, his native town, his country and soon after neighboring states too are oppressed, enslaved and

tyrannized in order to provide means for this man's bodily or spiritual voraciousness.

SECTION REVIEW

KEY TERMS

Josephus
Judaism
Exegesis
Stoic
Georgia
Cappadocia
Christology
Hermaneutics
Hebrew
Totalitarian Advantage

CRITICAL THINKING

- Why were not Philo's political or exegetical views accepted by his Jewish, Egyptian, Greek or Roman contemporaries?

- Explain the reason Philo's exegeses were widely accepted first by the Early Christians and then by the Orthodox Christian Church?

- What is the science of Hermaneutics?

- Which archetypal microcosm of human history does Philo use to condemn empires and to show the harm and evils of imperialism?

- How does Totalitarian Advantage differ from Competitive Advantage?

ROMAN ERA

MARCUS AURELIUS

"How can a man's life be made worse by what does not make him morally worse?"

MARCUS AURELIUS

BACKGROUND

Marcus Aurelius was a Roman Emperor from 161 to his death in 180 AD. He was the last of the *Five Good Emperors*. His reign was marked with thirteen years of grinding warfare with Germans. It is unknown where he found time to write his philosophical thoughts, but most likely he did it by utilizing every free second he had during these grueling war campaigns. His work is not a philosophical treatise or a rhetorically charged discourse. In fact Aurelius was a *stoic*, a practical man who had little regard for theoretical twists and turns of human psyche, and as he noted: "I bless the gods for not letting my education in rhetoric, poetry, and other literary studies come easily to me, and thereby sparing me from an absorbing interest in these subjects". His work is a compilation of his own thoughts and observations on human existence, both physical and spiritual aspects of life, and, if truth be told, originally it was never even titled, which makes us believe that he never intended it for public use. It has been simply known as *Meditations* of the Emperor Marcus Aurelius and lately as *The Emperor's Handbook*.

Marcus Aurelius' *Meditations* is a book of self improvement, action and practice, spiritual guidance, moral direction, ethical norms, political exploits, social obligations and the natural law. It is difficult to categorize these writings, but it can be easily said that they are full of honesty and real-life wisdom, which have no match in world history. They are keen observations of life by a great man. They are contemplations of afterlife by an unusually humble mortal. It is a book of Christian virtues and values, yet Aurelius was no Christian. Then how did he arrive ever so close to the teachings of Jesus? Christian scholars claim that it was through Holy Spirit and Divine Mercy. Historians, on the other hand, assert that he was basically familiar with Christian and Jewish faiths. As for us, we may only unassumingly suggest that he was simply a truth-loving human, who preferred humility over pomp, life-long keen observation of life over a lifetime of dull reading, practice over an empty talk and theorizing. A human who is truth-seeking and true to himself will undoubtedly at some point in his life arrive at common wisdom with Socrates, Plato, St. Basil the Great, Thoreau, St. Ilia, St. Augustine of Hippo or Plotinus, and even with Christ.

SOCIAL RESPONSIBILITY

According Marcus Aurelius social responsibility should be the primary goal of a conscientious human being. Sense of social obligation stems not from any kind of political contract, which a citizen may have with the nation, but the other way around – a political contract should commence from social responsibility, as the latter is encoded in every human mind as a natural law, called conscience. Aurelius argues that compassion is a primal form of social responsibility and that any social contract should be based on this. How close this is to the Christian doctrine "Love Thy Neighbor"! But Aurelius goes a step further – he recognizes and understands the stark reality that humans become corrupt and often deviate from their nature by becoming evil, and, when that happens, it is difficult to have compassion for them. Still, he argues, that it is a must for a true man to be compassionate to the fellow human being, even if this being is an ingrate, a liar, a schemer, a man with changed nature, an evil man in short, as wrong doers are still brothers to a good man via natural kinship. In fact, he prepares every good man for such a difficulty and, without any illusions of wishful idealism, warns them against such an intricate complexity of compassion and asserts that evil people who require compassion of good have become bad only due to ignorance of good and bad, otherwise they are naturally good too. For Aurelius there is only one way to start a day: "First thing every morning tell yourself: today I am going to meet a busybody, an ingrate, a bully, a liar, a schemer, and a boor. Ignorance of good and evil has made them what they are. But I know that the good is by nature beautiful and the bad ugly, and I know that these wrong-doers are by nature my brothers. To work against one another is contrary to nature, and what could be more like working against someone than resenting or abandoning him?" It is difficult to argue of Aurelius' Christianity, but after these words it is impossible not to see Christ by Holy Spirit in him, for how alike are his words to the most essential Christian prayer: "...and forgive us our trespasses, as we forgive those who trespass against us."

ON MORAL LIFE

Marcus Aurelius believes that a man's personal goal should be to become moral. Man's morality is what keeps him closest to his nature – human compassion, and his nature, in other words, compassion, is what keeps him closest to God. He argues that, for the sake of preserving his morality and remaining unwaveringly good, a man should endure patiently everything that life throws at him, and that the only true privation is moral privation: "Besides, how can a man's life be made worse by what does not make him morally worse?"

Aurelius looks at life as a moral resource to do good whether it is good for one's neighbor, country or humanity. He knows that life is all a man has to lose, so, if it is lost for a good cause, it may be considered as a small loss for a man. Yet, at the same time, man only has a life to live, in other words, only one lifetime to use for doing good: "remember that a man can lose only the life he is living, and he can live no other life than the one he loses". He reminds every citizen that one's days are numbered and one must keep a careful track of what is left, for time, measured in days, is a limited resource without which a human is no longer able to become good himself and to do good for others: "Don't act as though you'll live to be a thousand. Your days are numbered like everyone else's. In what remains of your allotted time, while you still can, become good."

REAL LIFE EDUCATION VERSUS READING BOOKS

Marcus Aurelius was by no means an anarchist who despised formal education, even though he writes strongly against overdoing anything, including reading books. Proof of his devotion to good education is in the very first page of his book, where he thanks his great-grandfather for having enough funds to hire private tutors for Aurelius instead of dragging him through public schools, where education was poor and learning scarce. At the end he adds that money spent on education is the best investment one can make: "I... learned that one cannot spend too much money on such things." Yet, as was earlier mentioned, Aurelius did not particularly like poetry, fiction and rhetoric, as these usually absorb too much human attention, disaffiliate a man from the real life and make him dormant and practically paralyzed for life.

Marcus Aurelius recognized the dominance of natural law in human existence and realized that a man's soul with its conscience and consciousness can contemplate and naturally arrive to many, if not all virtues and wisdom. He saw thinking as a natural ability which must be given enough room to exercise freely, and that over-reading subdues and eventually exterminates such a natural gift in men, but this realization came to Aurelius only due to his thorough knowledge of human existence in general and because he was a human himself, for a man is nothing more than a spirit, body and mind, and that anything added to it is against its nature: "What am I but a little flesh, a little breath, and the thinking part that rules the whole? Forget your books! They aren't any part of you."

Marcus Aurelius was a realist all his life. He practiced what he studied and theorized. He saw purpose in every action and never acted without a definitive aim. He saw purpose in learning too and purposeless learning he considered to be senseless. He asked, what is purpose of all learning except doing what is good? How can one do what is good, on the other hand, without an action? So the ultimate target of education must be good and beneficial action, not the developing of academic theories and pursuing vain debates and discussions. Any education which does not accomplish this, that is practical action, is useless and therefore harmful for human existence. Aurelius argued that useless books render a man paralyzed as they bring unrest and anxiety of endless mental dispute in his life, while action brings peace and satisfaction of a man's natural craving to do good for himself and for others: "Thirst no more for books, so that you will not die mumbling to yourself, but at peace, truly, and with your heart full of thanksgiving to the gods."

ON ACTIVISM

According to Marcus Aurelius, a man, with all his mental, physical and spiritual capacity, is designed for action, and there is no better action than social activism. Pain and pleasure should never hinder a man's activity. He argues that pain must be endured and thus life itself should submit and yield to the man's drive: "Be like a rocky promontory against which the restless surf continually pounds; it stands fast while the churning sea is lulled to sleep at its feet." As far as pleasure goes, Aurelius asserts that a man was made exclusively for action and therefore he could not at the same time be created for pleasure: "I'm getting up to do the work only a man can do. Was I made for lying warm in bed under a pile of blankets? Was it for enjoyment you were born?"

Marcus Aurelius envisions a hierarchy of the world and sees a man as its ruler. The role of a ruler is given to a man due to his unique ability to act with reason. Man, unlike anything else on earth, can act upon and influence all other subjects or beings. Aurelius envisages a man as the molder of the world, all he has to do is to obey his own nature and simply devote his time to activity: "Are you designed to act or to be acted upon …the work of welding the world? Why should you hesitate to do your part, the part of a man, by obeying the law of your own nature?" This is similar to how Spinoza describes a man as *natura naturans naturata,* that is, man as created nature that recreates nature by his actions.

ON SOCIAL PATERNALISM

In spite of an unwavering campaign for social activism and doing good for others, Marcus Aurelius opposes ***paternalism***, – a style of government or management, or an approach to personal relationships, in which the desire to help, advise, and protect may neglect individual choice, freedom and personal responsibility. He believes that one must do his utmost to help others and even use extreme patience when assisting the undeserved, but if the others are not willing to accept help or they hinder the benefactor from doing what is a common good and the right thing, then they become foreign and one must distance himself from ingrates of the kind: "I am obligated to do them good and to be patient with them, but if they prevent me from doing what I know is right, then they become as distant and indifferent to me as the sun, the wind, or a wild beast." Aurelius also recognizes the fact that some wicked people are simply incorrigible and therefore irredeemable. Their wickedness is their business and one must not sacrifice himself over such depraved individuals, and especially one must not use force to improve them, for often no force and no sacrifice is enough for helping evil to change: "To hope for the impossible is madness, and it is impossible for the wicked not to do wrong".

At one sight, issue of wicked being incorrigible does not seem to be of such an importance in the business of government or in a life of an individual, but it does bear a great deal of significance and important lessons. Aurelius recognizes that every individual is entitled to freedom and that entitlement comes as a part of human nature and it is derived from God himself. Taking away *freedom of choice* from a bad man is just as wrong as taking it away from a good citizen. A man must choose. Every human must decide for himself. It all seems quite simple, but in practice it is more complicated. It becomes difficult not to force or dictate when one is making a mistake. It becomes difficult not to force or dictate when you are in charge of a whole nation and the nation, due to its choice, its popular opinion, its utmost freedom, makes a series of wrong choices. History is full of instances, and especially modern history, when an educated man tried to impose his values, his rights and wrongs on nations and even continents. Communists always argued that paternalism was no *dictatorship*, and that their dictates were only for the good of the people. As we see, temptation to guide people by imposition existed even in Aurelius' days, but he too advises freedom of choice over the most thirsting desire to do good, because even the most well-intended imposing means depriving others of their natural freedom.

CONCLUSION

Marcus Aurelius is one of the greatest figures in world's political history, but he is even more outstanding as a human being, as a citizen, as a moral leader and a role model. His ability to think and act, to use theory and education for actual undertakings and exploits of the most benevolent form and purpose are worth studying, admiring and imitating. How was it that a man of such power remained uncorrupted with life's pleasures and desires? Or how was it that this truly learned man managed to foresee paralyzing consequences of over-reading and over-thinking? How did he manage to find time to write? Who did he write for when he wrote so cordially and humbly?

Today Aurelius' writings are studied by philosophers, religious scholars and political theorists alike, but, most importantly, they are still read by ordinary folks who have no pretensions for high offices or grand objectives, but simply want to become good and do good things for others. I strongly believe that Aurelius is of the most value to them.

SUMMARY

1. Marcus Aurelius was a Roman Emperor from 161 to his death in 180 AD. He was the last of the Five Good Emperors.

2. It is thought that it was sometime during his German campaigns, when he wrote a handbook of self-improvement and moral guidance. It was never titled, but today it is known as "The Meditations" or "The Emperor's Handbook".

3. Aurelius advocated social responsibility as the main goal of human nature and as the ultimate end in this world.

4. Aurelius' virtues are very similar to Christian doctrines. His love of humanity is close to Christian "Love thy neighbor" and his understanding of death as a natural and necessary event is close to Christian awareness of the demise.

5. Aurelius was a man of action. He saw education and theory only as means to action. It is with action that good and evil are ultimately committed.

6. Marcus Aurelius is an ultimate realist. He understands the difficulty of fulfilling social obligation and doing good when life is full of ill-disposed people, but he argues that nevertheless social good must be done, for even bad people are good by nature and it is ignorance of right and wrong, which causes them to transmute into something evil.

7. Marcus Aurelius believes that a man's personal goal should be to become moral. Man's morality is what keeps him closest to his nature – human compassion, and his nature, in other words, compassion, is what keeps him closest to God.

8. Aurelius assesses life as a moral resource to do good whether it is good for one's neighbor, country or humanity.

9. Aurelius' views on education are practical. He does not particularly like poetry, fiction and rhetoric, as these usually absorb too much human attention, disaffiliate a man from real life and make him dormant and practically paralyzed for life and useless for action.

10. Marcus Aurelius argues that the ultimate aim of education must be good action, and education, which does not accomplish that, is useless and therefore harmful for human existence.

11. Marcus Aurelius envisions a hierarchy in the world and sees a man as its ruler. The role of a ruler is given to a man due to his unique ability to act. Man, unlike anything else on the earth, can act upon all other subjects or beings. Man is the only *natura naturata* that can also be *natura naturans.*

12. In spite of an unwavering campaign for social activism and doing good for others, Marcus Aurelius opposes paternalism, – a style of government or management, or an approach to personal relationships, in which the desire to

help, advise, and protect may neglect individual choice and personal responsibility.

13. Marcus Aurelius is not only one of the greatest figures in world's political history, but he is even greater as a human being. His "Meditations" encompass basically all aspects of human existence. His philosophy is not just a philosophy on a topic or a theory. It is a multidimensional wisdom, proven by the author's action, as much as by his eloquence and logic. It is as multidimensional as life itself.

SECTION REVIEW

KEY TERMS

Dictatorship
Five Good Emperors
Freedom of Choice
Paternalism
Plotinus
Stoic

CRITICAL THINKING

- Explain Aurelius' conception of the social contract theory.

- What differences did Aurelius see with learning through experience and by books?

- Describe Aurelius' support for natural law.

- What are Aurelius' arguments for preserving freedom of choice even for the wrongdoers?

- In which countries can you still find political paternalism still in practice today?

THEOCRATIC PHILOSOPHERS

ST. AUGUSTINE

"What are kingdoms but great robberies?
For what are robberies themselves, but little kingdoms?"

SAINT AUGUSTINE OF HIPPO

BACKGROUND

For some Saint Augustine is a ***theologian***, – known as one of the earliest and greatest theologians of Christian religion. Indeed his writings are foundations of theological schools in both East and West, that is, in ***Orthodox*** and ***Roman Catholic*** churches. To others Saint Augustine is a political scientist, – known as an academic who analyzed, further developed and even preserved ***Cicero's*** thoughts and writings. Many see him as a rhetorician, who skillfully used and taught figures of speech and sustained and developed science of Rhetoric. To others Saint Augustine is a ***Neo-Platonist*** who criticized errors of the ***Academicians***, – students of Platonic school, and condemned faults of ***Peripatetics***, – pupils of ***Aristotelian*** school. To many Saint Augustine is the first autobiographer who, in his "Confessions", openly admitted his sins of youth and most humbly sought forgiveness of God and acceptance of the Christian church. And to others he is a historian, who cross referenced ***Marcus Varro*** and ***Eusebius***, and added and corrected ancient history. And yet to many he is a ***Biblical scholar*** who studied Jerome and analyzed Jewish, as well as ***Septuagint*** biblical texts. And then there are people to whom Saint Augustine is a bishop of the city of Hippo (modern day city of Annaba, Algeria), an African, who prominently represented all the talent and greatness of that continent in the world. In short, world history could rarely boast of true geniuses and extraordinary men like Saint Augustine. There is no gainsaying that his contributions to Christian Theology, Political Theory, Philosophy, academic thought, Rhetoric, grammar, science of history, Biblical scholarship and to every bit of the worldly and Heavenly studies are immense and even insurmountable.

POLITICAL FORMS OF GOVERNMENT

Although Saint Augustine in the most accurate and academic manner, without any lesser deliberation or elaboration than Plato in his "*The Republic*", Aristotle in his "Politics" or Tully in his "De Republica", describes all possible forms of government, both in theory and in practical examples, and not only in his contemporary examples, but in the most far-reaching historical precedents and contexts, nevertheless he believes in only one form of Government, – Kingship. But it must be emphatically stated that to Saint Augustine kingship does not by any means mean royalty. Saint Augustine in his "The City of God" shows a much greater appreciation of a man's free will and God's providence, than of the man-made system of inheriting throne to the worldly kingdom by hereditary means. In fact, he firmly believes that God himself, Heavenly Father as he is, with his omnipotence and by means of providence directly directs human affairs too: "Nevertheless power and domination are not given even to such men save by the providence of the most high God, when He judges that the state of human affairs is worthy of such lords." In order to justify his point further, he quotes an excerpt from the Holy text: "By me kings reign, and tyrants possess the land." That is not to say that tyrants are good, but that perhaps tyrants are best suited to certain societies, which have deteriorated to such common, but deadly sins as lust, avarice and envy. Indeed, societies so frequently digress in morality and so often become beastly by abandoning humane ethics, that instead of appointing a good king, according to God's will, by their foolishness and by some greedy person's evil desires, they are often taken over and kept under horrible dictates of a tyrant, as a punishment from God. To this affect, Saint

Augustine, being a holy scholar of the Holy Scripture thus quotes: "(He) maketh the man who is an hypocrite to reign on account of the perversity of the people" (Job xxxiv. 30.).

THE CITY OF GOD AND CITY OF MEN: HEAVENLY KINGDOM AND WORLDLY KINGDOM

Saint Augustine delves into world history commencing with Adam and Eve and Cain's murdering of his brother, Abel, and establishing the first City of Men by blood and fratricide and complete opposition of the City of God, which is peace and love. He then describes historical accounts of the first aggressor states of Babylonia and Assyria. He is the first scholar who not only accounts for the destruction of *Troy* and descent of proto-Iberian people, the indigenous population of southern European continent, its mixing with Greeks and Italians and the creation of Rome, the ascent of Greco-Roman race and Persian Empire, but, most importantly, he puts all these events in proper historical and *anthropological* context. He traces diminution of Caucasian race in Europe and subsequent Asiatic domination brought on by migrating Greeks and in these examples shows utmost differences between the Heaven and the World, Justice and Injustice, Peace and War. But in spite of these bloody historical evolutions and ethnic political turmoil, and perhaps in spite of the unjust aggressor nations' domination of more just and peaceful nations, Saint Augustine sees causality and God's vision. He firmly affirms that God, who has created heaven and earth, who has breathed life into human body and has given this same body to human spirit, this same God could have never abandoned human affairs on earth, be it a political or a social matter. He consistently proves that God is involved in social and political aspects of the nations and the world at large: "Therefore God supreme and true, with His Word and Holy Spirit (which three are one), one God *omnipotent*, creator and maker of every soul and of every body; by whose gift all are happy who are happy through verity and not through vanity; who made man a rational animal consisting of soul and body, who, when he sinned, neither permitted him to go unpunished, nor left him without mercy... – that God can never be believed to have left the kingdoms of men, their dominations and servitudes, outside of the laws of His providence."

HUMAN WILL

Saint Augustine, as much as he believes in Divine Providence, – the will of God, is a strong believer in the free will, – human will that is. He affirms that personal success of a man, as well as a political success of a state depends on freedom to exercise one's will. His idea of liberty rests precisely on an ability to exercise free will: "we will by free choice, in so saying we both affirm what is true beyond doubt, and do not still subject our wills thereby to a necessity which destroys liberty". Last words of this passage must be emphatically stated, as they have never been more relevant as in political and economic morass created by the increased degree of that same base necessity of materialism, which apparently also existed in Saint Augustine's day. And if necessity destroys free will, and the success of a political state rests on the free will, then necessity, this overbearing and ever-present necessity, also destroys a political state. Unlike Marxists and Socialists, Saint Augustine does not try to condemn materialistic necessity by taking away individual freedom, but to the contrary, he sees free will and its constant exercise as the preserver of social good and even of statehood, he sees free will as the means with which one can overcome necessity, as free will can induce exercise of strict temperance.

CITIZENSHIP AND INDIVIDUAL'S DUTY

The origin of government, according to Saint Augustine, is a logical consequence of the fall at Eden. Man disobeyed the law of God that was written in his soul at creation. That original sin was a rebellion against God's legitimate authority. The fall and the fratricide of Abel by Cain that quickly resulted showed that man had degenerated into a wicked, evil, selfish, conceited and ambition being incapable of being willfully law abiding. This compelled the introduction of public coercion, which is represented by state power needed for the maintenance of law and order.

Saint Augustine elaborates amply on the complicated issue of the relationship between an individual and a state. His opinion is that a state, as well as an individual, must live in harmony, not in opposition. He looks at this relationship as a citizen's willful and free partnership, not as a partnership by force, which not too long ago Communists of our era first tried to affirm theoretically and then even put in practice.

Saint Augustine's ideal relationship between a state and its citizen would be the one, which early Romans were instilled with. He quotes Sallust that in spite of many shortcomings, Romans were "greedy of praise, prodigal of wealth, desirous of great glory, and content with a moderate fortune" (Sallust, Cat. Vii.). Saint Augustine believes, and not without good grounds, that desire of great glory is what distinguished Romans from other nations and what made them powerful enough to dominate the world. Love of glory makes a citizen sacrifice his self interest for the interest of the nation. It makes man unselfish, and this unselfishness makes him brave against the state's enemies and caring with his fellow citizens. It even makes men die willingly for a national cause: "At that time it was their greatest ambition either to die bravely or to live free." This relationship between a citizen and a state differs from all other social arrangements, including the ones prevalent in Capitalistic states. During capitalism the highest value for citizens is capital, in other words, money. Glory, and intangible, immaterial achievements at best occupy a very insignificant place in capitalistic values. While a Roman citizen would die for glory, that is his personal glory, as well as glory of his country, a capitalist would call this action a *fanaticism* and, as adverse to dying as he may be, the only thing which could possibly motivate him to serve in military by free will, like a Roman would serve, would be some sort of compensation, in most cases money, either acquisition of the new or the preserving and protecting of the old, accumulated capital.

POLITICAL TEMPERANCE

As much as one may be inclined to accuse Saint Augustine of political fanaticism, when criticizing his ideas on citizenship, on individual's duties to the state and heroic sacrifices for the sake of glory and state, it would be almost an impossible task, considering that the very same Saint Augustine, without diminishing his belief in extreme patriotism and usefulness of the love of glory in order to obtain freedom for your country and the countrymen, preaches moderation and temperance in politics, as well as in personal affairs. He criticizes Romans, whose love of glory and bravery he greatly admires, when after actualizing their great and useful desire of glory, they often pursue domination, – excess of glory and vanity: "…but when liberty was obtained, so great a desire of glory took possession of them, that liberty alone was not enough unless domination also should be sought…." Moreover, Saint Augustine explores means of attaining glory. He strongly believes glory could be justified or condemned according to means by which it was achieved: "And what is meant by seeking the attainment of glory, honor and power by good arts, is to seek them by virtue, and not by deceitful intrigue," and by stating this ever so clearly and concisely he gives a definitive path to attaining not just Heavenly, but even worldly kingdom for a Christian leader. It must be mentioned that later, and admittedly much lesser in degree, political scientist, Niccolo Machiavelli, completely opposed fair and square path of attaining glory according to most honorable Christian doctrine proposed by Saint Augustine, and suggested every kind of hook and crook to our contemporary reader. But we must duly note that while Machiavelli's doctrines are composed in a way to ignore common good and to give best political tools for a political figure to obtain maximum power, in other words, while Machiavelli cares for one man's self interest to govern many, Saint Augustine, saintly as he is in his intentions as well as his name, cares for the common welfare and not for the welfare of a single selfish individual – a tyrant, he cares for many to be governed by a deserved one, and by doing so he also cares, and to a much greater degree than Machiavelli, for that One who is destined to govern, for governing by love and care is a better long-term strategy, than governing by self-care, which is usually ephemeral and unsuccessful, and ultimately results in the destruction of not just the common people, but of the governing body itself.

Augustine surely introduced a new paradigm into Western political thought after Rome. For him Rome fell because of its ungodliness and corruption, so any kingdom not based on Christian morality and fear of God will go the way of the Roman Empire. He argued that for an empire to survive and not to end up like the pagan Roman Empire, it must be governed with Christian love and fear of God. Since power comes from God, God's love is good for the survival of the state. Citizens of the City of God are at the same time citizens of the earthy kingdom of which they are residents. The temporal state must not jeopardize the ultimate goal of Christian existence. Hence, all rulers must govern according to the tenets of Christian love. Unjust kings and unjust laws are not acceptable in a Christian commonwealth.

CONCLUSION

It is difficult to discern how Saint Augustine managed to gain his ample knowledge, or even read so many books on diverse subjects, ranging from Theology to Political Theory, in his lifetime, which there is only one per person. As impressive as his erudition is, his humility and truthfulness are even more impressive. Many learned men throughout history and even in our days use their knowledge according to their selfish fancy and designs, and every so often, due to pride or *cognitive dissonance*, even endeavor to ground their expedient untruths on fundamental truths. Saint Augustine, on the other hand, always humbly offers academic factuality closely intertwined with Heavenly reality, whether it is in his personal "confessions" or the politically charged thesis of "The City of God" or the doctrinal book of "Teaching Christianity".

SUMMARY

1. Saint Augustine was the fundamental theologian in early Christian Church and his doctrines are still well in practice in both Orthodox and Catholic Churches.

2. St. Augustine found common grounds with Neo-Platonists, gave constructive criticism and thus reconciled Plato-Socrates to Christianity.

3. According to St. Augustine, the best political government is Kingship by merit of virtue and Divine Providence, and not royalty, which is hereditary, or democracy, which is misleading, or aristocracy, which is corrupt, or oligarchy, which is self-centered.

4. St. Augustine shares Plato's view expressed via Socrates, and asserts that political perfection is only achievable in The City of God and never in the Worldly City.

5. Freedom of choice is part of nature: Human will does not separately exist, and neither does the Divine Providence, instead human will coexists with the divine and plays a role in a man's success or failure.

6. A state and an individual citizen must live in harmony, not in discord and opposition.

7. Love of glory is politically useful for a state, as it makes its citizen to sacrifice his self interest for the interest of the nation.

8. Excess in love of glory leads to domination and, in general, political intemperance.

9. Love, social responsibility and virtuous leadership makes leaders successful in a long term, while rule by fear and domination, later mistakenly advocated by Machiavelli, sooner or later destroys the leader, as well as the state.

SECTION REVIEW

KEY TERMS

Academicians
Anthropological
Aristotelian
Biblical scholar
Cicero
Cognitive Dissonance
Eusebius
Fanaticism
Marcus Varro
Neo-Platonist
Omnipotence
Orthodox
Peripatetics
Roman Catholic
Septuagint
Theologian
Troy

CRITICAL THINKING

- When does world history begin for Saint Augustine?

- How is human will significant to the success of a state?

- How does Saint Augustine view a person's citizenship?

- According to Saint Augustine, what made the Roman Empire most successful?

- Explain how a love for glory must be held in check by political temperance.

THEOCRATIC PHILOSOPHERS

ST. THOMAS AQUINAS

"By nature all men are equal in liberty, but not in other endowments."

SAINT THOMAS AQUINAS

BACKGROUND

Saint Thomas Aquinas, also known as Thomas of Aquino or Aquin, was a Catholic priest in the **Dominican Order**. He was an Italian, namely Sicilian, and his genetic roots could be traced to Hohenstaufen dynasty of **Holy Roman Empire**. Prominent and impressive as this man's origins may be, his growth, development, cultivation of knowledge and scope of his mind, his legacy and his thoughts' constant presence in Western life, both spiritual and social-political, in short, the man himself is even more prominent and impressive. Much of modern philosophy in Western society has been conceived in an opposition or agreement with Saint Thomas' doctrines. **Thomistic school of philosophy** and theology influenced every bit of Western civilization inside or outside the Roman Catholic Church. Aquinas' achievements in Theology, Philosophy, Canon Law, Jurisprudence and even Political Science are impacting our daily lives and, by being further emulated and consistently considered by his succeeding thinkers, have powers over our very existence.

The works for which Saint Thomas Aquinas is best known for are "Summa Theologica" and "Summa Contra Gentiles." Summa Theologica, or simply Summa, is Saint Thomas' most acclaimed work, which he never finished. It is a textbook for beginners and contains all of his main theological teachings. Summa Contra Gentiles is a completed work and is usually classified as Saint Thomas' work on theological syntheses.

Saint Thomas Aquinas influenced many great minds even outside of the Catholic Church and he himself was influenced by his predecessor thinkers of both Christian and pre-Christian epochs. Although some influences could be ignored, one influence must be explicitly emphasized, – Saint Thomas was enormously affected by Aristotle. This influence is unique and rare. While a great majority of Christian theologians, such as Saint Augustine of Hippo, Shota Rustveli, Saint Basil the Great, etc. were more favorably disposed to Socratic ideas and to a greater degree agreed with Platonic school of thought, Saint Thomas was more inclined to Aristotle, who at his time was completely ignored and forgotten by the Christian churches, both in the Catholic and Orthodox parts of the world. Saint Thomas Aquinas not only showed his admiration for Aristotle and agreement with Aristotelian ideas, but he is widely credited, and rightfully so, for the revival of Aristotle and the **peripatetic school** of thought. In short, if the world credits Thomas Aquinas for developing Catholic theology, it must credit him for revival of Aristotle and reconciling the Catholic Church with Aristotelian school of thought as well, and the latter in a similar manner as Saint Augustine had already done for Plato.

THE LAWS

Saint Thomas Aquinas makes distinction between laws. He classifies the law into three categories: God's law, natural law and man's law. He tries to reason with the law, but sees that there is very little reason to be found in any of these three forms of law. He asks "Is law something of reason?" and quickly answers that "It seems that it is not". It is quite startling to realize that the law, especially man-made law, does not always appear to be logical and therefore does not belong to reason. The fact of the matter is that, it is not that the law lacks reason, but that the law does not even originate in human reason in the first place. Saint Thomas argues that law encompasses humans in a state of reason, as well as the state's unreasonable acts in human existence. Moreover, the law can be seen functioning in man's reasonable, as well as, unreasonable states: "Nor is it the act of reason, because then law would cease when the activity of reason stopped, as in those sleeping. Therefore law is not something of reason". And indeed that is a too obvious an example to ignore, – men sleep and their consciences are withdrawn, and yet natural law is in full force, political man-made law is still valid and the Heavenly law... well, the Heavenly law, according to Saint Thomas, never stops to be fully active.

Saint Thomas Aquinas, seeing no correlation between reason and law, then tries to explore the notion of the law in some other quality of a man and nature. He is well aware of the one power which is common among divine, natural and political laws, – the power to make things or beings act in a certain determined way according to the nature of the thing or the being and according to the nature of the environment with which that thing or being interacts. Aquinas realizes that such actions are brought about due to certain laws, but the instrument of bringing them about among humans is will, and hence he finds that to act rightly is caused by law and carried out not by reason, but by will: "Law moves those subject to it to act rightly. But to move to action pertains properly to will, as is clear from the foregoing. Therefore law does not pertain to reason, but rather to will, as the Jurist says: what pleases the prince has the force of law". Moreover, Saint Thomas explores the etymology of the word "law" and discovers that law is a binding force, while reason is the rule and measure of human acts only, and so even if human acts, to a certain degree, are guided by reason, overall existence is guided by the binding measure, which is the law: "law [lex] comes from 'binding' [ligando], because it obligates to act. But reason is the rule and measure of human acts, because it is the first principle of human acts."

As a consequence, the overall organizational chart of Law for Saint Thomas looks like this: "And first eternal law; then, natural law; third, human law; fourth, the old law; fifth, the new law, which is the law of the Gospel. As to the sixth, the law of sensuality..." There is no doubt which law is most significant to Saint Thomas, as he says: "There is only one eternal law", and then again he links the eternal law with divine will, rather than with reason, and asserts this idea by invoking Saint Augustine of Hippo: "Augustine says in *On Free Will 30* that: eternal law is the highest idea, which is always to be complied with." So the ultimate law, the law to which every other law must conform, including our political and social laws, is the eternal law.

ARISTOTLE AND THE SCHOOL OF PERIPATETIC THOUGHT

Saint Thomas Aquinas' theology takes into full consideration philosophy of Aristotle, the philosophy of the earlier school of thought. Of course, Christian philosophy does not fully agree with the **polytheistic** philosophy of Aristotle, but, in spite of differences, Aquinas concurs with the Peripatetic ideas and even borrows some of the ideas for the purpose of advancing Catholic understanding of the world, society, law and ethics.

Certainly there are many common grounds for Thomism and Aristotelianism, but one of the most important ones is the order with which this universe is created and with which this very same universe functions: "As the Philosopher teaches in the *Politics*, when several things are ordered to one, it is necessary that one is regulative or ruling and the others regulated and directed. This is clear from the union of soul and body, for the soul naturally commands and the body obeys". And indeed, Aristotle's teachings are in perfect unison with Christian faith: if speaking in absolute terms, God rules the universe, then everything obeys his order and everything happens according to his will demonstrated in divine providence; and if speaking in worldly terms, a ruler rules a country and people obey, he gives orders and laws and the public acts accordingly, the supervisor directs and workers comply. So Aristotle and Aquinas had the same notion of law and order and hierarchy, which is present in absolute, as well as in worldly matters, in Heavenly, as well as in social and political affairs.

Although Saint Thomas Aquinas is eager to find common grounds with his admired philosopher and he tries to revive his image among the people of Catholic faith, he does not draw back from criticizing Aristotle, when Aristotle's views oppose those of Christian faith, and therefore are wrong and unacceptable for Saint Thomas. One such example may be Aristotelian view on the world, which asserts that the world had always existed, independently of God and without God's creating it: "If we suppose, in agreement with the Catholic faith and contrary to what some philosophers mistakenly have thought, that the world has not existed eternally, and that its duration has beginning, as Holy Scripture which cannot deceive attests, a doubt arises as to whether it could always have been". Yet at the same time, in an effort to be fair, in an attempt to seek and reconcile the conjecture with the truth, Saint Thomas tries to find common grounds with philosophers and share, or even learn from them, what are commonly held by Christianity and Antiquity: "In order to get to the truth of the matter, we should first set down wherein we agree and wherein we disagree with our opponents".

Saint Thomas Aquinas is compelled to seek the truth and if the truth were hidden in Aristotelian doctrines, he would advocate these doctrines and would even advocate incorporating them into Christianity, but when those doctrines of Peripatetic are wrong then Saint Thomas would seek the truth somewhere else. His criticism of Christians' blind refusal to accept Aristotle's truths, which are indeed truths found in Christianity too, is as sharp and laud, as his criticism of those Aristotelian doctrines which are wrong and lead minds of people astray from the absolute truth. He calls the idea of world's existence prior to God and independently of God not just an error, but an abominable error: "Were it to be supposed that the world could always have been independently of God. As if something apart from him could be eternal and unmade by him, this would be an abominable error, not only in the eyes of faith, but also among the philosophers."

CONCLUSION

Saint Thomas Aquinas' legacy is truly immense. Virtuous theology expressed in his writings has affected a great deal of human existence to a great extent. Today some even claim that Saint Thomas' doctrines could be used to oppose harmful consequences of modern *utilitarianism* and Kantian *deontology*. More importantly, he is widely considered, and rightfully so, to be the developer and the climax of Catholic theology. His findings on laws, political theory and the conjunction in which social life and afterlife are bound, his unique interpretations of philosophy of *Antiquity*, especially of Aristotle, his overall influence on modern minds and modern thinker, both within and without Catholic faith... all and everything he has done, his persona itself is immense and great. "The Dumb Ox" as some of his contemporaries wrongfully called him and as *G.K.*

Chesterton often fondly and respectfully labeled him with, produced influence on the world of truly immense significance and enormous measure. Today, even when some speak against the Catholic Church or against Christian faith in general, they have a hard time speaking against Saint Thomas Aquinas and his theology on his God, which he asserted was the common and supreme God of all.

SUMMARY

1. Thomistic School of Theology serves as the philosophical foundation for the Roman Catholic Church.

2. St. Thomas Aquinas reconciled Aristotle to the Western Church: while a great majority of early Christian and Eastern theologians were more favorably disposed to Socratic ideas and to a greater degree agreed with Platonic school of thought, Saint Thomas was more inclined to Aristotle.

3. According to Aquinas there are three distinct classes of law:

    i.   God's Law,
    ii. Natural Law,
    iii. Man's Law (judicial law).

4. Law is beyond reason.

5. Aristotelian hierarchy of the subjective and objective nature, of the nature of a commander and compliant, of a ruler and a subject is shared by Aquinas and is exemplified in the rule of God and obedience of men, the rule of a soul and obedience of its corresponding body.

6. Aquinas opposes Aristotle on number of issues, including the matter of the origin of the world. Aristotle argued that the world had always existed, but St. Thomas maintained that the world never pre-existed independent of God. It was rather created by God and thus could not have preexisted before him.

SECTION REVIEW

KEY TERMS

Antiquity
Deontology
Dominican Order
G.K. Chesterton
Holy Roman Empire
Peripatetic
Peripatetic school
Polytheist
Thomistic school of philosophy
Utilitarianism

CRITICAL THINKING

- How did Saint Aquinas' political theory differ from his fellow Catholic predecessors?

- What are the three categories by which Saint Aquinas divided the law?

- According to Saint Aquinas, what human element makes law work?

- Which Aristotelian doctrine did Aquinas refuse to accept?

THEOCRATIC PHILOSOPHERS

AVERROES: IBN RUSHD

"Knowledge is the conformity of the object and the intellect."

AVERROES: IBN RUSHD

Note:

In this book we intend to present political philosophy from around the world. Humanity does not consist of only Western Europe or North America, and neither is human thought exclusively ubiquitous to those geographic regions. Philosophical ideas have been swapped, adopted and revised from one part of the world to another. Many scholars assert that Plato was familiar with the Torah before he wrote "The Republic", St. Ilia and Benjamin Franklin viewed the world in the same political and economic sense of pragmatism and "the Emperor's Handbook" of Marcus Aurelius reflects canons of Christianity and teachings of Jesus Christ. Some of these similarities may be due to coincidence, in which case they serve as a proof that all humans, in spite of their national or racial origins, are indeed equal, for they somehow arrive at analogous, if not identical, ideals. Some of these likenesses, on the other hand, are due to exchange of thought, which, not unlike commerce and trade, took place among the ancients and still is taking place today. In this light we intend to present you with Averroes, or Ibn Rushd in Arabic, – an Aristotelian of Arabic origin and of a very diverse background and very diverse knowledge and outlook on life. He is one of many representatives of the Islamic world who was well versed in Western thought and saw no conflict between religion and philosophy.

BACKGROUND

Ibn Rushd was an Andalusian polymath. Averroes is a Latinate distortion of his Arabic name and he is thus better known in the Western world. His background and origin, as well as his area of expertise, are most diverse. He came from ***Andalusia*** or Al-Andalus, – an Arabic name given to the parts of Iberian Peninsula governed by Arab Muslims in the period between 711 and 1492 AD. So he was an Arab who lived on the tip of Western Europe, loved Spain more than any other country, spent his last days in North Africa, practiced ***Islamic Theology*** and ***Maliki Law***, researched the science of medicine, unwaveringly believed in Aristotle and idealized Plato's Republic and after his death his writings influenced the greatest Catholic theologian, St. Thomas Aquinas, and Jewish philosophers, such as Gersonides.

Averroes' works are very valuable and offer a unique approach to philosophy, law, political theory, medicine, mathematics, geography, logic, astronomy and even psychology. Ibn Rushd was the last Muslim logician from Andalusia. As a physician, he wrote twenty discourses on Arabic medicine, which included seven-volume medical encyclopedia, "General Rules of Medicine." In physics he wrote works on the subject of mechanics and, more importantly, he was the first physicist who defined and measured force as the rate at which work is done in changing the kinetic condition of a material body. In politics he was a pioneering Muslim who claimed that men and women are created equal. He argued that men and women possessed matched aptitude and faculties, which made them equal in times of war and peace alike. To prove this theory he eagerly cited examples of female warriors from history of Arab, Greek and African nations. In short, Averroes' contributions encompass virtually every sphere of human endeavor, both in the category of physical science and metaphysics.

It is true that Ibn Rushd immensely influenced Arab and even Western world with his indigenous thought, but still his most significant contribution to human society is that he preserved and popularized Aristotle. It was Averroes' writings that led St. Thomas Aquinas to Aristotelian philosophy and physics. It was Averroes' writings on Peripatetic that was preached in the University of Paris and other medieval colleges. Averroism remained as the dominant school of thought in Europe through the 16th century, but Peripatetic, revived by the same Averroes, remains as the dominant school of thought throughout the world to this very day.

SECULARISM AND ANALYTICAL PHILOSOPHY

Ibn Rushd was devoutly religious, but he was just as devoutly a logician, who believed that analytical skills were just as important in human existence as faith. He saw no conflict between religion and philosophy, quite the contrary, – he strongly considered that both have one common goal, – to make men good. The difference, according to Averroes, was in the methodology: philosophy urged use of reason, while Muslim religion advocated use of faith. One of the most original accomplishments of Ibn Rushd is introducing analytical thinking in Islamic theology. In his work "The Decisive Treatise" he lays emphasis on the importance of analytical thinking as one of the main prerequisites for interpreting the Koran. This proposal was indeed revolutionary in his day, when *Ashari* theology was dominant in Muslim world. In Ashari analytical approach is almost completely disregarded and instead emphasis is placed on Hadith, which is extensive knowledge of sources other than the Koran. These sources are oral traditions relating to the words and deeds of Prophet Mohamed. Even though by all traditional schools of Islamic Jurisprudence *Hadith* collections are still regarded as important instruments for determining Muslim way of life, known as *Sunnah*, reasoning and analysis of the Kuran strongly advocated by Averroes has become a more dominant method of approach of texts in Islamic theology.

Advocating analytical method and lessening significance of Hadith is seen as the emancipation of science and philosophy from Ashari theology. Because of this, Averroism has been regarded as a precursor to modern *secularism*, and Ibn Rushd has been described as one of the founders of secular thought in Western Europe.

Law and Jurisprudence

Averroes' contributions to law and jurisprudence are truly great and immense. His approach to the subject of justice is distinctly unique, as it takes under consideration religious views and canonical texts. This consideration is not done on the basis of sheer faith, but it is rather based on reasoning and methodical analysis of the interpretation of laws under religious codex.

According to Ibn Rushd usury was to be deemed unlawful, except in a case of official credit. For this he cited Ibn Abbas, a companion of Muhammad, who never took interest in excess, as, according to him, the prophet himself had clarified that there was no *Riba*, usury, except in credit.

Averroes was one of the first to discuss concept of natural law in Islamic philosophy. In his treatise *"Justice and Jihad"*, as well as in his commentary on Plato's *"The Republic"*, he asserts that human mind in its consciousness has ability to know of the most fundamental unlawfulness. Natural law is so prevalent in human psyche that, according to Ibn Rushd, even an uneducated man is conscious of **Shariah**, Islamic Law, and its five **Maqasid** or purposes:

1. Religion,
2. Life,
3. Lineage,
4. Intellect,
5. Property.

It is arguable whether a man is conscious of any formal and methodically practiced system of laws, but one thing is certainly clear, that is, that all men have conscience and all men, deep down have a fairly good sense of right and wrong.

REVIVAL AND POPULARIZATION OF ARISTOTLE

The chief achievement of Averroes still remains revival and popularization of Aristotle not only in the Middle East or Europe, but all around the world, and not only in the medieval times, but throughout the world and throughout the ages. Just like his works, Averroes' approach to Aristotle and Peripatetic was quite unique and reflected deeply rooted religious traditions of Islam, which did not distort Aristotelian wisdom, but rather complemented it and contributed to it a great deal.

Averroes utilized the three levels of commentary: the **Jami**, the **Talkhis** and the **Tafsir**. The terms are taken from an Islamic methodology of interpreting Koran. Jami is a simplified overview. Talkhis is an intermediate commentary with more critical material. Tafsir is an advanced study of Aristotelian philosophy in an Islamic context.

Ibn Rushd wrote commentaries and analytical interpretations on all of the works of Aristotle with an exception of his "Politics". Averroes simply had no access to this book. Instead he substituted Aristotle's *"Politics"* with Plato's *"Republic"*, as the works are of the similar nature and treat basically the same subject.

CONCLUSION

Averroes' figure is truly great and yet his legacy is even greater. Some claimed that he contradicted the Talmud, which is a record of rabbinic discussions pertaining to Jewish law, ethics, customs, and history and it is a central text of mainstream Judaism. Others claimed that Averroism challenged Christian doctrines. Yet in spite of the criticism of Christian clergy and Jewish **Talmudists**, his writings were taught in all major universities in Western Europe and practiced in the Middle East even during his lifetime.

Legacy of Ibn Rushd is long lasting: firstly, because as long as there is study of Aristotle, there is Averroes; Secondly, because his personal writings are unique and overwhelmingly relevant notwithstanding the religion, ethnic background and era.

SUMMARY

1. Ibn Rushd, or Averroes as it is known in Latin, was a 12th century Arab polymath from Andalusia.

2. Averroes was devoutly religious, but he was just as devoutly a logician, who believed that analytical skills are just as important in human existence as faith.

3. In his work "The Decisive Treatise" he lays emphasis on the importance of analytical thinking as one of the main prerequisites for interpreting the Koran. Due to this Averroism has been regarded as a precursor to modern *secularism*.

4. Averroes' contribution in law and jurisprudence is immense. His legal views include the following:

    i.   Laws must take under consideration religious views and texts;
    ii.   Usury, or excess in interest rates on loans must be deemed illegal;
    iii. Natural law exists in humans in a form of conscience;
    iv.   Shariah, the Islamic Law, exists in Natural Law.

5. Averroes revived Aristotle and his school of Peripatetic, which was then virtually forgotten, in the middle ages in Europe.

6. Averroes, a devout Muslim and a devoted Aristotelian, had an immense influence on St. Thomas Aquinas and the Catholic Church, as it is due to Ibn Rushd that Aristotelian school of thought was preserved and later reconciled to the Western Church by Aquinas.

7. Averroes reconciled Aristotle with Islam.

8. Averroes' achievements are manifold:

    i.   Researches in medicine, physics, mathematics and other physical sciences;
    ii.   Contributions to Islamic Law;
    iii. Revolutionizing study of Koran by advocating analytical method;
    iv.   Reviving Aristotle in Europe;
    v.   Reconciling Aristotle with Islam.

SECTION REVIEW

KEY TERMS

Andalusia
Ashari
Hadith
Islamic Theology
Jami
Maliki Law
Maqasid
Riba
Secularism
Shariah
Sunnah
Tafsir
Talkhis
Talmud

CRITICAL THINKING

- Explain how Averroes argued for the equality of men and women.

- Explain how law applies to Islamic philosophy.

- How did Averroes contribute to the revival of Aristotelianism?

- Which Aristotle's work was inaccessible to Averroes?

SCIENTIFIC ERA

NICCOLO MACHIAVELLI

"It is necessary for a prince, if he wants to preserve himself, to learn how not to be good"

NICCOLO MACHIAVELLI

BACKGROUND

Few people in the history of political thought have achieved better name recognition than Florentine philosopher Niccolo Machiavelli. Machiavelli opened the doors to an entirely new political philosophy, one which completely disregards ethical behavior. Instead of judging actions by how virtuous they are, Machiavelli allows a good political goal to be an excuse for savagery. He is most famous for advocating a political theory based on the ends justifying the means. Machiavellian thought sets politics outside of the moral sphere, thus asserting that politics is *amoral* and not immoral.

A calm and orderly republic is the basic aim for many of his political stunts. Manipulating the populace is a tool Machiavelli supports to gain political ends such as a lasting government, national sovereignty and defense. Machiavelli was the first to speak of virtue in terms of expediency. He truly believed in using virtue to win the respect of the citizens so they can be used to keep a prince in power. His philosophy represents a complete break from all previous Greek and Christian thoughts. In fact, many philosophers prior to Machiavelli would consider his political theory to be a step backwards in terms of human progress. He essentially says it is okay to rule over a decrepit and morally destitute state as long as political stability is maintained. Therefore, the chief task for a prince is to prevent revolution and social change in exchange for keeping an everlasting peace in a state; improving the human condition is not a primary concern.

Machiavelli's most renowned work *The Prince* is a medieval masterpiece written during the Italian Renaissance. It stands today as the quintessential handbook for anyone aspiring for political office. *The Prince* is strikingly reliable since it is comprised of not only historical examples to back ideas but also because Machiavelli spent nearly two decades in politics. His career ended once Florence was conquered by Lorenzo de Medici. Machiavelli wrote *The Prince* while he was in exile as an attempt to ingratiate himself with the ruling regime. It was surely an exercise in sycophancy. Consequently, some consider the work to be a political satire because as a scholar who was not a natural aristocrat, Machiavelli couldn't have been truly sincere about the extreme ruthlessness as a means to perpetual rule, which he prescribed for Lorenzo de Medici. Maybe he was using *The Prince* to illustrate the ugly nature of ruthless dictatorship and how unacceptable it is. Nevertheless, it has stood the test of time and continues to be consulted by political leaders today.

VIEW OF HUMAN NATURE

Machiavelli takes a very harsh view on the nature of human beings. Nevertheless, it is one which has proven over the years to have a great deal of accuracy. He believes that humans are by nature selfish, greedy and stupid. In order to persuade the people of something, it must have an appeal to their self-interest. But even doing this can quickly become difficult. When people start to disbelieve what they have previously accepted as true, they must be made to believe again by force.

This immediately raises the question of whether it is better for a prince to be loved or feared. Judging by the aforementioned, one would guess that Machiavelli believes the latter to be preferable. This assertion is only half true. What he really advises is for a prince to be both loved and feared at the same time. However, he admits that in reality it is usually impossible for such an approach. The next best option, then, is for a prince to be feared. His reasoning for this is clear and concise: "Men in general are ungrateful...while you benefit them, they are entirely yours...but when you actually become needy, they turn away" (Prince, 17). Therefore, since the mass of men have no concept of love, which he describes as an obligation, they are incapable of serving their prince as well as he can serve them. Although it is choiceworthy for a prince to be feared instead of loved, he must be sure not to allow the fear to turn into hate. Machiavelli cites two things which a prudent ruler should abstain from taking so he does not offend anyone: another man's property or his women. As long as a prince follows this advice, the majority of the populace will remain content.

POWER POLITICS

A key for Machiavellian political thought is being stronger than one's enemy. Since Machiavelli believes in the ends justifying the means, a prince can never be too ruthless in attaining his goals. It is precisely because of this stance that Christian virtue has no room in his philosophy. In his view, too much concern with ethics makes a man weak and vulnerable to an attack. This position certainly is an antithesis of what is preached by Machiavelli's predecessors Plato and Cicero. Whereas such philosophers of the past imagined that a ruler has a solemn duty to act virtuously and honorably, Machiavelli insists that an ideal ruler must learn how to be sufficiently evil. "A man who wants to make a profession of goodness in everything is bound to come to ruin among so many who are not good. Therefore, it is necessary for a prince, if he wants to preserve himself, to learn how not to be good" (15). In short, a virtuous man will always be beaten by an evil man, so it is imperative that the virtuous man acquires the traits of the evil man.

While speaking of how to measure the strength of a state, he says, "It is necessary to consider...whether a prince has so much power that he can, in case of need, stand on his own, or whether he always needs the defense of others" (10). Thus he warns against depending too much on the help of allies. To Machiavelli, this is equivalent to leaving all of one's potential to win a war up to chance. He believes that the surest way to secure the defense of a state is to depend on oneself as much as possible. However, this should not be taken as if Machiavelli completely disapproves of outside help; it simply is a matter of maximizing a state's probability of coming out victorious. It follows that when a prince knows his own kingdom well enough he will consequently be capable of deciding how much assistance, if any, is necessary.

THE LION AND THE FOX

Ironically enough, Chapter 18 of The Prince opens with Machiavelli paying respect to integrity: "How laudable it is for prince to keep his word and to live with integrity and not by means of cunning...In the end, [men who are cunning] have overcome those who made loyalty their foundation." This observation leads him on to say, "It is necessary to be a fox to recognize traps and a lion to frighten the wolves" (18). Thus the *metaphor of the lion and the fox* almost completely sums up the whole of Machiavellian thought; priority is given not to what ought to be, but to what is. A prudent ruler will utilize a combination of the lion and the fox in practice. Machiavelli says that a prince that only recognizes plots against him or one that can only scare an enemy is not complete.

Surprisingly, the discussion of the lion and the fox comes about while Machiavelli is contemplating whether a ruler should keep his word. The inevitable conclusion here is that a prince must not keep his word if it will cause him any harm or when the conditions under which a certain promise was made change. This particular idea has perhaps been the most practiced of all in the history of politics. Time and again, the world watches in disbelief as politicians from all over the face of the earth break laws and pacts which they had previously agreed to in order to pursue a political end; when such events happen, look no further then Machiavelli for reasons to justify the outright injustice.

VIRTU AND FORTUNA

Machiavelli stresses the need for a successful ruler to possess *virtu* and *fortuna*. It is important to note that Machiavelli's virtu is vastly different from the traditional Christian virtue known to contemporaries. The most accurate translation of Machiavelli's virtu is skill or prowess. He suggests that a person with authority in a state must be a ruthless barbarian who implements draconian law to maintain order. A key example of this is his support of *authoritarian depoliticization* which can be defined as keeping the populace poor and destitute so they will not have enough strength to unite and revolt against the ruler. However, Machiavelli stresses the need for a ruler to balance these violent tactics by utilizing sound strategy in outsmarting the people. In his advisory remarks on how a ruler should ease the transition of a newly acquired state, he recommends that the ruler should keep the same laws and taxes which the citizens are accustomed to living under.

Having the right amount of virtu, however, does not mean a prince is equipped with all he needs to rule well. The second necessity for a prince is good fortune. Machiavelli describes fortune as a woman who must be beaten constantly to be kept in line. Although this is a harsh comparison, it is one for which he provides an adequate explanation. While fortune is out of everyone's control, it can be countered by being prepared for a disaster. This means a prince must be a dynamic being that easily adapts to change. A ruler is devoured by fortune when he becomes too comfortable with the status quo and is not ready for a disaster, which is sure to come. "I think it may be true that Fortune is the arbiter of half of our actions, but that she still leaves the other half of them, more or less, to be governed by us" (25).

THE ROLE OF RELIGION

While many historians argue that the decline of the Roman Empire was due, in part, to excessive entanglement with faith, Machiavelli thinks the opposite. According to him, a prudent prince will make sure that his state always keeps its religious foundations in place. However, this is not necessarily because he is a devout worshipper of any particular religion. He holds the position for practical reasons. First, he notes that an army is more manageable and willing to make sacrifices when it feels that it is fighting for a higher purpose. Secondly, keeping faith in high regard in a republic allows the prince to pass meaningful and effective laws. A prince who uses the *divine right of kings* as a justification for ruling and making laws will have a more favorable chance of the populace accepting his decisions without hassle.

Machiavelli is very critical of the Roman Church and holds it accountable for the lack of religious piety and also for Italy being divided, thus rendering it vulnerable to outsiders. He blames its leadership for setting bad examples for its followers. The lack of virtue and adherence to religious doctrines weakens the prince's ability to utilize religion as a means to bring about order in the state. Also, the fact that Italy was divided into several province each headed by its own governor, causes Machiavelli to lash out at the Church for facilitating the country's numerous occupation by invading armies. In his view, the Church should have either united Italy under a single ruler or stepped aside and allowed an outsider to bring the many provinces into harmony with one another.

CONSTITUTIONAL THEORY

Perhaps the biggest contradiction throughout all of Machiavelli's work is his vehement support for republican government. It is extremely hard to imagine how the same man who wrote the greatest authoritarian handbook of all times also happens to be a republican. Historians generally agree that Machiavelli's more balanced work *The Discourses* reflects his most profound beliefs on how the ideal government should be run.

The discussion of different forms of government closely parallels that of Aristotle; Machiavelli recognizes the same six constitutions that are enumerated in *Politics*. Also, he comes to the same conclusion as Aristotle in stating that a one dimensional government such as simple kingship or democracy easily deteriorates into corruption. Therefore, it is necessary to have a mixed government; one which blends all three authentic constitutions. Ideally, Machiavelli promotes a sort of *constitutional republic* headed by a prince who is held in check by the noblemen and people alike.

Despite the criticism many philosophers have written about Rome, Machiavelli considers its government to be one of the best examples in history of how a successful republic should work. He believes that the discord between the Roman senate and the citizens was very healthy and contributed to liberty in the state: "If one examines the outcome of these clashes, one will find that they did not result in exile or violence against the common good, but in laws and institutions that benefited civic liberty" (Discourses, 1.4). Thus Machiavelli stands as one of the most steadfast proponents of public debate. Furthermore, he holds that uprisings by the populace serve as important alternatives to show the government that it is overstepping its boundaries and must loosen its grip on power. As surprising as it may be to hear Machiavelli supporting revolts against leadership, he remains consistent with the thesis that the ends justify the means; no matter how much violence or bloodshed takes place it all is worth it as long as the desired political goal is reached.

CONCLUSION

No other philosopher ever attached so much importance to the ends justify the means as Niccolo Machiavelli. It is for this reason that his political thought is remembered in history as the epitome of *political realism*. His philosophy pays respect to what is, and not what ought to be; Machiavelli's ideal prince will waste little time contemplating virtuous deeds. Instead a typical Machiavellian ruler will use cut-throat tactics and as much unethical behavior as necessary to reach the purpose in mind.

The Prince provides any person aspiring for power an insightful and pragmatic perspective on how to hold on to authoritative positions. It is useful for ambitious politicians and any incumbent with devious ideas. Also, it has universal implications across the globe. After all, every corner of the earth has had its Machiavelli. Hitler, Stalin and Napoleon are a few from the past. To name some present day adherents of Machiavelli's mode of governance: Saddam Hussein, Hu Jintao and Robert Mugabe. Notwithstanding the harsh, amoral view that Machiavelli takes on governing, it has stood the test of time and remains a classic work of pragmatism and realism in political philosophy.

SUMMARY

1. Machiavelli served as a foreign diplomat in Florence for nearly two decades.

2. He believed politics have no morality and that the ends justify the means of anything.

3. He argued the only way to persuade someone of something is to make it appealing to their self-interest since men are naturally selfish.

4. Machiavelli asserted that is better for a man to be feared than loved since men are quick to forget any good done to them.

5. He believed that in politics good men must learn how to be deceitful.

6. Machiavelli believed in using religion as a means to make the populace easier to rule.

7. Despite writing a handbook for tyrants, Machiavelli heavily supported republican government.

8. Today's rulers continue to consult and practice Machiavellian politics.

SECTION REVIEW

KEY TERMS

Amoral
Authoritarian depolarization
Constitutional republic
Divine right of kings
Fortuna
Metaphor of the lion and the fox
Political realism
Virtu

CRITICAL THINKING

- How does Machiavelli's political thought represent a break from all prior philosophy?

- Why do some consider The Prince a political satire?

- According to Machiavelli, is it better for a ruler to be loved or feared?

- According to Machiavelli, what must a virtuous man do to succeed in politics?

- Explain the metaphor of the lion and the fox.

- According to Machiavelli, which two traits must a successful ruler possess?

SCIENTIFIC ERA

THOMAS MORE

"Everything will not be done well until all men are good."

THOMAS MORE

BACKGROUND

Many things can be said about Thomas More, but one word sums it all up, – "Utopia". It is hard to imagine a busy English lawyer relentlessly working on a trade commission in Bruges and negotiating agreements for King Henry VIII with Flemish Ambassador, finding time for dreaming up a perfect country and then putting this dream into words. It is even more difficult to comprehend that such a busy man involved in the very hub of not just simply worldly affairs, but in imperialistic concerns of the growing English Empire, still managed somehow to retain such a degree of idealism. And indeed, political philosophy of Thomas More is fully idealistic. Critics of More accuse him, at best, of wishful thinking, and some even go as far as to blame him for providing ideological grounds for the communist Soviet Empire. At any rate, it must be mentioned that the validity of such criticism is undermined by the very introductory letter to Utopia, in which More kindly warns his friend and the first reader of the book of such vile criticism of even viler men, calling themselves, on one hand, uneducated working class, who snub all the written word, and, on the other hand, literati, who look down on idealism, as they think it is lacking sophistication, – the very vile nature, which philosophers of ancient days condemned and feared, and which sophists ever so zestfully embraced: "Most people know nothing about learning; many despise it. Dummies reject as too hard whatever is not dumb. The literati look down their noses at anything not swarming with obsolete words". Therefore Thomas More's political philosophy is simple, but it makes sense. It is idealistic, but it is relevant to every reality, including today's. It is enchanting like a fairytale, yet it is true and not fabricated.

POLITICAL SYNCHRONISM: REALITY AND IDEALISM

It is true that Thomas More is an idealist and his political thoughts are perfectionist ideas, but this idealism is realistic, pragmatic and achievable, as it always takes worldly imperfection under consideration and synchronizes reality with idealism. More strongly believes that good people make a good state and that a state is not going to be thoroughly good, unless this first stipulation is met: "For everything will not be done well until all men are good, and I do not expect to see that for quite a few years." This idea is quite similar to the one expressed by Plato in his *The Republic,* where he asserts that goodness of all citizens must be strived to, although it is unlikely to be realized any time soon. Similarly Thomas More expresses the possibility of a perfect marriage between reality and idealism, between the fact that men in general are devoid of goodness, and the desire to make them good for self-good, as well as for the good of public.

COMMUNISM V. CAPITALISM

Thomas More's Utopia is clearly a Communist state, although it is not totalitarian like communist states of the 20th century. Moreover, More strongly believes in Capitalism, – industry and economic growth. The difference between Capitalism and Utopia is that in More's Utopia such industry and growth is devoted to public wealth and to social and common growth of the society at large, instead of individual gain. The author himself takes up a cause for Capitalism in a heated discussion and argues for certain strong points of private industry and capitalistic mode of life, which even to him at some point seemed convincing: "For how can there be any abundance of goods when everyone stops working because he is no longer motivated by making profit and grows lazy because he relies on the labors of others." In spite of this argument, he still supports socialism and common welfare, and believes that industry and hard work are just as present among citizens of a communist country, as they are among capitalists.

PRIVATE PROPERTY

Utopia is a country in which everyone has what he needs and no more than that. Desire of excess is greed and it is a ruinous practice both for an individual, as well as for a state. More loathes gold and jewelry, he sees no use in either, but recognizes the pressing reality of the majority of the public being fascinated by them and consequently citizens having a desire to obtain them. He comes up with a strange, but a viable solution, – Utopians use gold for shackling criminals and, because of that, social and consequently monetary values of this precious metal and its accompanying rare stones have dropped, as people commence to associate them with convicts and prisoners and start to dislike them and consider them to be stigmas of something bad and socially unpopular.

Besides gold and precious stones, Thomas More has well observed covetous nature of mankind and people's love of real estate. To him an Old English saying "my house is my castle" is nothing more than an abominable extract of greed and materialistic mode of thought. He sees dangers in human tendency of hording and even more dangers in human propensity to become attached to any kind of matter. So Utopians solve these social evils by rotating property on a cyclical basis, so that no one owns too much and no one becomes attached to his acquired good, especially the real estate, – Utopians swap houses and because of this practice they have become relatively free of materialism.

Granted Thomas More's Utopian anti-materialism may be a bit too much for any individual or a nation to bear and practice, as it is quite extreme and idealistic, but still one must admit that it has more than a grain of truth to it. It is a fact that in the past two centuries citizens of many wealthy nations have been suffering with overindulgence in material pleasures. Obesity, idolizing brand names and overspending are just a few problems out of a very long list, which have been caused by excessive materialism and which plague our free market societies today.

PUBLIC OFFICE

Utopians had unanimously passed their campaign reform bill long before Americans did it with a bipartisan support in the United States. Campaigning for an office is prohibited according to their laws. More believes that a public office is neither for honor nor for vanity. It is simply a duty of every good citizen to do public good and private motives should never induce a candidate for obtaining such a position. Public office is for public good and not for a private profit, show or vanity and therefore: "Anyone who campaigns for public office becomes disqualified for holding any office at all."

The ruler in Utopia has to pass the same criteria as any other public official, – he must administer in humility and be an equal member of the society. He must not be motivated with private gain of any kind to hold the office. His outward appearance must be plain and common. His clothes must not distinguish him from his constituents: "The ruler is not singled out by his clothes or a crown but rather by the sheaf of grain he carries."

THE LAWS

Thomas More was a lawyer by education and by trade, and he was very successful in the profession. He clearly saw social evil in unnecessary bulkiness and sophistication of the law. Volumes of laws and difficult language with which they were written in his contemporary England and continental Europe, coupled with high fees of a **barrister**, made full extent of the law and the right to a fair judicial system impossible to understand, it simply made justice expensive and unaffordable and therefore inaccessible for an ordinary citizen. On the contrary, Utopian laws are short and simple to understand, so that every citizen has time and ability to comprehend his rights and rights of others in the commonwealth: "They have very few laws, for very few suffice for persons trained as they are. Indeed, one of their primary charges against other nations is that endless volumes of laws and interpretations are not sufficient. But they consider it quite unjust to bind people by laws which are so numerous no one can read through all of them or so obscure that no one can understand them." Moreover Utopian philosophy considers a lawyer's profession dishonorable. More brands lawyers as devious rhetoricians and crafty interpreters of written rules: "they ban absolutely all lawyers as clever practitioners and sly interpreters of the law." Utopians, unlike Soviet era communists, strongly believe in freedom of speech, which, according to them, contains the truth in its simplest and most primary form: "They think it is practical that everyone should handle his own case and present facts to the judge as he would to a lawyer; in this way there will be less confusion and the truth will be easier to determine, since he tells his story without having learned any evasion from a lawyer."

Utopian law and its corresponding judicial system are impartial. There is no room for favoritism in either, for fairness must be a common value and everyone must have an equal access to it. More has a strong conviction that bias and avarice can ruin the best of states and such a ruin always starts in the judicial system first: "Wherever these two vices, favoritism and greed, get a hold on judicial decisions, all justice, which is the mainstay of the commonwealth, is immediately undermined."

INTERNATIONAL RELATIONS

Thomas More may be an idealist but by no means could he be called a romantic surrealist. His state of Utopia may be ideal indeed, but the environment is not. He knows that an ideal country still has to interact with not so idealistic and benevolent states, and that this interaction may be often imposed and frequently very violent. Even in today's relatively peaceful global environment it is a challenge to maintain international peace. Utopian society is well aware of such dangers and its strategy is based on self interests, as well as on a charitable notion to liberate oppressed nations and make the world more egalitarian: "They loathe war as positively bestial, and unlike almost all nations they consider nothing more inglorious than glory won in warfare. They are reluctant to go to war and do so only to defend their own territory, or to drive an invading enemy from the territory of their friends, or else, out of compassion and humanity, they use their forces to liberate an oppressed people from tyranny and servitude". Clearly this last notion is the notion with which America, may it be a capitalist country, is not unfamiliar. More commands a Utopian state to get involved in international affairs and help the oppressed nations. He commends intervention and he opposes political inaction.

CONCLUSION

Certainly it would be easy to argue that Thomas More's political philosophy is extremely idealistic and often impractical, but nevertheless it offers a fresh and unique prospective on political, economic and social issues which were relevant in his age and are relevant, if not pressing, today. It must be mentioned that in 1935, because of his humanism and deep devotion to Christianity, More was canonized by Pope Pius XI in the Roman Catholic Church and declared a *Patron Saint* of politicians and *Statesmen* by Pope John Paul II in 1980.

SUMMARY

1.   Thomas More was an English lawyer, whose legal accomplishments include working on a trade commission in Bruges and negotiating agreements for King Henry VIII with Flemish ambassador.

2.   More's "Utopia" is considered to be the first comprehensive thesis on Communisms. More is even credited with providing ideological grounds for the 20th century Soviet Union.

3.   According to Thomas More, good people make a good state.

4.   More advocated communism, but without totalitarianism, dictatorship and absolutism.

5.   It is more important to achieve social and common growth of the society at large than to attain individual gains.

6.   More believes that, on one hand, poverty is bad, but, on the other hand, desire of excess is greed and it is a ruinous practice both for an individual, as well as for the state.

7.   More has well observed covetous nature of mankind and their love of real estate, so his Utopians solve these social evils by rotating property on a cyclical basis, so that no one owns too much and no one becomes attached to his acquired good, especially the real estate.

8.   More completely opposes an idea of a political campaign, as he sees it as nothing more than a sophisticated form of ordinary flattery.

9.   More desired, at least in theory, to pioneer a legislative and judicial reform, as justice had become inaccessible for an ordinary citizen in his time, as well as in ours. He argued the following:

       i.   Laws are bulky and need to be made compact;
       ii.   Laws are written in a sophisticated tongue, so their language is hard to understand;
       iii. Lawyers' fees are high and should be negated.

10. According to Thomas More, war should be the last option and a state must resort to it for defensive purposes only.

11. More commands a Utopian state to get involved in international affairs under two circumstances:

       i.   When basic human rights are violated within a foreign state;
       ii.   When one foreign state is oppressed by another.

12. In 1935, four hundred years after his death, Pope Pius XI canonized More in the Roman Catholic Church. More was declared a Patron Saint of politicians and statesmen by Pope John Paul II in 1980.

SECTION REVIEW

KEY TERMS

Barrister
Patron Saint
Statesmen

CRITICAL THINKING

- How has the idealism in Utopia acted in the book's detriment?

- How does More use his idealism to counter reality?

- How does Utopia differ from real communist states, such as the USSR?

- What are some philosophical problems More has with a free market?

- Why did the Utopians forbid political campaigns?

SOCIAL CONTRACT THEORISTS

THOMAS HOBBES

"Covenants, without the sword, are but words,
and of no strength to secure a man at all"

THOMAS HOBBES

BACKGROUND

No one in the history of political thought has attached more importance to fear than English philosopher Thomas Hobbes. Since he was born during the Spanish Armada's pending invasion of England, Hobbes believed that he and fear were, in fact, twins. His innovative political theory came at the highest point of the scientific age. Hobbes sought to be the first to apply the same ideas of natural law which govern physics and geometry to politics.

Although Hobbes followed in the footsteps of his contemporaries such as Newton and Galileo, he can be credited with inventing a lasting and dominant political theory which still has great influence, namely, the social contract. In short, the social contract theory reflects a belief that government is artificial and comes about only when humans concede their natural rights for civil rights in order to achieve a given purpose. He argued that the concept of the sovereign or a king whom he described as a "mortal god" was created by humans out of expediency. Thus he was the first to clearly debunk the conventional deference to the divine right of kings. In Hobbes version, humans did this for their own *self-preservation*. He introduced the concept of **state of nature,** a condition in which man was wolf to man, *homo homine lupus.* This was prior to civil society when there was no order and everyone was out for his own good. So humans needed a king to protect them against themselves.

Because Hobbes bases almost his entire theory on human passions rather than incorporeal things such as God, it is no wonder he has been deemed over the years as the "beast of Malmesbury" for his implicit *materialism.* Even though materialism usually implies a *determinist* philosophy, Hobbes maintains that humans have a free-will but still choose to be ruled by feelings instead of reason. It is because of this that he believes humans are thinking most soberly when they choose to have a secure environment to live in over infinite liberties; personal safety is the *raison d'etat* which preempts all others.

STATE OF NATURE

Hobbes most famously said that without government life would be "solitary, poor, short and brutish." Unlike many philosophers before him, he does not believe man is by nature a political animal. Instead Hobbes thinks man's natural condition is selfish and concerned only with whatever brings about fear in life. In the *state of nature* man cares only about himself and how to maintain his property, elements such as sympathy and charity are nonexistent.

However, man in his original condition is so equal to his peers that fear is inevitable. "Nature has made men so equal in the faculties of body and mind...the weakest has strength enough to kill the strongest either by secret machination or by confederacy with others that are in the same danger with himself" (Leviathan, 1.13). Therefore, Hobbes' state of nature consists theoretically of an ongoing condition of war; every man is constantly looking for a way to obtain limited resources in order to survive.

THE SOCIAL CONTRACT

In order to secure peace among his fellow humans, man must endeavor to exercise his *natural right* which Hobbes defines as "the liberty each man has to use his own power as he will himself for the preservation of his own life" (1.14). The easiest way to strive towards everlasting peace is by giving up *natural liberties* for *civil liberties*. According to Hobbes, a man's natural liberty goes so far as to give every person a right to kill another in order to defend himself. Such an entitlement leads only to *vigilante justice* or every man taking justice into his own hands without consulting with a third party. This quickly becomes overbearing and anarchic since no man is a reliable judge of his own affairs. The need for a more objective type of justice gives reason for man to forge a *social contract* with his peers whereby he leaves the beastly state of nature for civilization.

The social contract gives way to what Hobbes describes as an artificial being – government. It is only through a government that man can strive towards his most fundamental and important natural right, namely, to seek peace and defend himself against all who do not. By electing a *sovereign* or someone who has authority to rule over a given geographic area the populace can ensure that everyone who breaks the law will face consequences. It must be noted here that without a sovereign power presiding over a state, the citizenry thereof will have no guarantee that every man will keep his word; therefore, recourse to fear is an invaluable necessity in any independently ruled territory.

Furthermore, Hobbes is quick to point out that when natural rights are given up they do not merely disappear. In fact, it is the natural rights conceded by the citizens which make up the power of the sovereign. Thus the state inherits the authority of the people to decide all cases arising from the breaking of a covenant. It is true that without a government justice has no meaning. By forming a civil society man creates a more powerful, though artificial, being than himself, one which has the capability to punish transgressors of the law by collectively utilizing every person's natural rights; hence the term *leviathan*, which is the name of a man-made monster in the Bible. In conceptualizing the social contract, Hobbes discovered a way in which a man can look out for his own self-preservation while simultaneously looking out for the good of others.

MODERN LIBERALISM

It is obvious that Hobbes believes man in his original state is not interested in helping his peers. His support for government to essentially force citizens to care for each other makes him the founder of *modern liberalism*. Modern liberalism says that all social and political institutions should serve the purpose of ensuring an individual's rights. In other words, government is the quintessential tool for a civilized and peaceful state. Modern liberalism is a big contrast from philosophers of the past such as Plato and Aristotle, in the sense that it makes them look utopian for having a belief that humans can function morally and economically without a regulating body. Modern day liberals believe that a larger government is needed for a state to have a prosperous economy and to maintain social equity.

The great fear of returning to the state of nature encourages man to accept each of his fellow citizens as equals. Once the social contract is in place, laws must be established to make certain that man does not regress into his natural state and break his pact with society: "Covenants, without the sword, are but words, and of no strength to secure a man at all" (2.17). This brings to light Hobbes' firm belief that humans are naturally selfish beings, capable of committing the greatest atrocities. Also, since man is ruled by passion instead of reason, he will always be engaged in incessant strife with the state. As mentioned earlier, Hobbesian political thought asserts that government is a sort of mortal god, brought into existence by men thus rendering it artificial. Therefore, a huge struggle comes into being between man's natural tendency to self-preservation and the civil laws which, while putting checks in place against the passions, they also guarantee a certain level of security for all.

THE SOVEREIGN

Hobbes' answer to such a dilemma is the creation of an all powerful sovereign. "The only way to erect a common power [which brings people into a civilized life] is to confer all their power and strength upon one man, or upon one assembly of men, that may reduce all their wills, by plurality of voices, unto one will" (2.17). To this end, Hobbes distinguishes between institutional sovereignty and acquired sovereignty. *Institutional sovereignty* is when a multitude of men agree to be commonly ruled by the same body. *Acquired sovereignty* is the condition of rule whereby the ruling body is in power simply because it has conquered the state.

While no man usually has a conscious choice to be part of a commonwealth and subject to the authority of a given sovereign, Hobbes believes anyone living under the protection of a government automatically agrees to adhere to all the laws in place. To put it simply, a citizen's obedience is exchanged for security. The sovereign has many powers to exercise such as making laws, the right to punish and to appoint whoever it wishes to carry out government functions.

Moreover, Hobbes believes no sovereign is ever subject to the civil laws since it is, in fact, he who makes them. Indeed, in his political theory Hobbes sets the ruling body above the rest of the populace. This merely reflects the absolute power a sovereign possesses in a state. In short, the ruling body can do no wrong and cannot be blamed for injury to its citizens since they have already surrendered their individual rights in exchange for civil rights. However, there is still one right of the people that may never be transgressed by the government – the right to self-preservation. This means the sovereign can never justly ask a man to harm himself physically or by depriving him of fundamental necessities required for survival.

FORMS OF GOVERNMENT

The optimal type of government in Hobbes' political theory is monarchy. The reason he gives to support this opinion is innovative and profound. Hobbes rates monarchy as the best possible government because it brings the private interest of the sovereign closest to the public interest. He recognizes that the sovereign is himself a man and is therefore subject to give in to his own passions rather than do what is best for the citizens. Accordingly, Hobbes says that by having only one person in charge at a time, the sovereign is most likely to govern in a way that looks out for the good of the people because he will have the greatest profit when the citizenry is prosperous and peaceful:

"The riches, power and honor of a monarch arise only form the riches, strength and reputation of his subjects" (2.19).

Not surprisingly, Hobbes believes the worst form of government is democracy. In a democracy the number of private interests is many and consequently the chance of the public interest being maintained is reduced. Since man is naturally selfish and constantly is on the lookout to make his own life better, Hobbes thinks it is best to have as few people share the power as is possible. Furthermore, he rejects the argument that without a democracy the liberty of the people is impeded upon. He believes those who support such an argument simply do not know the purpose of living in a commonwealth. After all, Hobbes' theory of government rests on the notion that if men are left in their natural condition of liberty, they will be detrimental to each other and cause nothing but harm. The cornerstone of the system is predicated on men being so fearful for their well-being that they enter into a social contract for security and to improve their self-preservation; liberty and freedom are sacrificed for mutual protection any day.

CONCLUSION

Thomas Hobbes' *Leviathan* is a revolutionary treatise in political theory. Hobbes was the first to find an alternative reason for government. He did not believe in the divine right of kings which dominated political thought up until his time, but instead invoked human passion as a new foundation for men placing themselves under the rule of a government. From all of the passions inherent in man, fear of a violent death and uncertainty for one's survival take priority over everything else. This fear which Hobbes describes is derived from a basic idea that all humans are more or less equal. Equality of ability, especially the ability to kill, translates into each man fearing for his life.

By submitting one's self to a sovereign with absolute powers, a social contract is brought about which has two main principles: one, to agree that whosoever is elected by a majority shall rule all, and two, to vote on a person or group which shall be granted the sovereign power. The powers of the sovereign come from each citizen giving up his own natural liberties for civil liberties. Doing this allows all men to feel a sense of security. Man's primary goal is self-preservation and by abiding by the civil laws in a commonwealth he is better able to attain it. Clearly, this is because anyone who intends to harm another will inevitably face punishment by the government for breaking the initial agreement to accept the protection of the laws. It is obvious that an offender will be more afraid of harming a person in a society rather than someone who remains in the state of nature since he will effectively wrong the entire commonwealth which consists of all citizens' wills in the form of a government.

Even in today's world dominated by continuous poverty, crime, hunger and seemingly unrestrained self-interest, Hobbes' political theory is near commonsensical. Everyone realizes that without laws and punishment imposed by a ruling body liberty would be at its peak; consequently a man's right to self-preservation would be very difficult to maintain. Therefore, government – an artificial creation, must be accepted as a necessary evil to counter the naturally evil disposition each man has toward his peers. Man must endeavor to be governed by the rule of law lest he should return to the degenerate condition of war known as the state of nature. Nature never seemed so ugly, that is, until Hobbes.

SUMMARY

1. Hobbes' political theory came at the peak of the scientific period.

2. Because Hobbes was born while the Spanish Armada surrounded England, he believed that he and fear were born twins.

3. Hobbes believed in a state of nature which predated modern civilization where man was naturally selfish and cared only about self-preservation.

4. He believed extreme equality can be dangerous, especially when each person has the equal ability to kill someone else.

5. He says man entered into a social contract in order to fulfill the need for an objective judge since no man is a reliable judge of his own affairs.

6. When a man enters into society, man gains civil liberties in exchange for his natural liberties.

7. Hobbes' sovereign had absolute power to do whatever he saw as necessary.

8. Hobbes believed that as a populace's freedom is increased, its security is reduced.

9. He based almost all of his political theory on a citizen's extreme fear of self-preservation.

SECTION REVIEW

KEY TERMS

Acquired sovereignty
Civil liberties
Determinist
Homo homine lupus
Institutional sovereignty
Leviathan
Materialism
Modern liberalism
Natural liberties
Natural right
Raison d'etat
Self-preservation
Social contract
Sovereign
State of nature
Vigilante justice

CRITICAL THINKING

- What new political theory did Thomas Hobbes invoke?

- According to Hobbes, why do people enter into the social contract?

- In the state of nature, why is extreme equality a reason to be fearful?

- Explain what is gained and lost by entering into a social contract.

- Why does Hobbes believe government is an artificial being?

- Why is Hobbes widely considered as the founder of modern liberalism?

- Why might Hobbes have given the sovereign absolute powers?

SOCIAL CONTRACT THEORISTS

JOHN LOCKE

*"No political society can be, nor subsist,
without having in itself the power to punish."*

JOHN LOCKE

BACKGROUND

Seventeenth century radical and political theorist John Locke was a controversial figure during his time. Following his alleged involvement in a conspiracy to oust King Charles II of England, Locke fled the country and became involved with helping other exiles. Before leaving, however, he had completed at least part of his highly influential *Two Treatises on Government*. In the work Locke sets forth his views on freedom and property while unveiling his own unique version of the social contract.

Locke belongs to a philosophical tradition known as ***empiricism*** which emphasizes the importance of sense experience on the human mind. While arguing against Descartes' theory of innate knowledge, Locke coins the term ***tabula rasa*** meaning "blank slate." He asserts the human mind knows nothing at birth and is waiting to be written on by worldly interactions; every experience for a person helps to shape their intellect.

The works of Locke are considered revolutionary for good reasons. Today's superpower The United States used his thoughts on the right to rebel as a justification to wage a revolution against the British Crown. How remarkable it is that an Englishman, of all persons, provided a precipitating factor for the enemies of his country to disobey their imperial masters! It goes without saying, then, that Locke played a leading role in introducing the most sacred ideals dominating contemporary political discourse.

THE SOCIAL CONTRACT

Locke begins his second treatise asserting that "all men are naturally in...a state of perfect freedom" (Second Treatise, 2.4). Out of this, he induces that all government is limited and only exists by the consent of the governed. Like Hobbes, Locke believes in a state of nature preexisting civil society. However, he differentiates himself because he thinks Hobbes underrates human intelligence to the extent that it is not dissimilar from that of an animal; Locke believes that man is ***res cognitans*** or a thinking being. Therefore, Locke's state of nature is not filled with the same degree of fear as in Hobbes' theory because man is naturally endowed with reason which allows him to be governed by natural law. This gives way to two rules which govern the state of nature: one, man is to preserve himself; two, man is to preserve mankind.

It is clear in Locke's theory that the state of nature is not synonymous with a state of war. He reasons that the same state of war which Hobbes focuses on in his state of nature is also possible in a civil society where the government does not do enough to mediate disputes between the citizens. Although Locke paints the state of nature rather benevolently, he maintains that it is best for man to join hands with those around him and create a civil government since man is not a good judge in his own disputes.

PROPERTY

One of the most commonly cited reasons for disagreements between men is property. Locke refutes the claim that all things are naturally common to all and that there is no such thing as property. He believes that such a condition is simply the original and must be improved upon for man to make use of what is naturally abundant. Property, then, comes into existence through the work of man. "Everyman has a property in his own person…The Labor of his body, and the work of is hands, we may say, are properly his" (5.27). Accordingly, Locke does not believe that property coming into being via labor will interfere with the property of others. "No man's labor could subdue or appropriate all; nor could his enjoyment consume more than a small part" (5.36).

Along with property eventually comes the invention of money. Money serves the very important purpose of allowing man to put to use his labor without an immediate usefulness. The truly useful, which Locke describes as items such as food and land, go to waste if not used within a reasonable time frame. By collecting money in exchange for labor, man may accumulate the ability to acquire what is necessary for survival, when needed, without having it spoil. Hence the creation of money enables man to save his labor already exerted for a future date.

THE ORIGIN OF CIVIL SOCIETY

According to Locke, man naturally is given the power to avenge wrongs done to him by punishing the transgressor. This quickly becomes problematic since all men have *self-love* whereby they maintain a certain degree of dignity and respect for themselves. This self-love will always prevent men from reasoning objectively in their own affairs. Consequently, the need for fair and unbiased judgment leads men toward civil society.

When this happens, man agrees to discard his natural rights for civil rights so that a political society may function. By doing so all adherents of the social contract consented to be ruled by the laws established by the commonwealth. The community becomes the ultimate judge in disagreements thus rendering the individual powerless in everything which includes a second party. "No political society can be, nor subsist, without having in itself the power to punish…Every one of the members hath quitted his natural power, resigned it up into the hands of the community" (7.87).

Every man who agrees to be ruled by the commonwealth also inevitably must consent to accept the decision of the majority. Without accepting rule of the majority, man would be in the state of nature again because he simply would be making judgments for himself; the entire social contract would be meaningless. "Every man, by consenting with others to make one body politic under one government, puts himself under an obligation…to submit to the determination of the majority" (8.97).

THE NATURE OF POLITICAL POWER

Locke believes strongly that Hobbes' idea of an absolute monarch is an unacceptable solution to get man out of the state of nature. In Locke's view, the political power of a state should rest within the laws thereof and not in the arbitrary judgment of a king. He thinks placing an all-powerful sovereign in charge of all of a state's matters does nothing to improve upon the state of nature from which man is seeking alleviation. His notion of rule under a monarch is identical to voluntary slavery, which no man can reasonably desire. Locke's main emphasis is on the importance of the rule of law since it involves no human passion. In this sense, Locke echoes what Aristotle previously said about the law: "Law is reason without passion" (Politics, 3.16.1287a33-34).

Locke's main thesis is that government is limited and exists only by consent of the ruled. In the ensuing social contract, to justify the power given to the government, it must, at least, protect life, liberty and property, the three natural rights of its citizens. In order to properly justify the sacrifice man makes when he concedes his natural rights, government must provide protection for his life, liberty and property. These three rights are owned by an individual and no one, not even the sovereign can may take them away. The advantage of having unbiased laws to turn to when an injury occurs, is never to allow man to take matters upon himself and avenge the offender.

Without a doubt, the most important branch of government for Locke is the legislative: "The great end of men's entering into society being the enjoyment of their properties in peace and safety, and the great instrument and means of that being the laws established in that society" (Second Treatise, 11.134). The ability to have recourse to the laws is the overall purpose of man submitting himself to a civil society. The laws of the state exist only because the citizens have appointed men to be trusted with the creation of rules to prevent man from degenerating into the state of nature.

Although much of Locke's exposition relates to positive law, it manages to attach significant meaning to natural law. The presence of civil laws does not force natural law out of the picture, instead Locke believes the two forms of law cannot only coexist but be mutually reinforcing: "The obligations of the law of nature cease not in society, but only in many cases are drawn closer" (11.135). Since the two laws governing the state of nature are for man to preserve himself and mankind, it is a fundamental rule that no civil law may transgress man's ability to carry out these two essential duties. Natural law and positive law are intertwined; positive law only carries a punishment for the offender.

THE RIGHT TO RESIST

Locke is the foremost champion of the people's *right to resist* against a government. He believes that a tyrant must be removed from power as soon as he begins to abuse his power. When a leader uses his power for any end other than the public good, he effectively destroys the government designed to protect man's property. The right to resist, then, is a means of saving a government's legitimacy, not its abolition.

Critics of the right to resist often cite the real possibility of the populace rebelling when displeased with the government, whether it is justified or not. Therefore, Locke is often looked upon as a catalyst for revolt and disorder in society. However, this is contrary to Locke's argument. Locke rather believes that those who invoke the right to resist are actually defenders of civil society, not its enemies. The purpose of overthrowing a government is by no means for the sake of man desiring to return to his original state but is a way of bringing about effective rule and good order.

CONCLUSION

John Locke was quick to realize that Hobbes' Leviathan did not recognize man as a thinking being; thus, a shift in the balance of power was necessary for government to work. He had a firm belief that Hobbes assigned too much weight to the element of fear and more attention needed to be directed toward human rationality. Needless to say, Locke took a much more optimistic view of human nature than his predecessor. Decidedly, he affirmed that man must give himself up to civil society, not so much because of fear, but as a means of addressing the need to defend property.

Locke attached more importance to man's property than anyone else. His definition of property goes well beyond corporeal goods and, in fact, includes two of the most highly valued ideals in Western civilization – life and liberty. Locke believed that man agrees to be governed by laws enacted in order to provide a sure defense against the unlawful taking of his property.

To this end, a government had to be constructed and given legislative powers; an act which Locke knew very well could put man into a condition of servitude. In order to avoid such an evil, Locke asserts that man has a right to resist bad government. When a tyrant usurps the power given to him, he becomes a liability to the common good; therefore, the people must act to salvage any government that fails to meet its fundamental duties, which is the protection of the three natural rights of its citizens. Locke's theory served as a counterweight to the absolutism which Hobbes so fervently endorsed. His social contract is viewed as a two-way contract as opposed to Hobbes' one-way contract.

SUMMARY

1. John Locke was a 17th Century radical who is said to have been involved in a plot to oust King Charles II.

2. He was an empiricist which means he emphasized the influence of sense experience on the human mind.

3. His works were among the most widely read by American revolutionaries who rebelled against England.

4. Locke believed Hobbes' political theory overlooked the fact that humans are thinking beings and therefore not capable of being so fearful.

5. Locke believed property rights are one of the most important reasons for government.

6. He believed that no political system can function without the power to punish.

7. He asserted that without rule of the majority the social contract would be meaningless.

8. Locke's main thesis is that government is limited and exists only by consent of the ruled.

9. Locke held that the populace has a right to resist the sovereign when the position begins to be abused.

SECTION REVIEW

KEY TERMS

Empiricism
Res cognitans
Right to resist
Self-love
Tabula rasa

CRITICAL THINKING

- How does Locke's theory of a blank slate demonstrate empiricism?

- What does Locke believe that Hobbes undervalued in his political theory?

- According to Locke, what gives a man ownership of his property?

- According to Locke, when is it okay for a populace to utilize the right to resist?

SOCIAL CONTRACT THEORISTS

JEAN-JACQUES ROUSSEAU

"Man was born free, and he is everywhere in chains."

JEAN-JACQUES ROUSSEAU

BACKGROUND

Although he was born in Geneva, Jean-Jacques Rousseau went on to become one of the most celebrated sons of France. His early life was quite rough, losing his mother almost immediately after birth and having to leave his birthplace alone at the age of only fourteen. As an adult, Rousseau gave up each of his children to foster care, an act at which his critics continuously scoff. This led Victor Hugo to write in his masterpiece *Les Miserables* that: "He abandoned all of his children, but in return adopted the entire country."

Many of Rousseau's political ideas are considered to be catalytic for the French Revolution. His belief that "man is born free and is everywhere in chains" (Social Contract, 1.1) illustrates his thoughts that government and society hinder man's naturally benevolent characteristics. Not only were his political ideas revolutionary during his time, but Rousseau was often at odds with much of Europe for his controversial thoughts on religion and the corrupting influence of culture or civilization. Nevertheless, he stands today next to Voltaire and Diderot as one of the three greatest philosophers of the *enlightenment.*

NATURAL MAN

The task of discovering the true nature of man is one on which Rousseau bases all of his subsequent political theory. He believes "as long as we are ignorant of natural man, it is futile for us to attempt to determine the law he has received or which is best suited to his constitution" (Origin of Inequality, preface). Clearly, Rousseau views the existing political order and social customs as unconnected to man's natural state which, in turn, leads to constant friction between the ruler and the ruled.

Man in the state of nature is governed by two main rules: one, to seek and obtain self-preservation; and two, to abhor seeing his fellow man suffer. In this, he closely mirrors Locke's interpretation of natural man. However, Rousseau goes into much detail in depicting man in his primitive state. Physically, he believes man evolves over time according to his conditions and particular needs. Since self-preservation is his primary concern, man's most fully developed faculties are those which contribute to his ability to attack and defend.

If this were Rousseau's complete depiction of natural man, it would not be anything more than that of an animal. Therefore, he is quick to show that besides the bodily similarities, man is endowed with a gift which separates him from beasts. Reason, according to Rousseau, allows man to think logically and have awareness that he is free to deny the commands of impulse: "Nature commands every animal, and beasts obey. Man feels the same impetus, but he knows he is free to go along or resist; and it is above all in the awareness of this freedom that the spirituality of his soul is made manifest" (Origin of Inequality, Part I). Early in the evolution of man, reason was only used to procure vital necessities for subsistence most efficiently. At the time, man desired only what he needed; the use of reason did not extend further until he became enlightened. The overall simplicity and innocence of man under the state of nature led Rousseau to refer to him as a *noble savage.*

THE ORIGIN OF INEQUALITY

According to Rousseau, man's downfall comes at the point when his mind begins to make distinctions such as large and small, slow and fast, weak and strong. Inevitably, when man starts paying attention to such differences he becomes egocentric and develops a desire to obtain not only more than his own survival requires, but also more than his fellow man possesses. During this stage of development, man acquires certain faculties which were previously foreign to him such as foresight and greed. Also, for want of a means to procure all his passions drove him to obtain man begins at this stage to construct the most fundamental civil society, the family. Family life, says Rousseau, gives way to an unnatural, though respectable, feeling of love. Nevertheless, since love is not a necessity required for survival, it breeds jealousy and discord which are each equally unnatural to man's character. Through such acquisition man becomes more and more reliant on his fellow man.

It is obvious, then, that Rousseau does not merely think inequality between men arises from property; it is the passions achieved by a degradation of the mind through the acquisition of knowledge which cause men to contrive the idea of property. Not surprisingly, Rousseau frequently attacks the enlightenment for removing man further and further away from the state of nature. When considered amongst the other two social contract theorists, Hobbes and Locke, he undoubtedly has the most benevolent view of the state of nature; if his predecessors think civil society is either necessary or even preferable, Rousseau thinks it is despicable.

THE SOCIAL CONTRACT

Man eventually degenerates to a point where his original state becomes a liability for him. Since he becomes so weak and corrupted by futile education, remaining in the state of nature would inevitably cause him to perish. Hence, he is obliged to form a civil society and must agree to be ruled. Rousseau's version of the social contract is unique in that it is presented in a way which allows man to be as free as he would be in the state of nature: "Find a form of association which defends and protects with all common forces the person and goods of each associate, and by means of which each one, while uniting with all, nevertheless obeys only himself and remains as free as before" (Social Contract, 6).

The key point in Rousseau's social contract is the formation of the *general will*. Each man places himself under the discretion of what the majority of citizens agree on. The general will must never be violated by anyone since it is a sort of equalizing force within society which gives the same rights to all and enforces the rule of law. The agreement to be ruled gives way to a sovereign power. Rousseau believes it is impossible for a sovereign to have any desire separate from the populace since they are also subject to the legislation they pass. Anyone that breaks the law is under the obligation to forfeit their citizenship or as Rousseau puts it "he will be forced to be free" (7).

While Rousseau laments the passing of man from the state of nature to civil society, he acknowledges one particularly admirable change in man – the transition into a moral being. Previous to civil life man relied on a type of instinctive justice similar to the proverb "do unto others as you would do unto yourself." Once man submits himself to civil society and government, he becomes privy of a different form of justice, one which allows the community to be the ultimate judge in human interactions and affairs. Thus through the socialization process man's physical impulses are replaced by a moral obligation to do what is right for others around him.

According to Rousseau, the transition from the state of nature to civil society entails both gains and losses: "What man loses through the social contract is his natural liberty and an unlimited right to everything that temps him and that he can acquire. What he gains is civil liberty and the proprietary ownership of all he possesses" (8).

ON PROPERTY

Rousseau believes the civil state's ability of protecting a man's property is pertinent to its right to rule. In the state of nature the main rule for ownership of land was the right of the strongest; whoever claimed land and defended it was able to call it his. This situation is filled with much uncertainty. According to Rousseau, "That first man who encircled a piece of land and said to others this is mine and found people simple enough to acquiesce to his claim started all the ills of private property.

In order to make property rights more reliable, the government must invoke what Rousseau calls the *right of first occupant*. The right of first occupant is governed by three main rules: one, land claimed by a man must not be already occupied; two, a man must not own more land than he needs for subsistence; three, taking possession of land must not be by means of a legal ceremony but by tilling the ground for harvest. The central thesis of Rousseau's theory of property rests on the notion that man must not take more than is necessary for his everyday subsistence so that everyone has enough to live.

CONCLUSION

There is no doubt that Jean-Jacques Rousseau had the most optimistic image of the state of nature. He believed all subsequent evolution of man and the creation of civil society degraded natural man and removed from him much of the innate benevolence. In Rousseau's view, the socialization process is corrupting and has the potential to breed greed, distrust and selfishness among men. He strongly asserted that man is naturally good and all of the malevolent passions within him are made during the transition from the state of nature into civil society. Immanuel Kant later wrote of Rousseau that he taught him to honor man and to make the cultural and political defense of human dignity his most important task.

Not only is Rousseau considered one of the few important forces behind the French Revolution, but he is also noted by modern day liberals as a true defender of human goodness. He believed that before one makes an accusation for a wrongful act committed by man, society must investigate the most underlying contributing factors. After all, man is by nature innocent and merciful but Rousseau paints a picture throughout his various works of the socialization process and his natural instincts pulling him in two different directions. The government most fit to rule is that which is closest to man's natural disposition.

SUMMARY

1. Rousseau was born in the city of Geneva and was left an orphan at age 13.

2. Rousseau's philosophy is considered a catalyst for the French Revolution.

3. He asserts that man is naturally good but is hindered by existing social orders.

4. Rousseau says that man was not selfish until he gained knowledge through society. He believed that such knowledge taught men to be greedy and selfish.

5. His conception of the general will calls for all citizens to accept majority rule.

6. Civil society, according to Rousseau, is the source of all human vices.

7. Man became a moral being at the same time he became a social being.

SECTION REVIEW

KEY TERMS

Enlightenment
General will
Noble savage
Right of first occupant

CRITICAL THINKING

- How does Rousseau's perception of natural man differ from Hobbes and Locke?

- What are the two rules which govern man in the state of nature?

- Explain how man's passions evolved as he became more dependent on his peers.

- How does Rousseau's social contract theory allow for the individual to remain free?

- Explain Rousseau's conception of the general will.

POLITICAL ECONOMISTS

ADAM SMITH

*"Every individual...generally, indeed,
neither intends to promote the public interest,
nor knows how much he is promoting it."*

ADAM SMITH

BACKGROUND

Adam Smith was a Scottish economist, philosopher and the founder of modern political economy as a science. Adam Smith would probably be considered as the first economic philosopher. Economy is a very important part of politics, considering that money is inevitably involved in political life as either a source of power – the resource with which political power is obtained, or the national capital, which the political governments, acting as trustees of their citizens, need to manage on behalf of the people. His *"Theory of Moral Sentiments"* is a masterwork on moral philosophy, while *"An Inquiry into the Nature and Causes of the Wealth of Nations"*, known in abbreviation as *"The Wealth of Nations"*, is his widely acclaimed *magnus opus*, and indeed it is the first thesis of its kind on political economy.

Adam Smith was a visionary, a creative thinker, an inspired futurist, – contrary to common misunderstanding of either his persona or the sciences of economics and political economy, Adam Smith was a Philosopher, not a mathematician. As immense as his contribution to modern science of economics may be, he was an ardent seeker of quality, not quantity. His political economy is not a dry **quantitative science** of **economic models**, **simulations** and complicated mathematical formulas, but a deep examination and true inquiry into human economy, both, in a singular, as well as in an aggregated, national or even global form.

Adam Smith's personal life reflected creativity and diversity of his mental vivacity. He was a socialite. He had a huge network of intellectual friends in his country as well as abroad. He was one of the most prominent figures of **Scottish Enlightenment**. He extensively collaborated with **David Hume**, – a Scottish philosopher, economist and historian, during this period. In later years of his life he took up a job as a tutor, which allowed him to travel all around Europe and meet intellectual leaders of his time.

ADAM SMITH AND MERCANTILISM

To understand Adam Smith, one has to understand the economic theory that influenced him. The prevailing economic philosophy during his time was mercantilism. In his *magnus opus*, *The Wealth of Nations*, Smith shows the dysfunctional nature of mercantilism as an economic philosophy. Nearly a century earlier, the French Prefect Cardinal Richelieu developed the economic philosophy of mercantilism during the reign of Louis XIII of France. Mercantilism, also known as economic nationalism, is the promotion of one country's prosperity at the detriment and expense of others. It is termed "beggar thy neighbor policy." The four basic tenets of mercantilism are:

1. Wealth of a nation is measured in gold;
2. A nation should export more than it imports;
3. A nation should import cheap raw material, but export expensive finished products;
4. A nation should control the source of raw materials.

Adam Smith rejected these ideas which he saw as recipe for war. Indeed, many wars among European powers at the time were blamed on the philosophy of mercantilism, as they fought over Africa and Asia to control sources of raw materials.

As an alternative, Adam Smith suggested a system, later termed Capitalism. Unlike mercantilism, which argued that wealth of a nation was measured in gold, Adam Smith contended that wealth of a nation is measured in its capacity to produce goods and services. The aggregate productivity of the nation's citizens is what constitutes the wealth of a nation. To ensure this a nation must create the right environment for maximum productivity. According to Adam Smith, productivity can only be maximized in a *laissez faire* political economy, – laissez faire meaning leave alone, that is, the government must leave the economy alone with little or no regulations. Instead the market should be self-regulating by the natural forces of free market or the invisible hand of the market.

It is the profit motive based on rational self interest that unleashes the creative energies of citizens to invent things and to supply to the needs of a society. It is the interplay of supply and demand that regulates the market to establish equilibrium prices. The profit motive is the driving force of capitalism.

With regard to international trade, not much has changed, especially regarding trade between developed and developing countries. The traits of mercantilism are still very visible in the huge discrepancy between imports and exports. Poor nations of Africa still suffer the trade imbalance caused by the weak prices of raw materials and agricultural products, which they export compared to expensive finished products they import from developed countries.

MICROECONOMICS AND MACROECONOMICS: INDUSTRIALIZATION

Adam Smith saw every economic issue in national or even global terms. He observed social and economic trends among individuals and applied them to national economy. He saw division of labor, technological progress, industrialization, social equality and inequality on grander and aggregated scale and only in conjunction with national economy. For example, his observation of industrial nations in comparison with underdeveloped nations addresses issues ranging from human rights to today's consumerism and modern day materialism. Subjects of his study are always social, or even personal, but their implications are national and even global. For example, Smith studied consumerism in conjunction with levels of industrialization in well-industrialized and unindustrialized countries. He found that in industrialized states consumers do not simply satisfy their needs and beneficial desires, but, due to greed and avarice, availability of goods and services and their ability to purchase, commence over-consumption, which is detrimental to them. In fact, in industrialized countries there are some who frequently consume ten times or even a hundred times more than other members of their society: "Among civilized and thriving nations... though a greater number of people do not labor at all, many of whom consume the produce of ten times, frequently of a hundred times more labor than the greater part of those who work". It is quite the contrary in unindustrialized nations, where all labor, but due to lack of industry consumerism is non-existent, and although certain social equality in ability to consume exists, overall poverty is so taxing and so prevalent, that such equality becomes equality in poverty and misery: "Such nations, however, are so miserably poor that, from mere want, they are frequently reduced, or, at least, think themselves reduced, to the necessity sometimes of directly destroying, and sometimes of abandoning their infants, their old people, and those afflicted with lingering diseases, to perish with hunger, or to be devoured by wild beasts."

Adam smith argues that industrialization, by providing competitive technological advantages, brings economic growth and wealth to a state, but such a competitive advantage cannot always be achieved with industrialization. Although in manufacturing industry modernization and mechanization provide a huge competitive edge, there are some industries, which are not as affected with industrialization as manufactures. In such industries labor efficiency remains unchanged when new technologies are applied. Smith asserts that farming is one of those industries and gives a comparative example of an industrialized and unindustrialized, largely agrarian country: "In agriculture, the labor of the rich country is not always much more productive than that of the poor; or, at least, it is never so much more productive as it commonly is in manufactures. The corn of the rich country, therefore, will not always, in the same degree of goodness, come cheaper to market than that of the poor. The corn of Poland, in the same degree of goodness, is as cheap as that of France, notwithstanding the superior opulence and improvement of the latter country. The corn of France is, in the corn provinces, fully as good, and in most years nearly about the same price with the corn of England, though, in opulence and improvement, France is perhaps inferior to England."

DIVISION OF LABOR

Adam Smith is a firm believer of benefits of division of labor. He argues that division of labor allows men to do one thing that they can do best and doing this one thing well systematically allows such men to be full of dexterity. He argues that "the increase of dexterity in every particular workman," along with "the saving of the time which is commonly lost in passing from one species of work to another" and "invention of great number of machines which facilitate and abridge labor, and enable one man to do the work of many" increases quantity, as well as quality of industry. Smith asserts that increase of dexterity is in direct correlation with increase in quantity and the division of labor is in direct correlation with the dexterity: "the improvement of the dexterity of the workman necessarily increases the quantity of the work he can perform; and the division of labor, by reducing every man's business to some one simple operation, and by making this operation the sole employment of his life, necessarily increases very much the dexterity of the workman." Smith also put forward the principle of division of labor as a way of maximizing productivity. He gave the precise example of pin factory showing how slow production would be if one person did everything as opposed to when different experts manned different phases of the manufacturing process.

POLITICAL LEADERSHIP, PROPAGANDA AND MARKETING

Adam Smith saw economics in conjunction with moral philosophy and political science. He was a true visionary in a sense that he was not devoted to a single academic discipline or a particular subject. He had a cross-disciplinary vision. Smith's political man is an economic animal and to him economic greed is twined with political ambitions, but at the end all is determined by human psyche, by man's lust for superiority and craving for social prominence: "Great ambition, the desire of real superiority, of leading and directing, seems to be altogether peculiar to man, and speech is the great instrument of ambition." Indeed, like Plato and his predecessor Socrates, Adam Smith saw speech, rhetoric and power of spoken words as prime instruments for achieving both, political and economic success. Ability to inspire and influence men, as a qualitative, emotional and thinking creature, was seen by Smith as the super-ability of the future. It did not take too long for his vision to come alive and for revolutionary disciplines of marketing and modern political science first to emerge and then to merge into cross-disciplinary tools during the past two centuries.

FREEDOM AND PUBLIC INTEREST

Adam Smith was no idealist by any means. As a matter of fact, he was a complete opposite – a man of pragmatism and expedience. His ideas reflect stark realism and practicality. Smith knows human race too well to be misled with wishful thinking about patriotism or egalitarianism, but, at the same time, he is convinced that bitter vices of human nature often produce a great deal of economic good. He argued for free trade and free national economy and believed in the success of a free society, not because of his trust was great in social honor, morals or propriety, but, to the contrary, precisely because he knew all too well that human dishonor, immorality and impropriety were, are and always will be part of social, political and economic culture of a nation and of humanity at large. But these vices, translated in human greed and rapaciousness for gain, will inadvertently and completely involuntarily serve well for public interest and provide economic verve and vivacity and consequent growth for people: "Every individual... generally, indeed, neither intends to promote the public interest, nor knows how much he is promoting it. By preferring the support of domestic to that of foreign industry he intends only his own security; and by directing that industry in such a manner as its produce may be of the greatest value, he intends only his own gain, and he is in this, as in many other cases, led by an invisible hand to promote an end which was no part of his intention."

FLAWS OF FREE MARKET

Adam Smith's vision for a *free market* society was never clouded with wishful thinking and enthusiasm. He is well aware of flaws of free market society and knows that, on one hand, overabundance of goods and, on the other hand, insatiable human appetite for material gain could also be harmful for economic growth and social harmony. He sees a right to private property as a foundation of market economy. He insists that private ownership is the foundation for private gain, and private gain itself, although inadvertently, yet still, does become the foundation for public benefit, but extremes of any kind are bad. He sees unchecked private ownership and greed as a detriment to public good, which is important for economic growth, for without public good there could never be public enthusiasm, desire to succeed and public dexterity. He shows examples of potentially dangerously extreme private ownership on renting: "As soon as the land of any country has all become private property, the landlords, like all other men, love to reap where they never sowed, and demand a rent even for its natural produce." And so Smith believes that free economy is a key to economic growth, but caution with extreme excesses is a key to a successful free economy.

CONCLUSION

Adam Smith debunked the claims of the inherently belligerent economic theory of mercantilism, leaving as alternative the enduring legacy of capitalism. It could be boldly said that without him science of economics, as we know it today, would not exist. In practice Adam Smith's theories and ideas were mostly translated and implemented, and the vision of a free market has been globally achieved. His philosophy and his notions not only seem practical, but are indeed practiced all over the world wherever freedom and democracy exist. Even solid communist strongholds could not resist at last to be naturally subjected to free market laws and market economy, which Smith saw as a liberating and self-regulating power for economic and political success of a state.

SUMMARY

1. Adam Smith was a Scottish philosopher and a founder of modern political economy as a science.

2. Smith discerned every economic issue in national or even global terms.

3. Adam Smith argued for capitalism and asserted that it was a more viable alternative political philosophy to mercantilism.

4. Adam Smith maintained that technology produces industry, industry produces prosperity and prosperity, in turn, produces consumerism with its high demand.

5. Adam Smith argued that citizens of industrialized states, due to common prosperity and abundance of goods, engage in over-consumption.

6. According to Smith, economic growth can only be achieved with human dexterity.

7. Adam Smith is a firm believer of benefits of division of labor. He argues that division of labor allows men to do one thing that they can do best and doing this one thing well systematically allows such men to be full of dexterity.

8. Adam Smith saw political science and economics as cross-disciplinary sciences. He argued that leadership, propaganda and marketing are common tools of political and economic success.

9. Adam Smith was a keen realist, not an idealist: he believed that a man was by nature a selfish creature and that social responsibility was therefore non-existent, but common good could be nevertheless achieved. He believed that these vices, translated in human greed and rapaciousness for gain, would inadvertently and completely involuntarily serve well for public interest and provide economic verve and vivacity and consequent growth for people.

10. Smith, although being an avid supporter of free market society, clearly saw flaws of capitalism. He recognized that unchecked greed can easily cause monopoly, in which case, he argued, in an example of agriculture: "As soon as the land of any country has all become private property, the landlords, like all other men, love to reap where they never sowed, and demand a rent even for its natural produce."

11. It could be undoubtedly admitted that without Adam Smith the science of modern economics would not exist, and that Smith gave a commencement and groundwork for many social economic theories to come, such as Keynesianism, Marxism and others.

SECTION REVIEW

KEY TERMS

David Hume
Economic models
Free Market
Quantitative science
Scottish Enlightenment
Simulations

CRITICAL THINKING

- According to Smith, what are the advantages of industrialization?

- Describe the relationship between industrialization and technology

- Explain Smith's idea of division of labor.

- Explain how Smith viewed economics in conjunction with politics and philosophy.

- Why did Smith believe that greed is useful in a free market system?

- What is mercantilism and how does it differ from capitalism as expressed by Adam Smith?

POLITICAL ECONOMISTS

KARL MARX

"In bourgeois society, living labor is but a means to increase accumulated labor."

KARL MARX

BACKGROUND

Karl Marx was a German philosopher, political theorist, *sociologist* and *revolutionary*. Although more than anything else he was the most pioneering *political economist*. Perhaps no philosopher, except Plato, has influenced the modern political world in the past two centuries as Marx did. It was not too long ago, when at least one third of the world not only firmly believed in Marxist ideas, but also rigorously practiced them on state and international levels. Communist ideology behind the *cold war*, which took place between the United States and the former Soviet Union, could also be duly credited to Karl Marx. Although nowadays Russian communist *imperialists* and even Chinese *Maoists* have abandoned Marxist theories, partly due to insatiable greed and appetite so commonly found in men of all nations, and partly because of sheer necessity of economic growth and impracticality of communist equality, even today there are nations and leaders of those nations who still place trust in socialist doctrines and communist values. In fact there has been a sort of revival of Marxist ideas, especially in the nations formerly ruled by oligarchs, where the middle class was rare and majority was economically oppressed by the rich who, besides having financial control, had also managed to obtain vast political powers, and also in the countries generally inhospitably disposed to the Western values and Capitalism. Today's Venezuela and Cuba's long standing resistance would be good enough examples to prove that to a certain degree human race at least in some parts of the world is still trustfully disposed to Karl Marx and Marxist dogmas and ideas.

It must be mentioned that Marxism is quite uniquely *paradoxical* in two very important ways: firstly, it has either a radical following or radical opposition. Its disciples adhere to Marxist doctrines frequently very blindly and often in large numbers, comprising of states, nations and even of greater international regions. Secondly, Marxist ideas are often supported or condemned, but very rarely read and seldom understood. It is a fact that neither working class, the so called *proletariat* of Russia or China, nor "catching up with the Joneses" type capitalists of North America or Western Europe ever studied or comprehended Marx, but nevertheless one always vehemently embraced Marxism, the other just as vehemently and just as always denounced it. So people either love Marx or hate Marx, but without ever reading a page of Marx.

Karl Marx was a student of Hegel from whom he adopted the idea of dialectic. Hegel had argued that human progress takes the form of dialectical idealism which he saw as the conflict of thesis and antithesis leading to a synthesis which then becomes a new thesis for the next stage of progress. Marx rather sees dialectical materialism, meaning that it is not a conflict of ideas but of material struggle expressed in class struggle. This is the constant battle between capital and labor over surplus value or profit. Marx argues that the lopsided distribution of profits clearly shows exploitation of labor by capital, which will inevitably result in class alienation. When this exploitation of labor reaches a saturation point, the working class or the proletariat will revolt, overthrowing the bourgeoisie and taking control of the means of production. This process leads to the demise of the state which Marx calls the executive committee of the ruling class. The ultimate result will be the emergence of the dictatorship of the proletariat and the establishment of a classless society, providing to each according to his ability and each according to his work. Marx calls religion the opium of the people and part of the exploitative superstructure, which is why Marxism is called an atheistic doctrine.

COMMUNIST MANIFESTO:
CAPITALISM, PRODUCTIVITY AND HUMAN RIGHTS

Nothing Karl Marx ever wrote was as controversial and yet as ground breaking as *Communist Manifesto*. It is a discourse, on one hand, about dangers of capitalism and its deficiencies, and, on the other hand, about usefulness of communism. The treatise was the guiding lantern of communist parties of Russia and China, and the same treatise was the subject of abhorrence of America and Western Europe. In short, global Communism itself commenced with this dissertation.

Marx compares bourgeois society and capitalism to a military machine, where everyone is employed in factories in the most soldierly and blind manner in order to increase productivity and with it accumulate wealth for the capitalist, – for the fat cat, who has already accumulated wealth and capital, and, out of sheer greed, desires to increase it even more. While the laborer, the poor proletariat, who was deprived of not only wealth, but of necessities, who lost all the property he ever owned when capitalism robbed him of what little property he inherited from a little lesser evil of feudalism, this former peasant, now bourgeois' hourly laborer, engaged in this productivity loses not only his property, but his freedom too, – division of labor, which increased productivity for the capitalist, also increased duration of a working day for the laborer. And hence, while the capitalist grows rich, laborer grows poor and poorer still, and on top of that his freedom, his existence, his time to grow and accomplish anything else in life is taken away: "In bourgeois society, living labor is but a means to increase accumulated labor." He warns that in bourgeois society modern industry demands a lot from the employees. It demands their very lives and existence. It tears families apart and breaks down all ties among individuals, as these individuals become articles of productivity and tools of labor: "by the action of Modern Industry, all family ties among the proletarians are torn asunder, and their children transformed into simple articles of commerce and instruments of labor." Certainly, there is a grain of truth in this warning, considering that in highly capitalistic countries an average labor week is 50 hours and an average yearly vacation is about 10 days, while in communist countries on the average per week a laborer worked 35 hours and his annual vacation time was comprised of 60 days. Karl Marx goes as far as to say that: "The bourgeois sees in his wife a mere instrument of production." This too, observing our today's gold-digging society could be said that at least partly makes sense.

Marx is not a mere critic, he also offers solutions and describes what can and must be changed in order for the people, for the working class to gain economic growth and personal freedom: "In Communist society, accumulated labor is but a means to widen, to enrich, to promote the existence of the laborer."

INDUSTRIALIZATION
V.
SEX AND AGE DISCRIMINATION

Karl Marx was one of the first to foresee that high level of mechanization and industrialization would bring about diminishing need for human labor. He also foresaw that this technological progress would cause equality of laborers, in regard to sex and age. Considering that youth and manhood make an individual strong and more expedient in power when compared to weaker sex or elderly, modernization with its powerful machines would diminish demand on powerful and youthful labor, and instead demand for an operative, for a routine, for a full conformist would drastically increase: "the more modern industry becomes developed, the more is the labor of men superseded by that of women. Differences of age and sex have no longer any distinctive social validity." This is one point over which perhaps no one would argue with Marx. Instead many would admit that his prediction was correct and it has taken place in modern Western society. Indeed, women and elderly now comprise a large number of our work force, but the point of jubilation is not that workforce of capitalism has grown, but rather that the good effects which it has had on human rights. Today everyone, man, woman or the elderly... a human, irrespective of any other distinctions, benefits of political and social equality and enjoys equal rights and fruits of economic growth.

GEOPOLITICAL AND SOCIAL POWERS OF CAPITALISM

Marx foresaw what great influence capitalism could have on every aspect of human existence. He believed that every sphere of human life, and, that is, human life globally and all over the world, would be somehow amply affected by capital. Social and demographic changes at home and geopolitical changes all over the world became evident to him long before they had taken place.

Karl Marx noticed shifts in demographics. He clearly saw population increase of big cities and towns and decrease of population in rural areas of the country. He also saw urbanization, which in an infantile state was already taking place in Europe and America: "The bourgeoisie has subjected the country to the rule of the towns. It has created enormous cities, has greatly increased the urban population as compared with the rural, and has thus rescued a considerable part of the population from the idiocy of rural life." But at the same time as these demographic revolutions were taking place, Marx was foreseeing negative effects which population growth of the cities and urbanization could have in the future. He anticipated depletion of the rural country, deprivation of it of farm labor, its lurking poverty and ultimately dependence of country people on the city. He saw this trend as a new sort of discrimination, discrimination not by sex, age or race, but rather by geographic area of residence. He goes further and applies this social phenomenon of a country to a greater *macrocosm* of the world, – global discrimination against agrarian, rural, technologically less developed nations by more industrialized countries: "Just as it has made the country dependent on the towns, so it has made barbarian and semi-barbarian countries dependent on the civilized ones, nations of peasants on nations of bourgeois, the East on the West." Certainly the second half of the past century and the very beginning of the 21st century have proved Marx right at least on this issue, – global poverty among less industrialized and technologically less developed nations, and not only poverty, but in many cases sheer starvation, is daily contrasted by weight-gain problems of an American corporate executive or a German electrical engineer.

GLOBALIZATION STARTED WITH AMERICA

Industrial economic growth of the United States of America did not go unnoticed by Marx. He saw this as an opportunity for expansion of both, Western European capital and Western values of productivity and money-making. He saw China's growth even in his time. But more than anything else, we must mention that Marx saw all this in terms of economic opportunity for increase of markets, both in number and volume, and their eventual globalization: "The discovery of America, the rounding of the Cape, opened up fresh ground for the rising bourgeoisie. The East-Indian and Chinese markets, the colonization of America, trade with the colonies, the increase in the means of exchange and in commodities generally, gave to commerce, to navigation, to industry, an impulse never before known."

CONCLUSION

Marx thought that capitalism was an unfair system, which would inevitably self-destruct. He argued that the proletariat or the working class would at last triumph in the struggle with the bourgeoisie.

Many consider Marxism's criticism of Capitalism as a bad thing, as an unfair and unnecessary picking on a perfectly well-rounded social, economic and political system, but one may argue that if we took some of the criticism of Marx to heart, we could make our systems, both, political and economic, as well as social... better and more just and even economically more efficient, and with our long-term success once and for all prove Marx wrong.

SUMMARY

1. Karl Marx was a German philosopher, political theorist, sociologist and revolutionary of the 19th century.

2. Perhaps no philosopher, except Plato, has influenced the modern political world in the past two centuries as Marx did. It was not too long ago, when at least one third of the world practiced communism according to Marxist doctrines.

3. Masses of people have almost blindly adhered or opposed Marxism during the past two centuries without clear knowledge of its principles.

4. "Communist Manifesto" is considered to be the most controversial and at the same time most pioneering work of Karl Marx.

5. Marx opposed and condemned capitalism on several grounds:

    i.   Productivity is demanding and it causes working men to lose:
         a.   Personal development,
         b.   Family life,
         c.   Education,
         d.   Property.
    ii. Increased capital makes a capitalist into a dominant force,
    iii. Division of labor, which increases productivity for the capitalist, also increases duration of a working day for the laborer.

6. Marx reasoned that high level of mechanization and industrialization would bring about diminishing need for human labor.

7. Marx predicted that technological progress would cause equality of laborers of the two sexes: "the more modern industry becomes developed, the more is the labor of men superseded by that of women."

8. Marx foresaw that capital would globally affect every sphere of demographic life of a man:

    i.   Demographically people would migrate from country to cities;
    ii. Discrimination would arise no longer from sex or age, but rather from one's geographic area of habitation;
    iii. Global discrimination against agrarian, rural, technologically less developed nations by more industrialized countries would be inevitable.

9. Marx claimed, and rightfully so, that globalization started with the discovery of America.

10. According to Marx, globalization would serve as a stimulus to industry, commerce and even science.

11. Communism so rigorously advocated by Karl Marx is readily challenged by today's political scientists, politicians, philosophers and economists, yet his keen observations and predictions on many shortcomings of capitalistic way of life have become evidently true.

SECTION REVIEW

KEY TERMS

Cold war
Globalization
Imperialists
Macrocosm
Maoists
Paradox
Political economist
Proletariat
Revolutionary
Sociologist

CRITICAL THINKING

- Explain the conflict between the proletariat and the bourgeois as told by Marx.

- How has technology made gender and age less of an issue?

- Explain the relationship between industrialization and urbanization.

- With what country did the globalization commence?

RATIONAL IDEALISTS

IMMANUEL KANT

"All subjects are equal to each other before the law
which, as a pronouncement of the general will, can only be one."

IMMANUEL KANT

BACKGROUND

Immanuel Kant stands today as the most influential philosopher of metaphysics since Plato and Aristotle. His work came at the end of the period known as the enlightenment. His Critique of Pure Reason is widely considered as one of the most thorough and complicated philosophical works of all times. The work reflects that of a very pensive and methodical man; it is often remarked that the women in his neighborhood could look at the clock and know the precise time at which Kant would take his evening walk. He spent most of life living in Kaliningrad teaching at a local university.

Kant believed that he had found common ground to one of the most pressing debates during his time. The rationalists and empiricists had contrasting opinions as to what constitutes human knowledge. The former, led by Leibniz and Spinoza, believed that all experience is subject to what is known as *Cartesian doubt* and is useless without the application of human reason. Empiricists like Locke and Rousseau thought that experience was sufficient enough to provide a firm foundation for knowledge. Kant's answer to the matter was that reason without experience is misleading and delusional; similarly experience without the application of the human mind is subjective.

Although the bulk of Kantian philosophy invokes the use of metaphysics and logic, Kant has nevertheless come up with innovative political contributions also. He is viewed as one of the earliest supporters of a league of nations and recognized internationally as a steadfast advocate for peace and freedom.

ON THE SOCIAL CONTRACT

Kant lived during a time in which Prussia was ruled by the very intolerant and harsh despot Friedrich Wilhelm III. The ruler believed that the presence of a variety of religions was harmful to the state. Anyone who questioned the legitimacy of Christian orthodoxy or even promoted the individual right for religious freedom was viewed as directly threatening the well-being of civil life. In his work: *What is Enlightenment?* Kant argues that human knowledge should never have to make room for faith since the latter is neither rational nor based on experience. In fact, Kant is widely viewed as one of the earliest supporters of a *marketplace of ideas* which encourages public discourse on matters such as religion, politics and morality. Clearly, these ideas undercut the religious zeal of the king.

His reaction to the state's hostility was quite surprising. Although Kant's popularity during this period was very high, he showcased a desire to not only avoid confrontation with authorities but also to practice a long-held moral belief – one which is based on the Hobbesian theory that a government is necessary to maintain civil order and to protect the lives of citizens. Kant felt an obligation to be submissive to the state and respect authority so that he would not set a dangerous precedent for others. Accordingly, he believed that it is utterly deplorable to disobey the orders of a legitimate government.

ON HUMAN NATURE

The entirety of Kant's works may be reduced to the following: man must acquire reason and learn how to utilize it in everyday affairs while avoiding the natural tendency to use it as a means to fulfill evil intentions. To this end, Kant also believes that reason is nevertheless limited in what it can achieve and part of a man's life is to learn that he is not all knowing and must find space for a sort of humility which will allow him to obtain pertinent knowledge for his existence.

Few philosophers before Kant have been so critical of the limitedness of human rationality. Yet there is a certain contradiction in his thought: although reason is limited in its abilities and sometimes deceptive, it is still the most thoroughly developed faculty which a man is capable of using for self improvement. Therefore, it is easy to understand why Kant strongly denounces the rebellion of a populace against its government: man is a *res cogitans,* a thinking thing, but reason can only take him so far. Government is justified, then, because reason is flawed.

With regard to ethics and morals, which must be integral parts of governance and exercise of power, Kant also becomes very relevant by his introduction of the concept of categorical imperative. The imperative says that we act not except if we can at the same time will that our action is a universal law, meaning that a moral action can only be evaluated by imagining a world in which everyone is doing the same thing. The imperative also decrees that we cannot see another person except as an end but never as a means. This exposes the inadequacies of most contemporary leaders who only exploit everyone in their route to power, and unscrupulously use people and public resources for their own benefits.

ON CIVIL SOCIETY

Similar to his thoughts on religion are his ideas of what constitutes human freedom. Kant believes no man may impose his views on what makes a person happy and contributes to their well-being; man simply does not possess the ability to objectively judge his peers. Instead Kant advocates a type of freedom in which no man prevents another from enjoying his own: "Everyone may seek his happiness in the way that seems good to him as long as he does not infringe on the freedom of others to pursue a similar purpose, such freedom may coexist with the freedom of every other man" (Theory and Practice, 8:290).

Also, Kant is a firm believer in the natural equality of man in the state of nature. Like Hobbes, Kant understands that natural man is more or less equal in almost anything, most notably in the ability to kill. Thus it is of the utmost importance for man to submit himself to the law conceived via the general will. "All subjects are equal to each other before the law which, as a pronouncement of the general will, can only be one... For no man can coerce another except through publicly-known law and through its executor" (8.292).

TO ETERNAL PEACE

Arguably Kant's most lasting contribution to political theory lies in his masterpiece To Eternal Peace. In it Kant lays fundamental conditions under which peace must be founded. The most basic ground rules include the following:

1.   No treaty of peace shall be held to be such, which is made with the secret reservation of the material for a future war.
2.   No independent state, small or large, may be acquired by another state through inheritance, exchange, purchase or gift.
3.   Standing armies shall disappear.
4.   No debts shall be contracted in connection with the foreign affairs of the state.
5.   No state shall interfere by force in the constitution and government of another state.
6.   No state at war with another shall permit such acts of warfare as must make mutual confidence impossible in time of future peace

The Definitive Articles for Eternal Peace:

1.   The constitution of each state should be republican in nature
2.   The league of nations should be based upon a federalism of free states
3.   The world law should be based upon universal hospitality

CONCLUSION

Clearly, much of Immanuel Kant's political philosophy was based on Hobbes' conception of the social contract and the need for a sovereign institution to check man's natural tendency toward evil. Despite writing at a time when enlightenment principles were at a peak, Kant remained true to his core belief of not disobeying his government. However, this is not to say that he viewed humans as not being able to rule themselves; he rather thought a ruling body is the better of two evils. Like Hobbes, Kant shivered at the idea of returning to the state of nature which, to him, is the equivalent to a state of war.

Consequently, for the sole reason that human rationality is limited is scope, Kant concluded that man must be ruled by the element of fear. Even though human reason is not sufficient for man to rule himself, it does not prevent him from striving toward what Rousseau called perfectibility. If Kant resembles any ancient philosopher, it is undoubtedly Plato. After all, it is he who held the belief that the beginning of knowledge lies in an awareness of being ignorant of everything. Immanuel Kant reawakened the modern world to the limitations of pure reason.

SUMMARY

1. Kant was a professor of logic and metaphysics at a university in Kaliningrad, Prussia.

2. Kant is believed to have solved the debate between the rationalists and empiricists during his time. Kant said that reason without experience is misleading, while experience without reason is subjective.

3. He is one of the earliest supporters of an international league of nations.

4. Kant believed in the Hobbesian view that government must be extremely powerful in order maintain social order.

5. He believed first and foremost that man must acquire reason and learn how to and utilize it in everyday affairs while avoiding the natural tendency to use it to fulfill evil intentions.

SECTION REVIEW

KEY TERMS

Cartesian doubt
Marketplace of ideas

CRITICAL THINKING

- Explain the debate between the rationalists and the empiricists.

- Explain Kant's view on human nature

- Why does Kant believe government is justified?

- According to Kant, what is man's condition in the state of nature?

RATIONAL IDEALISTS

JOHN STUART MILL

"The only freedom which deserves the name is that of pursuing our own good in our own way, so long as we do not attempt to deprive others of theirs, or impede their efforts to obtain it."

JOHN STUART MILL

BACKGROUND

John Stuart Mill was nothing short of a childhood prodigy. The young man was learning Greek and arithmetic at age three and was appointed schoolmaster at age eight. His father James Mill arranged to have him taught by his close friend and founder of *utilitarianism* Jeremy Bentham. Mill would later go on to formulate his own version of the philosophy and consequently become one of history's most vehement supporters of an individual's liberty.

At age twenty Mill started to realize the insensitivity that often comes with such intense studies. Mill became a pawn of reason and ceased to feel human. This experience reinforced utilitarianism in his mind. Indeed, Mill believed that at the core of human nature was nothing more than a consciousness which distinguished between pleasure and pain. Hitherto Mill had the idea driven into his mind that a person should strive to know as much as he can possibly know while suppressing all human sentiment inherent in the soul. This experience compelled him to believe that all things in this life should be judged on the basis of how happy they make a person feel.

ON LIBERTY

Mill's most renowned work *On Liberty* is a passionate exposition on the need for freedom of speech. He believes anytime an opinion is silenced or censored some element of truth is in jeopardy of being kept secret. It is freedom of speech, says Mill, which causes social progress and intellectual advancement. Any society with restrictions on what one is allowed to say must unavoidably be content with the status quo.

Central to Mill's discussion on liberty is the *harm principle* which dictates that no one should interfere with the actions of another as long as it does not adversely affect anyone other than the actor. "The only freedom which deserves the name is that of pursuing our own good in our own way, so long as we do not attempt to deprive others of theirs, or impede their efforts to obtain it" (On Liberty, I).

In light of this belief, Mill enumerates three essentials for freedom of the individual: one, liberty of thought and absolute freedom to voice an opinion; two, liberty of tastes and pursuits; three, freedom to unite for a peaceful purpose. These are the ground rules which he thinks are necessary to constitute a free society: "No society in which these liberties are not, on the whole, respected, is free, whatever may be its form of government; and none is completely free in which they do not exist absolute and unqualified" (I).

Perhaps the biggest reason for Mill's preoccupation with freedom of speech is the impact it has on individuality. Indeed, he believes that individuality is a key element of personal well-being. He asserts that man was put on earth with the object of improving himself by means of intellectual development. The presence of multiple opinions increases the opportunity for man to discover what is closest to the truth: "As it is useful that while mankind is imperfect there should be different opinions…It is desirable, in short, that in things which do not primarily concern other, individuality should assert itself" (III).

SOCIAL TYRANNY
V.
TYRANNY OF THE MAJORITY

Mill strongly believes that the subjects of a government should have considerable power to influence the decisions. This is an indispensable right the people must exercise in order to prevent a despotic government which will undermine the foundations of a society. To this end, the rulers of a state should have the same interests and concerns for the commonwealth as the people in order to prevent any abuse of power that may occur. This condition is known as *social tyranny*.

Conversely, Mill warns of the reverse situation known as ***tyranny of the majority***. When the people have too much power, the chances of more fortunate parts of the populace oppressing another are very high. "The will of the people, moreover, practically means the will of the most numerous or the most active part of the people; the majority…consequently may desire to oppress a part of their number and precautions are needed against this" (I).

UTILITARIANISM

The term utilitarianism refers broadly to an ethical viewpoint in which an action's moral worth is judged primarily on how well it contributes to overall happiness and pleasure. Mill's mentor Jeremy Bentham believed in the ***greatest-happiness principle*** which says that the goal of any action should be to obtain the most pleasure for the most people. This principle, needless to say, reflects a ***consequentialist*** philosophy because it evaluates an action on the basis of the outcome rather than the quality of the act itself. This line of thought varies considerably from Kant's ***deontological ethics*** or ethics of duty, which promote the opposite.

Mill's version of utilitarianism is vastly different from that of his teacher. He makes a distinction between intellectual pleasure and physical pleasure. The former, he says, is preferable to the latter because it generates true respect and is conducive to good moral scruples. Mill thinks the debate surrounding the two types of pleasure derives from a difference in human experience. Those who prefer physical pleasure over the intellectual kind do so because they are inexperienced and have no conception of what is genuinely good.

Mill admits that he had to read the poetry of William Wordsworth to rekindle his human emotions which were dulled by the strict mental regimentation his father forced on him. But most importantly it was his long term lady friend Harriet Taylor whom he later married that taught him valuable lessons about love, relationships and marriage. It is also true that his ideas about gender equity must have come from that association with Mrs. Taylor. Overall, Mill became a very liberal philosopher, advocating many radical reforms, such as universal suffrage, including women and the political rights of peoples of British overseas territories. He also recommends proportional representation, especially single transferable vote (STV), voting for a candidate rather than a party list as the best form of representation in a democracy.

CONCLUSION

Mill was born in a very fortunate predicament. His father James Mill trained his son John to act as a sponge and take in all the education that he would feed to him. James Mill also had a magnificent resource at hand in his friend Jeremy Bentham who taught Mill the concept of utilitarianism. Since Mill did nothing but live, sleep, and breathe education he was indubitably considered to be the genius of his day.

Mill's outstanding intellect and transcendental political philosophy was the immediate result of a well planned education and a dedicated parent. Notwithstanding his unrivalled brilliance, Mill learned throughout his life that there must be more than just cold, hard facts; a human simply must live a little in the process. In the words of David Hume, "Be a philosopher; but, amidst all your philosophy, be still a man."

SUMMARY

1. Mill was a childhood prodigy whose father arranged for him to be taught by a family friend, Jeremy Bentham.

2. He became one of the strongest supporters of utilitarianism.

3. Mill's harsh childhood reminded him that things in life should be judged by how happy they make a person feel.

4. Mill believed that freedom of speech causes social progress and intellectual advancement.

5. He held that no man's actions should be hindered unless they pose a direct threat to the well-being of another.

6. Mill believed intellectual pleasure is the highest pleasure of all. This assertion distinguished Mill from Bentham.

7. Mill cautioned against the tyranny of the majority, that is where or when a democratic majority forces its will on the minority.

SECTION REVIEW

KEY TERMS

Consequentialist
Deontological ethics
Greatest-happiness principle
Harm principle
Social tyranny
Tyranny of the majority
Utilitarianism

CRITICAL THINKING

- According to Mill, what is the catalyst for intellectual advancement and social progress?

- Explain how the harm principle relates to utilitarianism.

- What are the three essential freedoms for the individual?

- Explain the difference between social tyranny and tyranny of the majority.

- How does Mill's version of utilitarianism differ from Bentham's greatest-happiness principle?

HUMANISTS

HENRY DAVID THOREAU

"That government is best which governs not at all."

HENRY DAVID THOREAU

BACKGROUND

It is very rare to come across a great *polymath* like Henry David Thoreau not only in American history, but in history of any country. He was a renaissance man, a man of widest spectrum of intelligence and deepest understanding of many aspects of human existence. He is well known for many aspects of his gifted and dexterous life. Thoreau was a pioneering *transcendentalist* philosopher and a writer, a *tax resister* and *naturalist, civil activist* and a sage essayist, a lifelong *abolitionist* and an *environmentalist*, a *New Englander*, an American and yet he was a man before he was a *Yankee* or an American, and as he, per usual, so eloquently put it to all of us, Americans, and to the rest of the world: "I would remind my countrymen that they are to be men first, and Americans only at a late and convenient hour". In short, more than anything else, he was a *Christian humanist*, – a God-fearing and man-loving man.

It is a paradoxical fact that Thoreau's idealistic lifestyle is widely known to American public, but his idealism, overall usually unread by people, still remains as a powerful influence to a great number of democratic leaders and activists around the world. In his lifetime he influenced his best friend and an American essayist, *Emerson*. Most prominent and beloved son of America, a true champion of the *civil rights movement*, *Martin Luther King*, spiritual and political leader of India, *Mohandas Gandhi*, guardian of civil rights movement of South Africa and its most prominent son, *Nelson Mandela*, Georgia's first President, Dr. *Zviad Gamsakhurdia* and many others were tremendously influenced by Thoreau's writings and especially by his inspiring treatise, "Civil Disobedience", – an essay, which Thoreau wrote during his imprisonment for refusing to pay taxes, a warring essay, which seems to infuse peace and defuse violence whenever it touches men's hearts and minds. Peaceful protest is that powerful political instrument, which the world, among a great number of other things, has inherited from Thoreau.

SIMPLE LIVING

Thoreau was a New Englander. Simple living is evident in every bit of New England's life even today, – plain, whitewashed churches, cemeteries with thinly cut short gray tombstones, humble dwellings and wood stick fences indicate religious adherence of those folks to humility-invoking simplicity. Indeed Thoreau was a New Englander. Simplicity was the very soul of his soul. After much trials and tribulations in this life, he decided not necessarily to abandon human company, but rather to embrace nature in all its simple beauty and thought-provoking solitude. In July of 1845 he moved to a small, self-built cabin on the land owned by his best friend and essayist, Ralph Waldo Emerson, in a forest around the shores of Walden Pond, near Concord, Massachusetts. There he lived a great deal, farmed a little and wrote even less, but most importantly he lived… lived simply and, away from worldly clamor, simply lived. He completed the first draft of an elegy to his deceased brother, "A Week on the Concord and Merrimack Rivers". He started to work on the manuscript on his experiences of simple living on Walden Pond, which was completed and published in several years as "Walden, or Life in the Woods". It is a recounting of the two years, two months and two days he spent at the pond. "Walden" is a compressed account of this experience. It is a memoir, but, more than anything else, it is an account of the man's spiritual quest. It is a modern day "Odyssey", but instead of the man-made war and devastation described by Homer, it is full of natural beauty and peaceful war of ideals not only described, but also experienced first hand by Thoreau.

CIVIL DISOBEDIENCE

In late July of 1846 Henry David Thoreau came across Sam Staples, a local tax collector who demanded from Thoreau that he paid six years of delinquent poll taxes. *Poll tax* is a tax of fixed amount and uniform nature, imposed as a set amount of charge per individual usually on an annual basis. It was widely used until the 19th century after which it was substituted with Income Tax, which is not flat, but rather contingent on a size of an individual's income. Thoreau had not paid the poll tax because he did not want to contribute to the unjust government, which used the collected tax money for both, domestic injustice and international aggression, namely for slavery and Mexican-American War. On the spot Thoreau refused to pay the tax and he was immediately jailed under the charge of refusal to pay taxes. This experience had a huge influence on Thoreau. On January and February of 1848 he delivered brilliant lectures at the Concord Lyceum. The lectures called "The Rights and Duties of the Individual in Relation to Government" were groundbreaking advancements in political philosophy. Bronson Alcott, an American writer and teacher, attended the lecture and wrote extensively about it in his journal. Soon Thoreau reworked his lecture into an essay titled "Resistance to Civil Government", widely known today as "Civil Disobedience."

ON THE GOVERNMENT

Thoreau was one of the first and foremost of Americans who challenged the idea of a big government and especially of an interfering government. His dislike of the tight government rule and regulation was not because he abhorred the authority or the rule of law, but rather because he greatly loved people and valued individual freedom, and, on the other hand, he despised and completely opposed everything that was unjust, including the unjust government and the unjust law. "That government is best which governs not at all" was Thoreau's take on political rule. That was an advanced thought not only for his time, but even today some may make a case that no government and too much freedom would borderline sheer anarchy, but Thoreau's political vision was no anarchy. It was freedom for every individual to live simply and simply to live... to live without government's interference, without lawmaker's dictate, without *paternalism* of any kind. Many challenge his ideals and brand them as fruits of foolish optimism. It must be truly conceded that Thoreau was an optimist, but by no means a wishful one. He did not merely criticize the big, imposing and dictatorial government, but also offered a fine and well-tested solution, – conscience, which every man has, every man feels and if only every man exercises, America and the world at large would be a better place: "Must the citizen ever for a moment, or in the least degree, resign his conscience to the legislator? Why has every man a conscience, then?"

Henry David Thoreau was truly ahead of his time. He anticipated ruinous effects of excessive rule of law and confinement of human freedom, when men become subjects of big government and outdated, burdensome or even unjust laws, and that too especially in a democratic society: "I think that we should be men first, and subjects afterward. It is not desirable to cultivate a respect for the law, so much as for the right."

Thoreau foresaw devastating effects of the unjust laws and excessive number of lawyers. His warning for our generation sounded loud and clear long time ago: "The lawyer's truth is not Truth..." How relevant has all this become to us today needs no further deliberation.

According to Thoreau the law is nothing more than a dumb instrument, which often falls into the hands of the "selected" few, also known as the government. Under this circumstance the law loses its usefulness, as it becomes, on one hand, a license for the government to be authoritarian and, on the other hand, an instrument of civil slavery for the public: "The law will never make men free; it is men who have got to make the law free." He further states usefulness of good laws and proactively disproves his contemporary and even future critics' accusations of his supposed inclinations to anarchy: "They are the lovers of law and order who observe the law when government breaks it."

THOREAU'S DEMOCRACY

Henry David Thoreau valued every individual and individual freedom. In that sense he was truly a democrat, but on democracy, as well as basically on every issue this learned man touched his thought upon, he was beyond conventional understanding. His democracy was beyond his time's democracy. His democracy is beyond democracy of our time too. In his *Civil Disobedience* Thoreau challenges usefulness of the most democratic institution – voting. Thoreau believes that simply casting a vote is nothing, but a show of lack of interest in political life and in the future of the country. It is pessimism and inactivity. It is avoiding one's civil responsibility. A truly caring man must not just cast his vote, but he must rather actively pursue his citizen's duty: he must make sure that his vote is seen, his position or opposition is taken under consideration, that his voice is heard indeed and so and only so his vote may really count, and all this could only be achieved by civil activism and protest: "Even voting for the right is doing nothing for it. It is only expressing to men feebly our desire that it should prevail."

CITIZENSHIP

Although actions of Henry David Thoreau are peaceful, his language is quite exclamatory and patriotic. His love of the world is ample, but his love of America is ample still. It is not soft, "polite" or effeminate nationalism he has in mind, but, instead, out of love and care, just like Socrates or Cicero, he always offers tough words for his fellow citizens. He is puzzled with the devastating moral state of his nation and in an emotional soliloquy exclaims his concerns for America: "Our statistics are at fault: the population has been returned too large. How many *men* are there to a square thousand miles in this country? Hardly one. Does not America offer any inducement for men to settle here? The American has dwindled into an Odd Fellow."

There is something very unique about Thoreau's patriotism, – he loves America by loving humanity and the world even more. His doting on his country is mutually inclusive with adoration of mankind. He believes that not love of one's self, or family, or city, or even one's country, but rather love of humanity should be the ultimate purpose of all political instruments, such as governments, institutions and even the law: "No matter how valuable law may be to protect your property, even to keep soul and body together, if it do not keep you and humanity together." Love of one's country must not overpower and subdue love of the greater world according to Thoreau. Alas, in today's world of international politics and rivalry such a peacemaking concept is ignorantly overlooked and always ignored on all sides.

EVIL OF SLAVERY

Thoreau wrote two essays directly addressing slavery in America and evils of slavery in general. It must be noted that his condemnation of slavery was like a double-edged sword, as it contained a great deal of censure of the South, but even greater criticism of the North and especially of his beloved New England and native Massachusetts. Historical context is very important when one discusses Thoreau's position on slavery, – the South legally practiced slavery, while the North legally condemned it, but practically aided the South in this inhumane and shameful industry. New England's textile factories had huge contracts with Southern plantations and it seemed that the Yankee government had sacrificed its moral freedom for the sake of economic growth. The North aided the South by capturing and turning over the runaway slaves, by sharing economic fruits of slave-run plantations and, most importantly, by not expressing strong and definitive political will against this grave atrocity which was taking place in American history. Thoreau felt ashamed of being a member of such a state and firmly expressed his shame in a charged essay, *Slavery in Massachusetts*: "Let each inhabitant of the State dissolve his union with her, as long as she delays to do her duty", – duty of freedom and equality for all, that is! In another essay, "A Plea for Captain John Brown", he defends the freedom fighter and perhaps the greatest American hero to-date, Captain Brown and once again accuses his beloved New England of contributing to the Southern slavery: "The United States have a coffle of four million slaves. They are determined to keep them in this condition; and Massachusetts is one of the confederated overseers to prevent their escape." It was not uncommon for Americans to accuse Southern states of civil brutality, but even in accusation Thoreau had to be the pioneer, the champion, the seer of his nation's and humanity's welfare, – he clearly, loudly and unrelentingly accused and charged New England and its so called intelligentsia that was gaining and fattening up from Southern slavery.

CONCLUSION

Henry David Thoreau is indeed a radical, that is, his ideas are radically ahead of his time, as well as of the present time. Perhaps this is why many of our contemporaries unfairly brand Thoreau and assign to him a very obscure spot in American philosophy. It is also evident that his beliefs and idealism are difficult to practice, and that a few chosen activists who chose to lead their lives according to Thoreau's creed had ephemeral and tragic lives: Martin Luther King, Zviad Gamsakhurdia, Gandhi and John Kennedy would be sufficient to name. Although it must be admitted that such lives, tragic and short-lived as they were, are the lives which inspire us.

SUMMARY

1. Thoreau was a 19th century American philosopher, transcendentalist, Christian humanist, essayist, political activist and naturalist from New England.

2. Thoreau was a close friend of an American essayist, Ralph Waldo Emerson.

3. Thoreau spent two years in a self-built cabin almost in complete separation from social life at Walden Pond near Concord, Massachusetts, on the land owned by his best friend and essayist, Emerson. There he kept a diary and toiled as much on the soil, as he did on his writings.

4. "Walden" is Thoreau's book describing his spiritual Odyssey during his years of isolation at Walden Pond.

5. Thoreau was arrested in July of 1846 by a tax collector, as he was refusing to pay taxes to the government, which conducted unjust wars and oppressed its own citizens, referring to the Mexican-American war and the slavery.

6. Due to his short imprisonment, Thoreau writes "Civil Disobedience", a charged essay of a just citizen's conflict with his own unjust country.

7. Thoreau was one of the first Americans who challenged the idea of a big government and made a case against paternalism. He vehemently argued "That government is best which governs not at all."

8. Thoreau foresaw dangers of diminishing justice by the increase of powers of the legislators, judges and lawyers. He argued that justice system was a system of lies and deception, and a lawyer's trade was an art of flattery and sophisticated deception: "The lawyer's truth is not Truth."

9. According to Thoreau, democracy without an active involvement of virtuous citizens and political activism is not a democracy at all, but a pessimistic submission to the will of the ruling elite.

10. Thoreau believed that love of social responsibility and caring for the common good were what made a good man and a good citizen. In this sense, he argued that there were virtually no men left in America.

11. Thoreau accused the North of being just as guilty of slavery as the South on the several grounds:

    i. The North allowed Southern head hunters to catch slaves in the North;
    ii. Southern cotton, grown by slave labor, was used by the North in its textile industry;
    iii. The North did nothing politically to oppose slavery within the common country – America.

12. Henry David Thoreau is a beacon of political freedom, role model of citizenship and patriotism throughout many countries in the world, yet in the

United States his name is deliberately obscured and his legacy is dwindled to his hobbies of naturalism and transcendentalism, while his greatest and real accomplishments are largely unknown to American citizens.

13. Thoreau has been a role model to many prominent men, men of universal grasp of truth, good and humanism: Mohandas Gandhi of India, Dr. Zviad Gamsakhurdia of Georgia, Nelson Mandela of South Africa and our own Dr. Martin Luther King Jr. are just a few to name.

SECTION REVIEW

KEY TERMS

Abolitionist
Christian Humanist
Civil Activist
Civil Rights Movement
Emerson
Environmentalist
John F. Kennedy
Martin Luther King
Mohandas Gandhi
Naturalist
Nelson Mandela
New Englander
Paternalism
Poll tax
Polymath
Tax Resister
Transcendentalist
Yankee
Zviad Gamsakhurdia

CRITICAL THINKING

- Why was Thoreau jailed for a night?

- Why is Thoreau's refusal to pay taxes considered as civil disobedience?

- Explain the statement "the government is best which governs not at all."

- Explain Thoreau's views on voting.

- Which political activists of modern times were influenced with Thoreau's writings?

HUMANISTS

PRINCE ILIA CHAVCHAVADZE: ST. ILIA THE RIGHTEOUS

"People have forgotten that God himself has appointed only one Lord over men in this lifetime and that is their country."

PRINCE ILIA CHAVCHAVADZE:
ST. ILIA THE RIGHTEOUS

<u>Note:</u>
*Little is known about a small country of about five million people called **Georgia**, located at the juncture of East and West, Asia and Europe in the region of Caucasus. This is the country whose old name, **Iberia**, is still proudly bourn by the Iberian Peninsula at the very geographic commencement of the continent of Europe. This is the country, which culturally existed before the Indo-European Greeks marched onto the Iberian Peninsula and Italians settled on the Mediterranean. This is the country where Caucasian civilization was born with its **Golden Fleece** and **pre-Christian mysticism**. This is the country, from where **Prometheus** and other **Titans** descended and, according to the legend, where Prometheus is still currently chained. This is the country, which was the beacon of Eastern Orthodox Christianity with its prominent theologians and theosophist. This is the country, which yielded an entire philosophical pantheon of indigenous thinkers: St. Basil the Great, Peter the Iberian, Shota Rustveli, Anthim the Iberian, Davit Guramishvili, Ilia Chavchavadze, Zviad Gamsakhurdia and many others. In this book we intend to show unique contributions, which this nation has made to Western philosophy and political theory. We will do this by giving a short anthology of the greatest Georgian writer, poet, philosopher and political activist of the 19th century, Prince Ilia Chavchavadze, today* **canonized** *by Georgian Orthodox and Apostolic Church as St. Ilia the Righteous.*

BACKGROUND

St. Ilia the Righteous was born as Prince Ilia Chavchavadze in 1837 in a country called Georgia, which at that point had been conquered by Russia and remained a subject to the Russian empire under the brutal and oppressive occupation. He was first educated by a deacon of his native village, then attended a prestigious academy in the capital city of Tbilisi, and at last studied at the University of St. Petersburg to become a lawyer. Although his interests encompassed virtually every sphere of study, his attention was keenly drawn to learning Georgian and Western European literature and political science. It is difficult to cover St. Ilia's work and to describe contributions he made to Georgian national life. He virtually preserved the entire country from **Russification** and economic ruin, saved the nation from inner political instabilities and from very real devastations threatening to take place due to foreign **Imperialism** and occupation pressing from Russia. He was a writer, a publisher, a poet, a journalist, a theologian, a **grammarian**, a lawyer, a banker, a financier, a philosopher, a **theosophist**, an **apologist**, a **hymnographer**, a businessman and a man of innumerable talents and abilities. He was Henry David Thoreau for Georgian patriotism and **Benjamin Franklin** of the entire **Old World**. But most importantly he was a political theorist, as well as a practitioner, a political activist, in short, the one who without hesitation examined and reconciled the oldest Christian church to the oldest European statehood, – Georgian Orthodoxy to the political State of Georgia. But unlike an American or rather Anglo-Saxon protestant way, which is the separation of Church and state, St. Ilia did it by combination of those two. Georgian political model of St. Ilia has virtually no precedent in the political history of modern world.

Ilia Chavchavadze was assassinated, according to the orders of the Russian Emperor, Nikolai the 2nd, with a single bullet shot to his saintly forehead while he was traveling in a coach on the road outside of the city Mtskheta, – the religious capital of Georgia. This assassination was a direct blackmail aimed at every political activist in Georgia, – Russian empire desired an immediate submission of the freedom-loving nation to the "*Evil Empire*", as **Ronald Reagan** once rightfully and loudly called it.

SOCIAL OBLIGATION

St. Ilia was a Christian, so the rule, "love thy neighbor" became a part of his consciousness from the early childhood and remained a dominant force in his psyche to the very end of the days of his political activism. He believed that primary purpose of a human being is to praise God and the best way to do this is by doing good first and foremost for your countrymen and then for the entire humanity. He considered that it is crucial for a man to fulfill his social obligation; not doing so is contrary to human nature, and what is contrary to nature is harmful and even life-threatening to a man. Death itself could not harm an individual as stridently as escaping social contract with the nation and with mankind: "Death scares me not, as long as I leave a trace of my care for my fellow men behind me, so that future generations may look at my grave and whisper, – he has done his duty well." In this sense, Ilia Chavchavadze echoes to the words of Marcus Aurelius, when Aurelius too spoke of man's duty highly and described death as nothing more than a natural thing, and in order to encourage men to serve fellow human beings even at the cost of life, he added that: "we are dying from the day we are born."

At the dawn of capitalism, St. Ilia saw the dangers of unchecked moneymaking. He discerned that very frequently, if not always, private interest weakened sense of social responsibility in people and diminished patriotic sense collectively in a nation. Symbolically he compared the bourgeois nation to a communal slumber, which causes drowsiness of conscience and with it disappearance of man's God-given purpose and vanishing of human life's true meaning too: "O my God! Constant sleep and unremitting slumber! How long until we shall all wake up?!"

Social responsibility is not something done over a day or accomplished with a single good deed. It must be a constant effort on part of an individual citizen to benefit his fellow countrymen and humanity. For that Saint Ilia offers an advice, – make benefiting others your daily business and keep a good track of the deeds you do: "You become praiseworthy only by following one simple rule throughout the life: at the end of every single day ask yourself – how have I benefited my fellow men today?"

CHURCH AND STATE

Issue of Church and State is challenging for every modern nation, but especially for the nations of the Old World, where Church and State have centuries and even millenniums of history of coexistence, often in harmony and just as often in discord. This issue was especially problematic in the 19th century Georgia, when modernism, liberal thinking, foreign influence, economic crisis, political threats, all combined with imitators of unchecked license of Western bourgeoisie and of laziness of Middle Eastern nobility and direct aggression of Russian Empire's political and religious leaders against the independent state and its state religion… made a strong attack on Georgian Orthodox and Apostolic Church and threatened its complete annihilation. St. Ilia saw that one way Georgians always identified themselves as a politically independent nation was through their association with Georgian Orthodox Church. It followed that eradication of the church would consequently mean the extermination of Georgian statehood and independence, first, in the minds of its citizens and, then, in the awareness of the rest of the world. It was due to this pressing threat that Ilia Chavchavadze commenced a relentless political activity for protecting Georgian church and with it political freedom of the entire nation.

St. Ilia identified conditions which create a citizen in a singular sense and then an entire nation in an aggregate. His famous line still echoes in the minds of every citizen of today's Georgia: "Fatherland, Language, Religion", and perhaps the fact that presently they are citizens of an independent nation is owed precisely to this tri-dimensional definition of one's national identity. According to Ilia Chavchavadze, land is necessary as a fundamental resource to build a state and to support its statehood, hence the "Fatherland". Language is the mechanism with which uniqueness of a nation's thinking, its wisdom, its ethnos and matchless virtues are preserved and passed down from generation to generation, hence the "Language". Religion is the means by which a nation is congregated, united and strengthened. It fortifies people spiritually, but also politically, as it provides a powerful reason for citizens to associate themselves constantly, methodically and systematically, hence the "Religion". Although one must keep in mind that this particular state religion, which congregated Georgian nation and which St. Ilia advocated, namely Orthodox Christianity, is the religion of tolerance and love, even of other religions and cultures. State religion, according to St. Ilia, should not mean discrimination against other faiths and denominations. Quite the contrary! State religion meant congregation of every citizen under an umbrella of common good, which among Christians, as well as among other major faiths, is known under a simpler word, – love.

In spite of the fact that separation of Church and State virtually always existed in the United States, it must be noted that unification of these two according to the political model of St. Ilia is not completely foreign to American history. It was precisely due to religious freedom that this country's first settlers', pilgrims' political freedom commenced. And was it not religion, which united the first Americans on the Mayflower? The foremost of the founding fathers, Benjamin Franklin himself too preached social responsibility under the umbrella of religion. The very last advice in his "Thirteen Virtues" is humility, which is attainable only by imitating God and the God-fearing man: "Humility: Imitate Jesus and Socrates." African American slaves too found their minute freedom only in religious congregations and their will for political freedom was born in the church as well. So, small fragments of St. Ilia's political model of Church and State existed in our nation as well, which makes one think that in certain instances, especially when a country's political freedom and cultural independence are under a dire threat, unification, or at least a temporary amalgamation of Church and State is possible and even desirable.

PATRIOTISM V. BOURGEOISIE

St. Ilia was a ***pragmatic idealist***. He saw necessity of trade and finance, industry and technology. He even found pleasure in banking and agricultural studies. Yet he regarded unchecked private interest and life based solely on profit-making as nihilism and spiritual death of a man, of a citizen, of a country and at last of the entire humanity.

According to him, one way to oppose such a moral threat is to awaken patriotic sense in every citizen and to make him aware that the end of human existence is to benefit the country, and with it, of course, the entire mankind: "Young or old, no one feels heart ache of the nation anymore. People have forgotten that God himself has appointed only one Lord over men in this lifetime and that Lord is their country."

St. Ilia was disgusted by the bourgeoisie as these newly-hatched capitalists, whether they were old noblemen or freshly established merchants, oppressed working class and the educated alike by low wages, corruption of justice system and discrimination. He saw cheapening of learning. He condemned bourgeois thinking and pseudo-education: "I see not a single thought in their thinking." Ilia Chavchavadze foresaw spiritual emptiness, which follows greed and materialism, and the fact that once the materialist has oppressed others, he then starts oppressing his own soul, his own consciousness, his own life and this very life itself becomes one living emptiness: "Unbearable is his life, colorless and empty. It is neither life, nor tastefulness, and becomes repulsive, so that there is nothing enviable left in it. In such a life of human rapaciousness one day follows the other in utmost monotony."

Unbridled greed and unrestrained capitalism has many social implications, which we, through Ilia Chavchavadze's words, described in the previous paragraph, but the pinnacle of its wrongdoings is that it deprives a nation of its political freedom. It corrupts justice and legislation. It rewrites social values by setting wealth as the top value, accumulation of wealth as the top priority and the ability to hoard as the top virtue. At last, greed compels a man to sellout, – on one hand, by losing humaneness he sells an individual fellow human being and, on the other hand, by losing his patriotism he sells the entire country: "They exchange their feeling for gold; they sell their chastity to put a smile on boss' face; and they trade their nation's political freedom for rusty shackles of invading empires."

CONCLUSION

St. Ilia combines a layman and a priest-philosopher, pragmatism and idealism, tangible and intangible even in the duality of his name, – St. Ilia and Prince Ilia are twined and used interchangeably even in this book. His legacy is ample and multidimensional, but there is one point in his accomplishments, which shines the most, that is his political vision of Church and State coalesced in one body and creating perfect harmony in a democratic state. It is absolutely impossible to find a mortal man in world history whose accomplishments encompassed so many spheres of human and divine affairs and whose reach was so deep and profound on every issue. It is difficult to pinpoint St. Ilia's area of expertise, for he was a philosopher, poet, novelist, journalist, publisher, banker, financier, venture capitalist, project manager, agriculturist, farmer, theologian, theosophist, businessman, curator, humanist, philanthropist, lawyer, political scientist, activist, hero and a Saint all at once and all at all times. To his countrymen he is best known as Father of the Nation, to the world as St. Ilia. If other philosophers dedicated their entire lives to searching correct virtues, he found them fast and, without wasting valuable time, simply practiced them. If others wrote books on political theory and over-scrutinized issues of social contract, he wrote tombs on political science and kept renewing his social contract by his activism. In fact, at the end he signed the very contract with his blood when he was shot to death by the enemies of his country.

Today Prince Ilia Chavchavadze is widely regarded as the foremost founding father of modern Georgia. He was canonized as Saint Ilia the Righteous by the Georgian Orthodox Church. Today, Georgians revere Ilia Chavchavadze as ***Pater Patriae***, Father of the Fatherland of Georgia.

SUMMARY

1. Ilia Chavchavadze was a 19th and early 20th century Georgian political activist, philosopher, writer, poet, Orthodox Christian hymnographer, apologist, acclaimed critic, journalist, lawyer, banker, financier, venture capitalist, public servant, theosophist and theologian.

2. According to St. Ilia, social responsibility is a part of human nature and one must practice it daily.

3. Ilia Chavchavadze deemed patriotism as one of the most fundamental forms of social responsibility. He maintained that a man must extend his duty to his country and then to the entire humanity.

4. St. Ilia viewed death very similarly to Marcus Aurelius. He considered it to be a light burden to a man who has served the country and humanity well.

5. At the dawn of capitalism, Ilia Chavchavadze saw the dangers of unchecked commercialism. He discerned that very frequently, if not always, private interest weakened sense of social responsibility in people and diminished patriotic sense collectively in a nation.

6. Main creed in St. Ilia's social political philosophy is simple, yet profound: make benefiting others a daily task. In this lies a man's honor, argued St. Ilia, and, not unlike Marcus Aurelius or Plato-Socrates, he wrote: "You become praiseworthy, only by following one simple rule throughout the life: at the end of every single day ask yourself – how have I benefited my fellow men today?"

7. St. Ilia was a strong proponent of unification of church and state. He saw national identity most strongly expressed through Christian religion and argued that a Christian nation's liberty is closely hinged with its freedom of choice to practice Christianity, and that it was Christianity, which best preserved all the insignia of Georgian statehood, – Georgian language, alphabet, land, ethnicity, tradition, poetry, prose, morality and ethics.

8. St. Ilia identified three premises, which create a citizen in a singular sense and then an entire nation in an aggregate:

    i.   Fatherland – a physical land area;
    ii. Language – an original language of indigenous citizens;
    iii. Religion – Christian Orthodox religion, which unites people under an umbrella of eternal love and infinite virtue.

9. Ilia Chavchavadze argued that the purpose of a human life is not a self-benefit, but to benefit others, hence unchecked moneymaking is contrary to the God-given purpose and represents a deep perversion and transmutation of healthy human will into unhealthy desires.

10. St. Ilia made a distinction between true liberal education and trade. A man educated in a particular profession is no educated man: "I see not a single thought in their thinking."

11. St. Ilia argued that greed compels a man to sellout, – on one hand, by losing humaneness he sells an individual fellow human being and, on the other hand, by losing patriotism he sells the entire country.

12. Prince Ilia Chavchavadze was canonized as Saint Ilia the Righteous by the Georgian Orthodox Church. Today Georgians revere Chavchavadze as ***Pater Patriae***, Father of the Fatherland of Georgia.

SECTION REVIEW

KEY TERMS

Apologist
Benjamin Franklin
Canonized
Evil Empire
Georgia
Golden Fleece
Grammarian
Hymnographer
Iberia
Imperialism
Mysticism
Old World
Pater Patriae
Pragmatic Idealist
Pre-Christian Mysticism
Prometheus
Ronald Reagan
Russification
Theosophist
Titans

CRITICAL THINKING

• Explain St. Ilia's way of combining church and state.

• Describe Russification as a form of modern Imperialism.

• According to St. Ilia, how far does a man's social obligation extend? Does it encompass one's nation or does the obligation to benefit men extend beyond one's nationality?

• How does Ilia Chavchavadze's view on death and patriotism coincide with the views of Marcus Aurelius?

• What conflict did St. Ilia foresee between unrestrained capitalism and political freedom?

• Explain the term "pragmatic idealist."

• In your own words, paraphrase Ilia Chavchavadze's rule on social responsibility, which every person must put to own self in a form of a question at the end of every day.

ORIENTAL POLITICAL THEORISTS

CONFUCIUS

*"Exemplary people understand matters of justice;
small people understand matters of profit."*

CONFUCIUS

BACKGROUND

Confucius was a Chinese thinker and philosopher of the 5th century BC. It would not be an exaggeration to say that his teachings have defined Chinese social culture and in many ways the ideological character of Chinese civilization. Confucius' teachings have also deeply influenced thought and life of Korean, Japanese, Taiwanese and Vietnamese people.

Confucius is unique because his philosophy is social. It considers a single human only as a part of greater humanity. Unlike *Taoism*, which focuses on achieving individual spiritual peace, Confucius teaches that justly and honestly performing social responsibility is the source of attaining ultimate good for an individual.

Confucius did not consider himself a philosopher or an author of any philosophical doctrine or school of thought. He rather saw himself as a recipient and conveyor of the ancient learning developed over the centuries before him, and yet not by wise individuals, academics or individual philosophers, but rather by people and society – folk wisdom that is. Confucius' ideal was *social idealism*; therefore his philosophy too was *social philosophy*. In order to understand Confucius' strong drive towards common good and social enlightenment one must understand the time in which he lived and the events which preceded that time.

Confucius was born right after the death of *Guang Zhong*, the famous political philosopher and the prime minister of the state of Qi. He grew up fatherless in a state of Lu. The country was torn by many years of wars and political instability. Confucius supported himself by taking odd jobs. By the age of fifteen he had already developed deep interest in classical education and philosophy. By the age of thirty he had served as a teacher and then as an official of the state of Lu. In his early fifties he was made, first, a governor of the city and then the chief of constabulary. In his middle fifties he set out on a fourteen-year journey. He traveled through and lived in at least nine states of the old Zhou confederation, and returned home in the state of Lu in 484 BC. It was through this journey that Confucius strengthened his philosophic outlook on life and saw vividly that everywhere and anywhere an individual's good is attainable only through common good and that philosophy must be ultimately concerned with social rather than personal issues. Confucius was not a mere dreamer or a wishful thinker. He truly believed that common good was achievable. He based his belief particularly on one *historical precedent*, – government by virtue, which Confucius himself aspired and thought to be the only way to social good, had already existed in Chinese history, legends and folk tales. And what is even more important, remembrance of such a government and yarning for it still existed in Chinese people's collective consciousness. From that point on Confucius had one vision, – to revitalize the culture which was once epitomized during the liberal reigns of several memorable leaders of ancient China, which dated as far back as the 24th century BC. Chinese history has preserved well the names of the first three of these leaders, who governed by virtue, – Yao, Shun and Yu. Confucius' yarning for the past was due to progressive reasons rather than pessimism. His yarning was not for taking his people back in time, but rather for taking his people fully ahead with old virtues reborn and practiced anew.

Confucius' teachings are arranged in the *"Analects of Confucius"*, which is a collection of aphorismic fragments of his spoken wisdom passed down from generation to generation often by heart rather than by writing. The "Analects of Confucius" were compiled many years after his death and historians do not believe that the philosopher himself had written any segment or even any specific chapter of it. Instead it is considered that Confucius' aphorisms were socially popular, memorized by heart, and passed down through ages as folklore.

SOCIAL INDIVIDUALISM: EXEMPLARY INDIVIDUAL

Confucianism, when considering subject of its study, has a lot in common with Platonism and Neo-Platonism. It endeavors to find the purpose of human existence, the end and aim for which men are created and procreated. Confucius asserts that an individual must be exemplary and that his goodness must be applied to common good. Being exemplary means observing one's life and cultivating virtue. At this point one cannot help but think of Socrates' famous line and connect Confucius' views with Socrates' outlook on life, which the Greek philosopher summarized in one phrase: "The unexamined life is not worth living." Hellenistic Platonism was geographically far removed from ancient China. Confucius era too was some three quarters of a century ahead of Socrates. Yet ideology of both, Confucius and Plato-Socrates, were quite similar: an individual must examine his life, cultivate virtues and serve the society. Confucius strongly believed that such an "exemplary life" was especially necessary for the ruling class, as, firstly, it is in charge of governing people and then it is a role model for the public: "I examine myself three times a day: have I been unfaithful in planning for others? Have I been unreliable in conversation with friends? Am I preaching what I haven't practiced myself?"

ON RELIGION

It would be unbelievable to claim that an ancient Chinese man who passed away in 479 BC was a Christian, but it is not at all unbelievable to say that his wisdom had a lot in common with Christian teachings. "Love thy neighbor" is fully and repeatedly expressed in "Analects of Confucius". According to Confucius there is only one way of serving the higher being and it is by doing good for fellow men: "As long as you are unable to serve people, how can you serve ghosts?" Similarly Confucius asserts that one may attain Heaven only when one lives a well-examined life, first, here, on earth: "As long as you do not know life, how can you know death?" Indeed, even his religious views tend to be social rather than individualistic. An individual, according to Confucius, becomes pious only by being humane with his fellow humans, and this too is quite frequently preached and practiced among virtually all Christian denominations.

One virtue which Confucius places over others is faith. According to him without faith people depreciate to nothingness, but with faith, on the other hand, men connect to the inexhaustible source of the divine power: "If people have no faith, I don't know what they are good for. Can a vehicle travel without a link to a source of power?" And thus Confucius many centuries before the Christ's first coming once again connects with Christ and Christianity, for nowhere is Faith considered to be of such a principal virtue as in Christian teachings.

CONFUCIAN UTOPIA

Confucius' vision of an ideal state is based on a possibility of virtuous government. It is as much of an idealistic view, as it is pragmatic. Confucius is fully aware of the dishonesty which exists in every state and which frequently becomes an insurmountable obstacle for even the most virtuous rulers to govern justly and consistently. Yet he finds a way to deal with offenders, and once again it is a social remedy, not an individual one, – if a state appreciates exemplary lives of the honest and endorses such good citizens, then the dishonest will see benefits of being honest, will follow the suit and they too will become exemplary members of the society: "Promote the honest, placing them over the crooked, and you can cause the crooked to straighten out."

ON ECONOMIC GROWTH

Confucius acknowledges that economy is a part of human existence and that one needs to have some degree of material gain in order to exist. This is yet another proof of this philosopher's realistic idealism and his acute, rather than wishful, understanding of life. Human desire, which drives social economy, is indeed present and necessary for mankind, but such desires can be kept in check by practice of moderation and temperance: "…desire without being greedy." Being exemplary also requires doing charity, but even this must be done prudently, so no wastefulness begins to take place among people and ultimately among the state for it is harmful for the economy: "Good people are generous without being wasteful." Confucius also acknowledges necessity for toil, for realizing one's desires and satisfying basic human necessities require work, so no man has the right to resent labor: "they are hardworking without being resentful."

Although Confucius has no problem acknowledging reality of economic necessities in human, and especially in social existence, he strongly opposes greed and unchecked capitalism. His belief, and not without firm grounds, is that profits devoid of moral benefit oppose justice, and that commendable people are concerned with justice, while mere profits, profitable business which entails no honor that is, matter to petty folks only: "Exemplary people understand matters of justice; small people understand matters of profit."

Confucius is truly a social philosopher and his ultimate aim for an individual is to serve common good, but at the same time he values individuality and uniqueness of every human life. Social good does not mean blind conformity and annihilation of a person, of a human entity and eventually of a man. Confucius foresaw dangers of high economic growth and productivity, which often turn an individual into a number or a machine or an instrument of some economic goal: "An ideal person is not a tool." Keen relevance of this one phrase to our modern existence can be easily seen at a conveyor belt of an assembly line or of any for-profit institution which itself is one large conveyor belt of this or that industry today and has turned many men into an operative, a human subject and indeed into a profit-producing tool of some sort.

CONCLUSION

Confucius' legacy is truly enduring and extensive. He influenced thinking mode of the entire Far East Asia. After being introduced to the Western civilization by a

Jesuit Matteo Ricci, the first Latiniser of the name "Kong Zi", Confucius in his Analects clearly showed that the Asians, having many common social issues of the time with the Hellenic or the Caucasian West, also had common grasp of such issues and common outlook on social, political, economic and spiritual aspects of human existence. The aphorismic analects demonstrate that Socrates and Plato, or at least their comprehension of the world and their devout devotion to bettering men, existed in other parts of the world... in China it was perhaps under the name of Confucius, in ***Caucasia*** under the name of St. Ilia Chavchavadze or ***Shota Rustveli***, in Africa under the name of St. Augustine. In short, Confucius' philosophy united, not divided, the world's thinking, as it showed common social problems being thought of by such uncommonly virtuous men as himself and in different parts of the world and at different times by a few others, which we have just enumerated above.

SUMMARY

1. Confucius was a Chinese thinker and philosopher of the 5th century BC.

2. Confucianism is a philosophic school of thought, which has defined Chinese social culture and ideology. It has also heavily influenced principles of Korean, Japanese, Taiwanese and Vietnamese people.

3. Confucius' creed is social philosophy, – a man's personal good is common good, a man's life must be spent, not in private interest, but in acquiring this social good. This philosophy is called social idealism.

4. Confucianism opposes Taoism, as Taoism is practice of relative withdrawal from social life, while Confucianism, acknowledging hardships one may be subjected to during his social endeavors, still strongly advocates for a social engagement of a virtuous man.

5. Confucius teachings are arranged in "Analects of Confucius", which is a collection of aphorismic fragments of his spoken wisdom passed down from generation to generation in an oral tradition.

6. Confucius' social philosophy and its creed of common good is quite similar to the one advocated by Socrates and Plato.

7. Confucius shares many common values with Christianity, even though it would be a *pragmatic anachronism* to claim that Confucius borrowed these values from the Christian creed. Doing good to thy neighbor is one of the doctrines Confucius shares with and through Jesus Christ, as he argues that the best way of being religious is by making yourself socially beneficial: "As long as you are unable to serve people, how can you serve ghosts?"

8. Confucius believes in only one form of a political government, which is government by virtue.

9. Confucius acknowledges necessity of economy, but he argues that its growth and consumption must be done with moderation and without any waste.

10. Aim of Confucius philosophy is social good, but he values individuality of a man. He is an ardent opponent of oppression of an individual's free will and free choice, and argues that a man is a thinking being: "An ideal person is not a tool."

11. Confucianism today is practiced in China and South-East Asia most rigorously and his legacy has also immensely influence Western Thought.

SECTION REVIEW

KEY TERMS

Caucasia
Confucianism
Guang Zhong
Historical precedent
Jesuit
Pragmatic anachronism
Shota Rustveli
Social idealism
Social philosophy
Taoism

CRITICAL THINKING

- How does Confucius' political thought differ from Taoism?

- What is the goal of Confucianism?

- How does Confucius balance idealism with pragmatism in his philosophy?

- Who Latinised the name Kong Zi into Confucius?

ORIENTAL POLITICAL THEORISTS

LAO TZU

"Loving the people and ruling the state: can you avoid over-manipulation?"

LAO TZU: LAOZI

BACKGROUND

Lao Tzu is an honorific form of two words "old" and "master". Laozi is a central figure of **Taoism**. Tao simply means "way" in Chinese and refers to the way of peace and harmony, which a human can attain in this world. Taoism is a collection of spiritual and philosophical concepts and traditions, and is practiced like a religion.

There are no reliable historical sources to which origin of Lao Tzu can be traced, but in Chinese tradition and later historical documents in some instances he is thought to be from the sixth century BC and a contemporary of Confucius, and in some cases it is told that he was not a single individual, but rather a mythical figure, or a synthesis of multiple historical figures of ancient times. Some also assert that Lao Tzu lived in the 4th century BC during the **Hundred School of Thought**, a great cultural period in Chinese history, which flourished from 770 to 221 BC.

No other philosophical movement is more prevalent and significant, with an exception of Confucianism, in China and its surrounding domain than Taoism. At the same time these two movements are completely different in practice, although in theory their authors or rather their preaching philosophers, Lao Tzo and Confucius, never intended such a stark opposition. Both Lao Tzu and Confucius sought the way to be good and to live in harmony. It would be an over-simplification to state, but still, Lao Tzu saw "the way" in retiring from worldly affairs, from social corruption and political deviousness, and in finding the inner peace. Confucius envisioned accomplishing the same result, but by different means. He taught that being good and living in harmony could be accomplished not by withdrawing from the world, but rather by actively participating in it and by promoting good over bad, justice over injustice, truth over deception even under the most difficult and problematic circumstances. In spite of the differences in the means, it is quite clear that both, Lao Tzu and Confucius had the same goal – for a man to become morally, socially, politically and spiritually good.

GREEK SOPHROSYNE IN TAOISM

Even though **Sophrosyne** is a concept which was practiced in ancient Greece and popularized in the post-Christian era through Plato's writings, its concept was expressed in "Tao Te Ching" by Lao Tzu. Greeks upheld the ideal of Sophrosine, although it is difficult to translate it in any of today's modern languages, including English. Sophrosine roughly means quality of prudence and moderation. It derives from the two most famous maxims of the **Oracle of Delphi**: "Nothing in excess" and "Know thyself".

Lao Tzu too asserts that for inner peace and personal harmony moderation is a key: "An over-sharpened sword cannot last long. A room filled with gold and jewels cannot be protected." Lao Tzu values moderation over any knowledge when it comes to governing a political state. He considers it to be a mysterious virtue and a key to successful administration: "Loving the people and ruling the state: can you avoid over-manipulation? ...Excel, but don't take charge. This is called Mysterious Virtue." Moderation is a must in every aspect of human existence if one desires harmony, peace and rapture. Moderation, unlike greed and ambition, besides making happiness more attainable also makes it more durable: "...we always pay a great price for excessive love and suffer deep loss for great accumulation. Knowing what is enough, you will not be humiliated. Knowing where to stop, you will not be imperiled and can be long-lasting."

Prudence, which one must acquire, first, by "knowing thyself", is a common key point in Platonism and Taoism. Lao Tzu advises that everything must begin with one's self, whether it is examination of life or overcoming challenges: "If you overcome others you are powerful. If you overcome yourself you have strength." Lao Tzu is a strong proponent of observing and knowing inner-self, but he is just as much an advocate for studying the social surrounding, economic environment and political world. Knowledge of own self provides one with virtue, knowledge of the world gives one the world of virtues: "Cultivate it in yourself and virtue will be real. Cultivate it in the world and virtue will be everywhere. Therefore, take yourself and observe yourself. Take the world and observe the world."

Lao Tzu's approach to the ideal of Sophrosine is very unique and far-reaching. He understood that the two parts of this ideal, moderation and self-awareness, are interdependent and exist in constant *correlation* and *causation*. Lao declares that excess is caused by lack of self-knowledge and moderation is brought only by thoroughly knowing thyself: "Natural disasters are not as bad as not knowing what is enough. Loss is not as bad as wanting more. Therefore the sufficiency that comes from knowing what is enough is an eternal sufficiency."

POLITICAL GOVERNMENT

Lao Tzu promoted inner peace and withdrawal from worldly flaws. Confucians often argue that Lao did not recognize social duty and common good. Alas, they are mistaken. Lao's withdrawal was from the evils, wrongs and decadence of the world, not from the world itself. "Tao Te Ching" is full of advices on management, administration, kingship and on governing a political state. Lao offered several suggestions on political administration. He asserted that frugality is one way men fulfill their social obligation. In fact, frugality benefits a private citizen, just as much as it profits an aggregate, a nation, and ultimately the practice of frugality leads to acquisition of virtue: "In governing the country and serving Heaven there is nothing like frugality. Only by being frugal can you recover quickly. When you recover quickly you accumulate virtue."

Lao Tzu offers an advice for large political states and suggests that they must be sort of a mixing bowl of the world, where diversity is nurtured: "The great state should be like a river basin. The mixing place of the world..." This certainly has relevance to social-political history of the United States. Arguably its political and economic success is precisely due to the diversity, which it achieved by being, as many like to say, a melting pot of all cultures and variety of backgrounds.

Lao Tzu opposes government by force and fear. Unlike Niccolo Machiavelli's model of governing expressed in his famous quote "it is better to be feared than loved", Lao asserts that true greatness of power should no longer inspire fear, which is politically paralyzing and mutually damaging: "When the people do not fear your might then your might has truly become great."

Lao Tzu foresaw the usefulness of a ***decentralized government***, where more power is granted to the local administrators who are more knowledgeable about local issues than the federal centrists. Lao saw utmost necessity in preserving certain personal freedoms and thought it essential to decrease interference of a government in personal matters. He saw that increased individual freedom would be beneficial for a country as a whole. Millenniums before modern times, he saw that political micromanagement would be felt as an oppression by the people: "Don't interfere with their household affairs. Don't oppress their livelihoods."

EDUCATION AND VIRTUE

Lao Tzu shared common view on education with Western philosophers. Socrates always ironically spoke in Plato's writings that he was never rich and fortunate enough to have formal education. Descartes claimed that one did not need to be educated in Socratic dialogues to achieve Platonic virtues. Lao Tzu asserted something quite similar – that one only needs to be educated just enough, not being overeducated that is, in order to be able to retain room for clear and uninfluenced thinking: "The one who really knows is not broadly learned. The extensively learned do not really know."

CONCLUSION

Lao Tzu's legacy can easily be seen in China and South-East Asia. Its non-aggressive and peaceful way, Tao, leads men to success in many areas of life. Lao Tzu's wisdom is just as much applicable to spiritual matters as to political issues, social and economic concerns. Taoism advocates softness over hardness, quiet over riot, less over more and thus and only thus advocates achieving long-lasting, not a short lived, triumph. Although it still remains astonishing that the 6th century BC Chinese master had ideologically so much in common with the 5th century BC Athenian philosopher, or that his creed clearly coincided with Sophrosyne of the Oracle of Delphi. This must certainly be looked at as yet another proof of human rights, that all men, in spite of their nationality, race, geographic location... are created truly equal and that we, as humans, must always have something in common, – humaneness.

SUMMARY

1. Lao Tzu was an ancient Chinese philosopher of the 6th century BC. He is a central figure of Taoism. Lao Tzu means an Old Master in Chinese.

2. Taoism is a collection of spiritual and philosophical concepts and traditions, and is practiced like a religion.

3. Taoism alongside Confucianism is the most influential school of thought in China and South-East Asia.

4. Taoism advocates withdrawal from worldliness, which is a contradiction to Confucianism that promotes social involvement for the men of virtue.

5. Taoism shares values with the Greek concept of Sophrosyne: moderation and close examination of one's own life. Lao Tzu too asserts that for inner peace and personal harmony moderation is a key: "An over-sharpened sword cannot last long", says Lao Tzu on moderation. "Cultivate it in yourself and virtue will be real. Cultivate it in the world and virtue will be everywhere. Therefore, take yourself and observe yourself. Take the world and observe the world", says Lao Tzu on examining one's life.

6. Lao Tzu sees large states as mixing bowls of the diverse cultures and encourages them to promote personal freedom and diversity: "The great state should be like a river basin. The mixing place of the world..."

7. Lao Tzu is a proponent of a decentralized government where, more power is granted to the local administrators who are more knowledgeable of local issues than the federal centrists.

8. Lao Tzu valued education, but ultimately saw its limitations and argued that "The one who really knows is not broadly learned. The extensively learned do not really know."

9. Taoism is a non-aggressive school of thought, which advocates inner peace and relative withdrawal from social affairs. Lao Tzu's legacy is significant, as Taoism has promoted peace among billions of people in Asia.

SECTION REVIEW

KEY TERMS

Causation
Correlation
Decentralized Government
Sophrosyne
Hundred School of Thought
Oracle of Delphi
Taoism

CRITICAL THINKING

• Compare and contrast the theories of Lao Tzu and Confucius.

• Explain how the moderation preached by Lao Tzu may be useful for a head of state.

• Explain the concept of Greek Sophrosyne in terms of Taoism.

• What is Lao Tzu's view on education?

• Why did Lao Tzu disagree with Machiavellian form of ruling by fear?

AMERICAN POLITICAL PHILOSOPHY

MARTIN LUTHER KING, JR.

"I have a dream..."

MARTIN LUTHER KING, JR.

BACKGROUND

Although Dr. Martin Luther King, Jr. never in fact held a political office, he is remembered as one of the most renowned figures in the history of American politics. The prominent African American civil rights leader held various positions as a Baptist minister, attorney, orator and political activist. He is known worldwide as a *human rights* icon and even recognized by two Christian Churches as a *martyr*. King is also the recipient of a *Nobel Peace Prize* for his work to end *racial segregation* and discrimination through non-violent means such as *civil disobedience*.

King is widely considered in the United States as the single most important African American leader in American history. He is credited with changing the lives of millions of Americans, both white and black; indeed, he quickly became the face of the *civil rights movement*. Despite not being a politician, his beliefs and ideas eventually shaped the American political landscape into what it is today.

A MYRIAD OF INFLUENCES

It is somewhat difficult to say that King championed or believed in just a single political theory or ideology. He was an intellectual who sought to comprehend the full range of effects of his actions on the general public. Politically, King strived to instill egalitarian thinking into a society dominated by *capitalism* and segregation. Such philosophies included *Protestantism, Ghandian thought, social democracy, Marxism* and *republicanism*.

Over the years few have paid attention to King's political thought mainly due to the fact that he was not a student of politics, that is the academic discipline of political science; however, this also has to do with the fact that his most profound ideas and theoretical contributions were expressed in famous speeches, public appearances, and interviews rather than in extensive *manifestos*, academic treatises or theoretical inquiries. It is fair to say one of the most vital characteristics that made King successful in his travails was his ability to obtain weighty insight on the political world which he sought to affect.

FREEDOM AND POLITICAL PARTICIPATION

A large part of King's mission was to reshape conventional understandings of the term freedom. In his view freedom includes equality among those who are free and the opportunity to participate in social and political action. In addition, King believes political agents are free if they have completely equal rights, are neither forced into nor excluded from politics, and have more or less decent economic and social standings to participate proudly without having to endure any hardship. Therefore, freedom includes the ability to participate in meaningful action.

Furthermore, King's political theory essentially looks at political participation as a necessity for all citizens of the country to possess if complete equality is to be achieved and used to better the lives of the populace. The importance King attached to political participation implies an acceptance of the political system in which he sought to be a part. His support of such a system, which at the time denied blacks the same rights as whites, separates him from other black leaders of the civil rights era such as *Malcolm X* who steadfastly denied that the system could serve blacks justly. Hence King embraced a policy of *inclusion* instead of *anti-formalism*.

Dr. Martin Luther King, Jr. believed the right to vote would enable blacks to live a decent life in two ways: one, by dignifying the black community; and two, by being able to improve their lives in the manner of their choice. In short, King's theory does not only require that African-Americans merely gain the right to participate meaningfully in politics, but to expand and convert such participation into gains in policymaking – without that no truly meaningful participation in politics could exist.

NONVIOLENT RESISTANCE AND POLITICAL ORGANIZATION

As noted earlier, King was politically savvy and was a strong proponent of civil disobedience. The first major example of this was in 1955 when *Rosa Parks* was arrested for refusing to give up her seat on a bus in Montgomery, Alabama. This set off *The Montgomery Bus Boycott* which lasted for 385 days. As the primary leader of the boycott, King had his house bombed and even spent time in jail. Eventually, the standoff ended with a United States District Court ruling in *Browder v. Gayle* which banned racial segregation on all Montgomery public buses.

In 1957, King co founded the *Southern Christian Leadership Conference (SCLC)* in order to create moral authority and to organize the power of black churches to conduct non-violent protests for the civil rights reform. He felt that organized and non-violent protests against racist *Jim Crow laws* would eventually lead to a plethora of media coverage for the black struggle towards equality and voting rights. King believed the images of blacks being beaten and suffering would over the course of time sway the broad public to develop a sympathetic opinion of the battle for equal treatment under the law. Overall, King and SCLC utilized the principles of nonviolent protest with great success which obviously frustrated the enemy.

In August of 1963, King represented the SCLC in Washington, DC at the *March on Washington for Jobs and Freedom*. The march made various demands such as an end to racial segregation in schools, meaningful civil rights legislation, protection of civil rights workers from police brutality and a $2 minimum wage for all workers. It was at the march that King delivered his "I Have a Dream" speech which is considered one of the most famous speeches in American history.

CONCLUSION

Today King is recognized internationally as a symbol for modern era political martyrdom and civil rights movement. He used his talent and the political opportunities with which he was endowed to achieve equality and civil rights for all Americans regardless of color, ethnicity, political affiliation or social standing. He recognized the need to achieve human rights not only theoretically, on paper, but, more importantly, to acquire economic wealth which empowers people politically. In 1983 President Ronald Reagan signed a bill creating a national Martin Luther King, Jr. day in the United States.

Also King's statue stands in the Gallery of 20th Century Martyrs at Westminster Abbey in England. He is remembered as the most famous face of the Civil Rights Movement. King was assassinated on April 3, 1968 by James Earl Ray in Memphis, Tennessee.

SUMMARY

1. King is remembered as one of the most renowned figures in the history of American politics. He was a Baptist minister, attorney, orator and political activist.

2. He was the key leader of the civil rights movement.

3. He was heavily influenced by Protestantism, Gandhian thought, social democracy, Marxism and republicanism.

4. Instead of writing books or essays on certain issues, King expressed most of his ideas through public speaking.

5. King believed freedom meant having the legal right to participate in politics and having the economic means to participate without experiencing hardships.

6. King was a savvy political organizer and a strong proponent of civil disobedience.

SECTION REVIEW

KEY TERMS

Anti-formalism
Browder v. Gayle
Capitalism
Civil Disobedience
Ghandian Thought
Human Rights
Inclusion
Jim Crow Laws
Nobel Peace Prize
Malcolm X
Manifestos
March on Washington for Jobs and Freedom
Martyr
Marxism
Protestantism
Racial Segregation
Republicanism
Rosa Parks
Social democracy
Southern Christian Leadership Conference (SCLC)
The Montgomery Bus Boycott

CRITICAL THINKING

- Despite not being a career politician, which characteristics contributed to King's success?

- List the philosophies that influenced King.

- Why have many ignored the political theory of King?

- Explain King's idea of freedom and equality.

- How did King's ideology differ from other black leaders during his time?

AMERICAN POLITICAL PHILOSOPHY

HANNAH ARENDT

"Political questions are far too serious to be left to the politicians."

HANNAH ARENDT

BACKGROUND

Hannah Arendt (1906-1975) was a German Jewish political theorist, and one of the most famous political philosophers of the twentieth century. At a youthful age of twenty seven she fled Nazi Germany in 1933 and spent eight years in Paris, helping Jewish refugees and victims of the *holocaust*. She later immigrated to the United States in 1941, and shortly after became an influential member of the New York academy. She taught in several American Universities, publishing among other things, two major works in political philosophy.

In her first major work: The Origins of Totalitarianism (1951), she analyzed the nature of *Nazism* and *Stalinism* in Germany and former Soviet Union respectively, and in the second, The Human Condition,(1958), she explored the nature of work, labor and action – the three principles she believes define the essence of humanity. She also published other essays on revolution, freedom, authority, tradition and the modern age. She also wrote The Life of the Mind, which dealt with thinking, willing and judging.

POLITICS

For Arendt, politics has an existential connotation, because it is only in public life that freedom can really be actualized. Like Cicero, she argues that true living is to live for the public good and this is what they both took from ancient Greece. Arendt was attracted by life in ancient Greek poleis, where the citizens are routinely involved in direct democracy, and come together to deliberate on the common good. Real politics is where people unite deliberation and dialogues to articulate and execute what is in their public good not an arena for domination and absolute control.

Arendt believes that the real meaning of human life can be found in immortal propositions and actions, through continuous communication with others. Mankind as *homo laborans* emphasizes work as the essential condition of human nature, whose primary purpose is to cater for the biological needs. This is similar to Marx's *homo faber*, that is, the manufacturing man working for his material sustenance.

NATURAL DEMOCRACY

Arendt places very high premium on natural democracy as the most genuine version thereof, especially because of its spontaneity. She was attracted to instances of direct democracy such as the New England Town Meetings, the Paris Communes, the council of workers and soldiers in Russia and Europe especially during times of revolutions. She also cherished the spontaneous US students' movements of the 1960s. Obviously, Arendt would felt equally elated by the traditional and *consensual democracy* of many pre-colonial African societies, such as the Igbo. Mass society, she argues has destroyed this self-governance and autonomy of the people as individuals.

Hannah Arendt clearly articulates the separateness of public and private spheres of human existence and actions. She separates the world of the home from the *res publica* in the **Greco-Roman** traditions. Cicero had earlier argued in favor of this separateness by defining corruption as the co-mingling of public property or affairs with private interests.

ARENDT V. TOTALITARIANISM

Arendt was horrified by totalitarianism which she calls the modern form of domination. She argues that it reduces the authenticity of the individual and his unique contribution to history. By assuming absolute control of society, totalitarianism whether under Nazi-style fascism or under Marxist- Leninism, politically diminished the individual. Such regimes rob the individual of his essential human characters. In other words, the omnipotent totalitarian state renders the individual both superficial and superfluous. This destruction of individuality is one of the most invidious characters of totalitarianism. Mass society is an inadequate replacement of individuality and the naturally sanctioned history-making character of humans as individuals. Politics though a gregarious activity, it cannot be deprived of individual its individualist contents. For Arendt, true power is a political product evolving from the united actions of individuals.

The natural character of **humans qua humans** is to learn from mistakes while striving towards getting it right. Living is a comprehensive struggle to get things right. Politics is the most practical expression of this struggle. Democratic politics is politics **par excellence.** According to Schattschneider (1965) democracy is neither perfect nor omniscient. The attraction of democracy is that it is a system of governance organized by people who recognize that they are not perfect. It is a freedom-based enterprise.

Furthermore, mass societies of totalitarianisms rob people of their primary qualities as autonomous thinking, working and judging entities. It is this usurpation that facilitates the evils that are inherent in such dehumanized regimes, causing them to act like machines without conscience and susceptible to atrocious actions such as the holocaust and other crimes against humanity. This is why Arendt sadly viewed politics as an ongoing conflict between freedom and tyranny. Arendt would agree that mass propaganda, wholesale power, and mass killing machines have made modern totalitarianism more dangerous than the tyrannies of the past. The alienation of individuals from public life has resulted in the enthronement of mass deceit as the basis of modern politics.

Arendt rejected the irreversible fusion of the three essential qualities of man as individuals, namely: labor, thought and action. Work has become mere labor through mass production of the assembly line. She did not see totalitarianism as benign gesture to improve the human condition but calculated efforts by what Liam O'Sullivan (1984) referred to as **demagogic** illusionism aimed at destroying the true meaning of humanity.

Arendt subscribed to the Greek notion that the true meaning of human life is achieved through perpetual acts appreciated in the infinite discourses of others, and especially infinite posterity. The common sense that is imbued in realism is the antidote against deliberate imposition of false world views. She was reacting to the systematic lies and distortions that were endemic in extant totalitarian systems that sought to create utopias or fairytale worlds where everything was possible. The modern world according to Arendt is quick to promoting imagination over reality. One might argue that modern democracies are not immune to similar mass deception, but unlike totalitarian regimes, democracies are always subject to popular control through regular competitive elections.

CONCLUSION

Hannah Arendt is an *atypical* conservative scholar whose incursion into political philosophy is somewhat radical in itself. She ventured into male dominated intellectual arena, and quite audaciously challenged the two awe-inspiring ideologies that made the twentieth century the bloodiest in human history. In a unique way, Arendt was liberal and conservative at the same time. She challenges totalitarianisms of the right and of the left. She fought against the fascism of Nazi Germany, a right-wing totalitarianism, as well as, its left wing opposite, Soviet communism. Challenging these new forms of political corporatism of both the right and left that usurp individual rights and freedoms could be considered the core of Hannah Arendt's political philosophy if not its *raison d'etre*.

As a pro-Hellenist scholar, Arendt vouched for the ideal of Greek political philosophy with its emphasis on popular democracy, while rejecting the commandeering of individual freedom and liberties by arrogant dictatorships pretending benevolence. For her, the rise mass societies engineered by the aforementioned liberal and conservative totalitarianisms have trivialized the essence of humanity as they attempted to nullify the import of individual citizens' aggregate strivings of individual engaged in concert with one another. Only in public life can true freedom be realized. Extant difficulties are consequences of the negation or closures of avenues of self expression, occasioned by the inordinate ambitions of tyrants playing God and assuming omniscience. It is only publicness that is imbued with the illumination of common experience and realities that can prevent the unnecessary search, by an arrogant few, for unrealizable utopias that appallingly result in man-made calamity such as the Holocaust.

SUMMARY

1. Hannah Arendt (1906-1975) was a German Jewish political theorist, and one of the most famous political philosophers of the twentieth century.

2. At a youthful age of twenty seven she fled Nazi Germany in 1933 and spent eight year in Paris helping Jewish refugees and victims of the holocaust. She later immigrated to the United States in 1941, and shortly became an influential member of the New York academy.

3. In her first major work: The Origins of Totalitarianism (1951), Arendt analyzed the nature of Nazism and Stalinism in Germany and former Soviet Union respectively, and in the second, The Human Condition,(1958), she explored the nature of work, labor and action-the three principles she believes define the essence of humanity.

4. Arendt believes that the real meaning of human life can be found in immortal propositions and actions, through continuous communication with others.

5. Arendt places very high premium on natural democracy as the most genuine version thereof, especially because of its spontaneity.

6. Hannah Arendt clearly articulates the separateness of public and private spheres of human existence and actions. She separates the world of the home from the res publica in the Greco-Roman traditions.

7. The natural character of humans qua humans is to learn from mistakes while striving towards getting it right.

8. Arendt rejected the irreversible fusion of the three essential qualities of man as individuals, namely: labor, thought and action.

9. Hannah Arendt is an atypical conservative scholar whose incursion into political philosophy is somewhat radical in itself.

SECTION REVIEW

KEY TERMS

Nazism
Stalinism
Consensual democracy
Homo laborans
Homo faber
Humans qua humans
Par excellence
Demagogic
Holocaust
Atypical
Raison d'etre
Res publica
Greco-Roman

CRITICAL THINKING

* Why can it be said that Hannah Arendt was liberal and conservative at the same time?

* How does Arendt's view of politics differ from the conventional view?

* What did Arendt see as the major problem of totalitarianisms?

* In Arendt's view are totalitarians benign why not?

* What went wrong with modern governance, according to Hannah Arendt?

* What was Hannah Arendt's attraction with the politics of ancient Greece?

AMERICAN POLITICAL PHILOSOPHY

JOHN RAWLS

"The principles of justice are chosen behind a veil of ignorance."

JOHN RAWLS

BACKGROUND

Born in Baltimore, Maryland in 1921, John Rawls perhaps, lacks the exotic origin, which characterizes most philosophers in this collection. Arguably, to us, Rawls also falls among the modern thinkers so contemporary that their values have not matured like old wine. Yet Rawls makes tremendous impact on political philosophy not only by his thirty years of teaching at Harvard but also by his impressive scholarship that culminated in the publication of several quality essays in philosophical journals and especially his masterpiece and Magnus Opus titled, "A Theory of Justice". This book instantly became a must read for nearly all political theorists in America and beyond, mainly because of its originality.

John Rawls, like Plato of antiquity, rightly identifies justice as the quintessential attribute for a legitimate political society. As a true philosopher, Rawls also seeks to establish a new beginning for a just society. Essentially, John Rawls is concerned with justice as fairness. This just society has to be deliberately constructed to deliver fairness to all of its members.

SELF-INTERESTED RATIONAL PERSONS, VEIL OF IGNORANCE AND RATIONAL CHOICES

Rawls posits three guiding principles, namely: original position, self- interested persons and a *veil of ignorance*. Like other seminal figures in the history of political philosophy, especially those of the social contract tradition such as Hobbes, Locke and Rousseau who articulated the concept of the *state of nature* as that primordial moment in the origin of state, John Rawls posits the *original position* as the crucial moment in the founding of a just society. This original position represents that moment in time at the birth of such a state during which *self-interested rational persons* decided to create a just society.

Why the idea of a self-interested rational persons? Self-interestedness means that everyone would choose what is in their best interest. Rawls principle of justice cannot operate in a political space inhabited by people who are ignorant of their interest. Instead, it is one involving *rational choices* of self-interested rational persons who if given the choices of good and bad would opt for what is in their best interest while leaving others with the raw deals. Corruption results from cheating the public for selfish interests and gains. To forestall this, the advantages and disadvantages of members of this new society must be neutralized by denying everyone prior knowledge of where they stand and how they can benefit more than others, through a veil of ignorance according to John Rawls.

The veil of ignorance becomes the equalizer under which these self-interested persons would be subjected. The veil means that none would be aware of his or her condition or status while deciding according to Harold Lasswell, who gets what when and how in society. Under the veil of ignorance everyone would think about what would happen if they were the disabled members of the society. Where would the one like to be, and how would one like to be treated? On the one hand, knowledge of the fact that you will always be wealthy predisposes you to argue against high taxes to cater for the poor.

On the other hand knowing that you will always be poor makes you a natural supporter of high taxes to cater for the poor. A veil of ignorance neutralizes these self-protecting prejudices. If people knew their conditions and circumstances, they naturally make policies that would benefit people like themselves and make sure that people like themselves have the best of all things.

Therefore, the rational thing to do is to ensure that there is unmitigated justice for all, as this would be the only way to ensure that everyone would get justice no matter their station in life. If, for instance, I knew before hand that I would never be handicap, I could foreclose any policy that would benefit those who would handicap. This is what one's self-interestedness would suggest, but because people are precluded from such vantage positions due to the veil of ignorance they logical thing to do would be to create level playground for all irrespective of status and condition.

MODUS VIVENDI

In justice as fairness, Rawls sees justice as the first virtue of social institution. His original position resembles the state of nature of the social contract theorists and those who seek a zero point at which a *modus vivendi* is established. In this case the moment of laying the foundation for social relationships in which all would feel comfortable. Prior knowledge of one's talents and privileges can prevent or even blind the one from seeing the advantages one enjoys and the disadvantages others suffer. So a veil of ignorance becomes necessary to preclude such prior knowledge of one's situation and condition. With this ignorance, one can legislate fairly and entrench situations which would be inherently fair to all. The postulation is that only a self-hating or oblivious imbecile would jeopardy his own wellbeing when given the chance. Hence, the self-interested rational arbiter would only create conditions that would be beneficial to him no matter where he falls on the social spectrum.

Rawls posits two basic principles of justice as fairness. First, everyone should have as much freedom as is compatible with similar freedom for everyone else. Second, if there are benefits to be shared from social cooperation, they should be distributed in a way that the most disadvantaged person has to be as well off as possible. For instance, "chances to acquire cultural knowledge and skills should not depend upon one's class position, and so the school system, whether public or private, should be designed to even out class barriers."

Conservatives may find fault with this as distributive justice, but is must be noted that Rawls was not speaking of absolute equality of all, just that social advantages and disadvantages should not be predetermined. Rather any forms of inequality among people should only come from individuals' special efforts and the lucky breaks like being at the right place at the right time while possessing the best talents for the particular situations, not by any calculated corrupt human interventions.

Furthermore, Rawls justifies *civil disobedience* arguing that only a just state is entitled to the citizens' obedience. Like St. Thomas Aquinas before him, and even Reverend Dr. Martin Luther King Jr., Rawls argues that unjust laws are no laws. Disobeying an unjust law is a civic duty aimed at not only exposing the failings of the state but also to dissuade the authors of such laws from making them.

CONCLUSION

Rawls recreates an ideal condition for the establishment of a just society. In this situation no one knows their position and their disadvantages. Hence a blind order is created which benefits everyone no matter where they eventually fall in after the veil of ignorance is removed. This order is supposedly created by people who love themselves and care for their own interests, and would choose the best outcome if given the choice. The goal therefore is to establish a universally good order as the only way to ensure that they would not be adversely impacted by any situations that happen to be their lots. Justice as fairness means determining of benefits in society based on the condition that a neutral order is created in which everyone would get what they get without a preconceived and biased intervention of human elements. In other words, all must comply with the principle of *the golden rule* by not giving to others what they would not accept for themselves. John Rawls theory of justice is like Anthony Dawns, theory of rational choice.

SUMMARY

1. John Rawls was an American political theorist born in Baltimore, Maryland in 1941.

2. Rawls, perhaps, lacks the exotic origin, which characterizes most philosophers in this collection. Arguably, Rawls also falls among the modern thinkers so contemporary that their values have not matured like old wine.

3. John Rawls, like Plato of antiquity, rightly identifies justice as the quintessential attribute for a legitimate political society.

4. Rawls posits three guiding principles, namely: original position, self- interested persons and a veil of ignorance.

5. In justice as fairness, Rawls sees justice as the first virtue of social institution. His original position resembles the state of nature of the social contract theorists and those who seek a zero point at which a modus vivendi is established.

6. Justice as fairness means determining of benefits in society based on the condition that a neutral order is created in which everyone would get what they get without a preconceived and biased intervention of human elements. In other words, all must comply with the principle of the golden rule by not giving to others what they would not accept for themselves.

7. John Rawls theory of justice is like Anthony Dawns, theory of rational choice.

SECTION REVIEW

KEY TERMS

Veil of ignorance
Original position
Self-interested rational persons
State of nature
Modus Vivendi
The golden rule
Rational choice
Civil disobedience

CRITICAL THINKING

• What are the two basic principles of justice according to John Rawls?

• How does Rawlsian justice conform with or differ from the golden rule?

• What do Rawls, Aquinas, and MLK Jr. have in common in their philosophies of justice and proper citizenship?

• Compare Plato's theory of justice with that of John Rawls.

• How is Rawls theory of justice analogous to the theory of rational choice?

• Is Rawls theory of justice utilitarian?

EUROPEAN REALISTS

LEO TOLSTOY

"The purpose of every man is to strive toward moral perfection."

LEO TOLSTOY

BACKGROUND

Leo Tolstoy was a Russian writer whom many consider to be the world's greatest political novelist. His masterpieces *"War and Peace"* and *"Anna Karenina"* represent, in their scope, breadth and vivid depiction of 19th century Russian life and attitudes, the peak of realist fiction and philosophy. Tolstoy's further talents as essayist, dramatist, political philosopher and educational reformer made him the most influential member of the aristocratic Tolstoy family. His literal interpretation of the ethical teachings of Jesus, centering on the *"Sermon on the Mount"*, show him as a pioneering Christian political theorist. His ideas on nonviolent resistance, expressed in such works as *"The Kingdom of God Is Within You"*, were to have a profound impact on such pivotal twentieth-century figures as Mahatma Gandhi and Martin Luther King, Jr.

CHILDHOOD AND ARISTOCRATIC "EDUCATION"

Leo Tolstoy or Count Lyev Nikolayevich Tolstoy was born on September 9, 1828 in Yasnaya Polyana, which means "Bright Field" in English, – the family estate in the Tula region of Russia. The Tolstoys were a well-known family of old Russian nobility. He was the fourth of five children of Count Nikolai Ilyich Tolstoy, a veteran of the crusade of 1812, and Countess Mariya Tolstaya (maiden name Volkonskaya).

Tolstoy's parents died when he was young, so he and his siblings were brought up by relatives. Tolstoy himself describes of what sort of bringing up that was in his semi-autobiographical story *"Childhood"*. In those days Russian noble families used to hire Central and Western European governesses who worked relentlessly to impose academic studies on the youngsters for the purpose of turning them into perfect aristocrats. But this resulted in subduing and eventually completely eradicating that naturally free and creative spirit which is present in every child. The end effect of this "education" was the external luster of an individual with all its noble propriety, decorum and cultured appearance, which were necessary attributes of noble men and women. In the result true talents of an individual were destroyed. Tolstoy's inner gift was ever so great that even though he experienced all of this academic *"lobotomy"* ever so ubiquitously present in his society, he still remained true to his nature and was able to retain and develop his genius – his ability, and for that the ability of every human being, to think freely.

In 1844 he began studying oriental languages at Kazan University; soon after he changed his major to law and jurisprudence. Although his teachers described him as "both unable and unwilling to learn", Tolstoy was an ardent reader of Montesquieu and Jean-Jacques Rousseau. Their writings had a tremendous impact on the young man. He once said, "I worship Rousseau!" In the middle of his studies, Tolstoy, quite disappointed in the dogmatic ways of the formal education, left the university, returned to Yasnaya Polyana and endeavored to better existence of Russian peasants. He described his country experience in his literary work, *"Landlord's Morning"*. Alas, the young idealist was faced with lots of obstacles, which compelled him to leave the country and seek his fortunes in big cities. He spent much of his time in Moscow and Saint Petersburg. In 1851, after running up heavy gambling debts, he went with his elder brother to the

Caucasus and joined the army. Around this time, he started to write, and it could be said that in Caucasus, namely in Georgia, his Muse was born. Whether it is a coincidence or not, the same happened to many Russian writers and philosophers – Georgia was that mystical land which cradled not only Georgian talent, but the talent of the tyrannical empires which attempted its conquest. Georgian experience inspired Russian playwright and composer Alexander Griboyedov, the foremost Russian poet Alexander Pushkin, prominent Russian Romantic writer, poet and painter Mikhail Lermontov and many others.

TOLSTOY V. SOCIAL ETIQUETTE

Tolstoy's first work, *"Childhood"* was published in 1852. This is an autobiographic novel with very heavy political undertones, which was written outside of Russia, when the young writer was serving as a military officer in Tbilisi, Georgia. Soon after its sequels, *"Boyhood"* and *"Youth"* followed. The hero of all three novels is Nikolenka Artenyev. He is no ordinary child. He sticks out in the Russian aristocratic society as he refuses to share the same common value with it – *etiquette* which is designed for a false show and keeping up appearances. In these novels Tolstoy unveils decadence of Russian aristocracy. Its "propriety" is nothing more than posing and pretension, much like actors do during a play. Generations are enslaved with this false show, and there is not a soul among them who is willing to speak up and put an end to this everlasting pretending, and the idleness, impotence and redundancy which follow.

Russian, and not only Russian but European Aristocracies were so consumed with mannerism and etiquette that it eventually caused effeminacy of generations and political demise of well-established and powerful empires. Tolstoy uses literary and metaphoric forms to convey elementary truths of plain and simple living, which have been the bases of political philosophies of many successful countries. He gives an advanced warning, – political life of a nation is strictly business, where there is no time for decorum.

The keynote idea of these three novels of Tolstoy is based on proven principles of personal, as well as national lives throughout history. Useless etiquette, and *hedonism* which always follows, are detrimental in two ways: First, they extinguish human nature within an individual and with it they smother human life – a human being becomes a mutilated mutant who, as it keeps following the unnatural *protocol* imposed by the society, is losing his touch with reality and his human nature. Second, this etiquette is of utmost detriment strictly from utilitarian point of view: political success of an individual, as well as of a state, could only be achieved with plain, truthful and upright lifestyle, and any sort of false show and excessive mannerism are a waste of precious resource – the time.

"Vivere Militare Est" – "To Live is to Fight", the doctrine advocated by Seneca; Job 7:1 of Vulgate Latin Bible states: "Militia est vita hominis" – "the life of a man upon earth is a warfare". These are the proven statements which we can use for individual, as well as national pedagogy, as they compel us to abstain from excessive pleasures and redundancy. They are the pillars on which individual, as well as common success has been and can be built. To these Tolstoy added the third philosophical decree which is also intended to preserve and help succeed both individual and national lives:

"The purpose of every man is to strive toward moral perfection." And in this striving there is no room for either hollow etiquette, or effeminacy, or hedonism.

FALSE PATRIOTISM

Crimean war started in 1853 and Tolstoy was assigned to Dunai Army. He served as a second lieutenant. He wrote several novels with loud political nuances. These novels are masterpieces of literary work, but they are also magnum opus of political science. Tolstoy was one of the first political theorists who saw the war in its true colors, abandoned romantic style of his contemporaries, as there was no romanticism to be found in any of the gory battles, and showed the war in its only true color – the color of blood. His audacity itself was pioneering and revolutionary in political outlook of European nations – no romanticism, no empty optimism, no liberal false hope, but neither depressing pessimism, – just pure reality of dirty politics and war which often follows.

Tolstoy is sure that a war is the most unnatural event in human existence. It is initiated by humans who have mutated into mere brutes. They are tyrannical people who will undertake any political intrigue, scheme, deception and conspiracy to satisfy their ever-increasing appetites. Birth of a war is always preceded with degradation of humans, who become leaders of nations, rob their own citizens and, with ardent desires to rob others, commence the war on the neighboring states. Tolstoy calls them people who have lost touch with nature and become immoral.

Tolstoy discovered one intricate detail of a war which unveils depth of human psyche and its psychology – vainglory. Even though to the great majority an unjust war is an unnatural event from which one must shy away and even experience fear of death, there are some who out of excessive desire for glory suppress natural fear of loss of life and become quite brave, although the reason of such bravery is quite foolish – conceit and vainglory, desire to distinguish themselves even at the cost of losing the life in an unjust war which only serves interests of a tyrant.

CIVIL DISOBEDIENCE IN EUROPE

Leo Tolstoy's conversion from a dissolute and privileged society author to the non-violent and spiritual anarchist of his latter days was brought about by two trips around Europe in 1857 and 1860-1861, a period when many liberal-leaning Russian aristocrats escaped the stifling political repression in Russia; others who followed the same path were Alexander Herzen, Mikhail Bakunin, and Peter Kropotkin. During his 1857 visit, Tolstoy witnessed a public execution in Paris, a traumatic experience that would mark the rest of his life. Writing in a letter to his friend V. P. Botkin: "The truth is that the State is a conspiracy designed not only to exploit, but above all to corrupt its citizens... Henceforth, I shall never serve any government anywhere."

His European trip in 1860-1861 shaped both his political and literary transformation when he met Victor Hugo, whose literary talents Tolstoy praised after reading Hugo's newly finished "Les Miserables". A comparison of Hugo's novel and Tolstoy's "War and Peace" shows the influence of the evocation of its battle scenes. Tolstoy's political philosophy was also influenced by a March 1861 visit to French anarchist Pierre-Joseph Proudhon, then living in exile under an assumed name in Brussels.

WHY CAUCASUS AND GEORGIA?

Last years of Tolstoy were full of disagreements and conflicts with his friends and acquaintances. Russian Empire and its high society could not allow the great genius freedom of thought and freedom of speech. Tolstoy felt smothered. Decadent Russian Empire had become a jail to him. He had to find the way out.

So elderly, yet still brilliant Tolstoy makes yet another astonishing move – at the age of 82 he makes a decision and at once abandons his friends and family, without even giving them explanation or information about his removal. He departs for Caucasus with the plans to spend the remaining life in Georgia – in the ancient Christian country conquered and deride by the despotic Empire which his own country had become. Tolstoy never reached the destination. He died at the Ostapovo train station on November 20, 1910.

CONCLUSION

It can be stated with almost no assumption that, after Peter the Great, Tolstoy was the most prominent and at the same time most pioneering figure in the development of Russian political thought. But he was beyond that – Tolstoy was the man who could state the truth, political and other kind too, and earnestly depict life's realism for the entire mankind. His political philosophy is simple, yet startling – individual, as well as social and national lives must be filled to the brim with upright and truthful actions, and there is no room for any excess in it – complicated social niceties, etiquette, tyranny, academic dictate – they are all unnatural and therefore harmful for a man and the society in which he lives.

SUMMARY

1. Leo Tolstoy was a Russian writer whom many consider to be the world's greatest political novelist.

2. Tolstoy's ideas on nonviolent resistance, expressed in such works as *"The Kingdom of God Is Within You"*, were to have a profound impact on such pivotal twentieth-century figures as Mahatma Gandhi and Martin Luther King, Jr.

3. Tolstoy's Muse was born in Georgia, and not, as many presume, in Russia. He started to write while serving in military in Tbilisi, Georgia. Whether it is a coincidence or not, the same happened to many Russian writers and philosophers – Georgia was that mystical land which cradled not only Georgian talent, but the talent of the tyrannical empires which attempted its conquest. Georgian experience inspired Russian playwright and composer Alexander Griboyedov, the foremost Russian poet Alexander Pushkin, prominent Russian Romantic writer, poet and painter Mikhail Lermontov and many others.

4. Russian, and not only Russian but European Aristocracies were so consumed with mannerism and etiquette that it eventually caused effeminacy of generations and political demise of well-established and powerful empires.

5. Tolstoy was one of the first political theorists who saw the war in its true colors, abandoned romantic style of his contemporaries, as there was no romanticism to be found in any of the gory battles, and showed the war in its only true color – the color of blood.

6. During his 1857 visit to Europe, Tolstoy witnessed a public execution in Paris, a traumatic experience that would mark the rest of his life. Writing in a letter to his friend V. P. Botkin: "The truth is that the State is a conspiracy designed not only to exploit, but above all to corrupt its citizens... Henceforth, I shall never serve any government anywhere."

7. Russian Empire and its high society could not allow the great genius freedom of thought and speech. So the elderly, yet still brilliant Tolstoy makes yet another astonishing move – at the age of 82 he makes a decision and at once abandons his friends and family, without even giving them explanation or information about his removal. He departs for Caucasus with the plans to spend the remaining life in Georgia – in the ancient Christian country conquered and deride by the despotic Empire which his own country had become.

SECTION REVIEW

KEY TERMS

Lobotomy
Etiquette
Hedonism
Protocol

CRITICAL THINKING

- Which 20th century public leaders were influenced by Tolstoy's philosophy?

- Where was Tolstoy's muse born?

- Explain correlation between mannerism, etiquette and effeminacy.

- Which war reinforced Tolstoy's political realism and completely removed him from romanticism?

- How can vainglory be mistaken for patriotism?

EUROPEAN REALISTS

ANTON MAKARENKO

"Our children must be raised in such ways as to become fine citizens, good fathers and mothers."

ANTON MAKARENKO

BACKGROUND

Anton Semyonovich Makarenko was a Ukrainian and Soviet educator and writer, who promoted democratic ideas and principles in educational theory and practice. As one of the founders of the Soviet pedagogy, he elaborated the theory and methodology of upbringing in self-governing *child collectives* and introduced the concept of productive labor into the educational system. Makarenko is often reckoned among the world's great educators, and his books have been published and used as guidelines for holistic education globally.

Makarenko was born on March 13, 1888, in a Ukrainian town Belopolie. In a small town of Kremenchug, near the tracks which lead passengers from Poltava Region to Kirivograd Region, there is a tiny railroad station, Kryukov... That's exactly where Makarenko started his pedagogical career in a two-year school which has just a handful of pupils and is in the middle of nowhere. This school is a museum nowadays. The building has retained the main character which it once shared with its prominent educator – plainness. This in the middle of nowhere museum has a tour guide, Mrs. Ludmila Kirienko. To this date she explains to the visitors in the most stoic manner: "...in 1938 Makarenko's literary and pedagogical book, *'Banners upon a Tower'* was published, and a year before – his patriotic-pedagogical work *'The Book About the Motherland'*, in which the great theorist discusses issues of family education." Such were the humble beginnings of Anton Makarenko – the man who many described as the world's greatest educator, and just as many – as the academic tyrant and lunatic.

SOVIET LEADERS V. SOVIET EDUCATOR

In 1911 Makarenko opposes the principal of the tiny Kryukov school after becoming ever so popular among the country folk that people were lining up at his door steps to solicit his advice on raising and educating their children. After that life-changing incident he holds quite a few positions as a school teacher, and also as a principal at various schools throughout Ukraine.

During the Russian Revolution Makarenko actively participated in the Eastern School Convention – a transnational movement in Ukraine and Russia which uncompromisingly supported the Revolution. In the aftermath of the Revolution he established self-supporting orphanages for street children, including juvenile delinquents, left orphaned by the Russian Civil War. Among these establishments were the Gorky *Corrective Labor Colony* and later the Dzerzhinsky *Labor Commune* in Kharkiv, where the famous FED photo camera was produced. Makarenko writes his world renowned *"Pedagogical Poem"* and actively participates in planning the Soviet education system and its pedagogy. Even though his pioneering methodologies were accepted by the Soviets, they did not go without fair amount of criticism. As Makarenko's methods were very advanced for his time, both communists and non-communists often argued against them, and Makarenko remained quite misunderstood throughout his lifetime. The recognition by the Soviet leaders came only after his demise.

SOCIAL DIVERSITY

Makarenko's idea of a perfect education system was a communal participation, but at the same time he was a huge opponent of collective education present in Ukraine and Russia back then, which entailed gathering children in a military-style public school, subduing individuality and creating obedient operatives who would serve the country and the ever growing communist empire blindly. Makarenko's methods indeed evolved around communal participation and social togetherness, not unlike Spartan ways, but he also wanted to nurture creativity and diversity of talents both, within a single individual, as well as in the entire community.

Makarenko used to argue: "We must remember at all times, this one important circumstance, – does not matter how much it seems that a man is a complete and whole creature, he is still a collection of diversified talents which needs to be taught and flourished."

PEDAGOGY, PSEUDO-PATRIOTISM AND SOCIAL ENGINEERING

Makarenko understood patriotism as the main goal of education. He argued that every individual must be raised in order to benefit the society and hence the national cause. Although he fully supported nurturing the feeling of personal interest in an individual, by creating personal incentives, not only in schools, but throughout the lifetime of an individual, still he firmly believed that the ultimate purpose of a human being was to serve the country. This was the focal point of his pedagogy, for which many accused him of social engineering. He asserted: "You are parents raising your sons or daughters not only for your own delight, but you and your families are in charge of raising the future citizens, future social activist, future warriors."

It must be taken under consideration that serving a nation is a fine and honorable goal, and that Makarenko's patriotic education would have been not only a successful undertaking, but an admirable one too. But Makarenko applied his methods not to a country, but to the ever-growing Russian empire. Because of that he and his communes were abhorred throughout the nations which were under the Russian tyranny, as for many "serving the nation" would have meant serving the Russian Empire, and not their native countries.

Makarenko saw patriotism intertwined with the world and its entire humanity. According to him the mission of a model citizen begins with personal goals, moves on to the family, to the country and ultimately to the entire mankind: "Our children must be raised in such ways as to become fine citizens, good fathers and mothers. But even all that is not good enough: our children – they are our old age. Proper upbringing – that is our pleasant old age, while bad upbringing – that is our future grief, that is our tears, that is our crime against another human being, against the whole world."

INCENTIVE-BASED COMMUNISM

Makarenko found planty of enemies among the communists. He supported an idea of a social commune, but he was a firm believe of an incentive-based system, where one gets promoted by merit only. He also argued against cruel punishment. Yet, at the same time, he supported punishment, and argued against such liberal approach where no pupil and no individual is held responsible for the actions – ideas quite frequently entertained and practiced in some European countries in his days: "I am personally convinced that punishment is not that great a good. But at the same time I am also sure that wherever punishment is need, the teacher has no right to withhold it. For punishment is not just a right, but also a responsibility."

Makarenko saw the necessity of incentive-based upbringing and he argued that a citizen's life must constantly evolve precisely around the **_merit-incentive correlation_**. For that he was often accused of Americanism and Capitalism, but Makarenko stood steadfast and defended his idea. He argued that merit-incentive correlation was cause-and-effect correlation, which was, is and will always be the fundamental principle of life and human existence – the most natural correlation between an action and its consequence.

CONCLUSION

It is a matter of some speculation, but it could be argued that if the Communist East had better used some of Makarenko's ideas and based its education, as well as the economy on a sound principle of "cause-and-effect" – deeply rooted in human nature, it would have avoided the ruinous course of pseudo-socialism which eventually bankrupted the Soviet Union and caused its demise. It can also be argued that had Makarenko been born in a country, rather than in an empire, his ideas would have actualized – his patriotic education and egalitarianism would have found a more popular following. One thing is certain – many positive results of Makarenko's impact on the Soviet education to this date can still be discerned in Ukraine and Russia. Perhaps it was Makarenko's realism that saved the Eastern Block from the complete socialist lunacy and preserved a certain degree of common sense even in the Evil Empire.

SUMMARY

1. Anton Semyonovich Makarenko was a Ukrainian and Soviet educator and writer, who promoted democratic ideas and principles in educational theory and practice.

2. As one of the founders of the Soviet pedagogy, he elaborated the theory and methodology of upbringing in self-governing child collectives and introduced the concept of productive labor into the educational system.

3. Makarenko understood patriotism as the main goal of education. He argued that every individual must be raised in order to benefit the society and hence the national cause.

4. Makarenko saw the necessity of incentive-based upbringing and he argued that a citizen's life must constantly evolve precisely around the merit-incentive correlation. For that he was often accused of Americanism and Capitalism, but Makarenko stood steadfast and defended his idea.

5. It is a matter of some speculation, but it could be argued that if the Communist East had better used some of Makarenko's ideas and based its education, as well as the economy on a sound principle of "cause-and-effect" – deeply rooted in human nature, it would have avoided the ruinous course of pseudo-socialism which eventually bankrupted the Soviet Union and caused its demise.

6. Perhaps it was Makarenko's realism that saved the Eastern Block from the complete socialist lunacy and preserved a certain degree of common sense even in the Evil Empire.

SECTION REVIEW

KEY TERMS

Child Collectives
Corrective Labor Colony
Labor Commune
Merit-incentive correlation

CRITICAL THINKING

- Explain the idea of child collectives, corrective labor colonies and labor communes.

- According to Makarenko, what should be the main goal of education?

- Why was Makarenko accused of social engineering?

- Explain the idea of Incentive-based Communism.

TRADITIONAL AFRICANISM

IGBO POLITICAL PHILOSOPHY

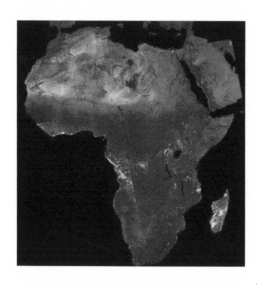

Igbo political philosophy:
When theory meets practice

IGBO POLITICAL PHILOSOPHY:
THE CASE OF THE IGBO OF SOUTH EAST
NIGERIA

POLITICAL THEORY

Political theory is the *raison d'etre* or what gives meaning to the practice of politics. Political philosophies attempt to provide *a priori* foundations for our empirical expressions of the struggle for power. To understand any political system it is imperative to understand the principles that give it meaning and significance. Simply put, political philosophy attempts to answer the questions about the goals of politics, who should govern and why? These questions are as perennial as they are universal. Answering them provides insights into the political values and traditions of people everywhere. The answers also provide the necessary insight into the beliefs and values of the various peoples and cultures of Africa. In the special case of Africa, insights into their traditional political philosophy will also hopefully provide explanations for the failures of modern African political economies.

AFRICAN POLITICAL PHILOSOPHIES

Traditional African political philosophies are numerous and various. Prior to the advent of European imperialism, most of the nations of Africa who now share common statehood had very little or no interactions with one another. They had their cultural and political boundaries clearly defined by both language and geography. As a result of European colonialism, they now exist like strange bedfellows in the forced political unions in the so-called modern states. A truly comprehensive study of African traditional political philosophies would ideally require a complete anthology of all the extant traditional African political cultures, but such an exercise would be impossible given the sheer number of such cultures. However, in spite of their large number, certain things were common to all traditional African societies. These include: **communalism** and spiritualism. **Communalism** ensured they were their brothers' keepers, while spiritualism made them accountable to and for one another, thus moderating their behaviors in dealing the less privileged members of the society. Spiritualism also compelled traditional African leaders to be intuitively or naturally cautious in their actions. To illustrate these traditional African political values, we chose one African political culture, the Igbo of South East Nigeria as a case study. We conclude by suggesting possible remedies for the current seemingly intractable political problems of modern African states.

Since most of traditional African cultures remain largely oral, African philosophies are found in other genres like novels or fictions, rather than conventional philosophical writings. In his work in literary analysis, Okolo (2007) provides an insight into the conflict between contemporary and traditional African politics. He provides African writers' commentaries on how the intrusion of Western colonialism disrupted the African way of life.

CHINUA ACHEBE

One such writer is the Nigerian Igbo novelist, Chinua Achebe whose works have provided consistent political criticisms of modern African states, especially Nigeria. For his very first novel, Chinua Achebe appropriately chose the title: *Things Fall Apart* (1958), signifying that: the Europeans had put a knife to what held Africa together. Hence African cultures have fallen apart. In *Things Fall Apart*, Achebe also illustrates with the life of his protagonist Okonkwo that: among the Igbo, the individual's right to act politically on behalf of his community must be based on a majority decision, and in fact consensus, in line with their traditional democratic disposition. Achebe in *No Longer at Ease* (1960) illustrates that the disintegration in African communities was caused by the European intervention that disconnected the African from his traditional values. In the *Arrow of God* (1964) he uses Ezeulu to illustrate the all important Igbo philosophy that no man no matter how great is greater than his community; no man ever wins a judgment against his clan p. 230. In *A Man of the People* (1966) Achebe exposes the genesis of the corruption that was engulfing modern Nigerian polity, and almost prophetically foretold the military coup that toppled the civilian government of Nigeria that year. Yet turning his sight on the locals Achebe in the *Trouble with Nigeria* (1983) issues a total condemnation of Nigeria's political leadership, arguing that the "leaders' inability to act as role models is the single most important factor blocking political progress."

Inherent in Achebe criticisms of modern Nigeria is the postulation that the modern had failed because it was not connected with the past. For him, the efficacy of traditional Igbo political system and philosophy illustrates that traditional African political systems and values did exist, and that their non-incorporation deprived contemporary Africa of its logical and natural transition from traditional to developed political economies. It is also pertinent to provide a theoretical link between the failures of post-colonial Africa and the abandonment of her traditional systems, which is also a goal of this work. The approach is to use the Igbo society to explain some of the universals in African political philosophies, since we cannot provide the full compendia of all the thousands that are African nationalities. Although this may never capture all nuances but it is hoped that it would be a good beginning in the compilation of the great corpus of African political philosophy.

AFRICAN POLITICAL SYSTEMS AND CULTURES

As indicated earlier, pre-colonial Africa had many political systems and cultures. Like societies everywhere some were hierarchical and highly structured with established ruling groups and even ruling families. Others were less structured and more autonomous or non-cephalous. Political culture encompasses political values and the types of institutions they engender. Political philosophy is mainly about why and how a society bestows, distributes and utilizes power, as well as, who benefits from power and who checks its excesses. According to David Apter (1965), African traditional political cultures can be categorized under three types in terms of authority structure, namely: hierarchical, pyramidal, and segmental, and two types – instrumental and consummatory on the basis of political values.

The table below is a summary of some of the political systems of traditional Africa. There are others, but too many to list here. But the grid represents the extant political structures and the political values or attitudes. **Hierarchical** societies are just like European monarchies with highly differentiated structures and elaborate

246

bureaucracies. The traditional Buganda kingdom of Uganda ruled by the Kabaka is representative of this kind of system in Africa. The **pyramidal** type is like confederation of authorities. It involved local semi-autonomous sovereignties that still maintain quasi-relationships with the larger nation based on common origin. The Yoruba of western Nigeria represent this kind of political structure. The **segmental** system as represented by the Igbo is completely autonomous village sovereignties with no centralized authorities.

Table 1

Social attitude	Political Structure	Political Structure	Political Structure
	Hierarchical	Pyramidal	Segmental
Instrumental	Buganda (Uganda)	Yoruba (Nigeria	Igbo(Nigeria), Kikuyu (Kenya)
Consummatory	Fon (Togo)		Nuer (Sudan)

From Vincent Khapoya's book: *The African Experience*. Prentice Hall 1998.p.61

IGBO POLITICAL CULTURE

The traditional Igbo political culture as explained in Kapoya (1998) was republican in nature. Henderson (1974) describes the Igbo as a culture with "king in every man." The Igbo society was an intricate system where aggressive individualism was mitigated by communal sense of propriety and sanctions. It was where one drove or controlled one's destiny *(onye kwe chi ya ekwe)*, and yet subscribed to the world view that community is strength *(umu nna wu ike)*. When a young person washed his hands clean he dined with elders *(nwata kwopu aka o soro ndi okenye ree nri)*. Yet honor and courtesy compelled that when a young man threw his father in the air he was blinded by his loin cloth *(nwata tuo nna ya n'elu ogodo wupia ya anya)*. This was congruous with their general disposition that the most experienced members in the society, the elderly must be part of decision-making at least at the advisory level. They considered experience a critical element in decision-making. A healthy polity for the Igbo was run by a grassroots assembly of the people working through a consensus to reach rational decisions to which the community's elders would readily give their imprimatur.

The Igbo valued mutual respect with their neighbors, the same way they mutually respect themselves because no one had natural claim to deference. Hence they asserted that the hero of one community has a counterpart in other communities *(eshi amuru dike na mba wu eshi amuru ibe ya)*. They also asserted their fierce sense of independence by shunning any attempt at subjugation. An Igbo would readily ask you to break that dish with which you fed him, signaling that he would rather go hungry rather than accept servitude under any guise of benevolence *(ite ahu i ji enye m nri kuwaa ya)*. Evidence of this freedom loving nature of the Igbo was ubiquitous even during trans-Atlantic slavery. According to Sieber (1989) for almost two centuries an unreported mass drowning of "Ibos" in the creek has been claimed by African-American residents. As it turns out, a rebellion and freedom march at the creek site took place in May 1803, involving a group of Igbo from the ancient West African civilization of Igboland. The above event is popularly known as Ebo (Igbo) landing in colonial America during which several Ebo slaves committed mass suicide by self-drowning, confirming the "freedom-loving peculiarity of this West African people, the Igbo, who lost 1 million persons to the intercontinental slave trade" (Sieber, 1989).

With regard to political responsibility and accountability, for the Igbo when your people put their confidence in you to attempt the impossible, you must do your best to deliver *(onye umu nna ya sina oga eje Chukwu ga eje)*. None is omniscient *(odighi onye nya akpa ako)*. No one person constituted the public *(otu onye anaghii awu nnam oha)*. This was the principle that made dictatorship and despotism unnatural among the Igbo. The most fundamental political pronouncement among the Igbo is their unequivocal declaration that they have no king *(Igbo enweghii eze)*, and that only the almighty God is king *(Chi wu eze)*.

The Igbo also believed in pluralism and diversity, that is, the validity of the other. They demonstrate this by their readily acceptance that different cultures do things differently *(okwa mba na achi na olu na olu)*. Obviously, this natural disposition of the Igbo towards pluralism and diversity is antithetical to the intolerance that seems to characterize interethnic relationship in contemporary Nigeria and Africa. The Igbo have always been outgoing people, who readily appreciated other cultures. In deed they still have a high propensity to adapt to the cultures of their neighbors rather than impose theirs on them. They readily learn the language and cultures of whomsoever they interact with. This is indicative of the **instrumentalism** of the Igbo, which according to Apter (1965) made the mastery new ideas, including other cultures, a cause for bragging among them, because of the very high premium they placed on personal achievements.

POLITICS, MORALITY AND SPIRITUALITY

In traditional Africa there was a very strong link between politics, morality and spirituality. The interwoven link between the political and the spiritual among the Igbo and Africans generally is reminiscent of theocracy under the Holy Roman Empire of medieval Europe and Islamic empires and monarchies around the world. But the Igbo were not about the rule of God, but rule of men with fear of God. There is no question that European political and legal evolutions infused their societies with strict moral standards and values. Their populace learned to obey their laws as a result of brutal enforcement. The rigorous and brutal execution of their law overtime instilled in Europeans the lasting fears of their laws and values. In traditional Africa, such ruthless sanctions were the order of the day, and thus ensured that morality and order were preserved even in societies that did not have elaborate law enforcement agencies. For instance, traditional Igbo villages often lived away from their farmland. They had community yam barns and cassava firms. Their livestock roamed freely and safely. Yet stealing and corruption were very rear in traditional Africa. These vices are common in modern Africa today. Why? This is because unlike traditional Africa, modern Africa states were founded by European imperialists who unhinged the natural link between politics, morality and spirituality. Capitalism as a means of social organization was alien to Africans and so were the values that came with the amoral political structure Europe bequeathed Africa as a result of colonialism, and now perpetuated under **neocolonialism**.

Modern states everywhere rely almost exclusively on physical coercive power to maintain order. In some cases especially in old **nation-states** of Western Europe their long culture of rule of law has given their societies some semblance of moral imperative to good citizenship. This is so because their modern state systems emanated from their political traditions, and they have united their cultures and morality with the secular principles of modern governance. On the contrary, traditional Africa mainly relied on the moral coercive power of the society. Moral coercive was expressed by means of ostracism and other forms of communal sanctions. However, the formalism of the Eurocentric state model caused them to offhandedly reject the informal or semi-formal nature of traditional African institutions. This accounts for why Europeans inaccurately claim that some African nations, not tribes, like the Igbo had stateless or non-state systems.

A stateless system is really a misnomer, because no society can truly be stateless. The absence of a written constitution that spells out formal structures of government does not automatically mean statelessness. Statelessness can only be seen in the so-called failed states of the twentieth century such as Somalia. No one can say that traditional African societies were anything like Somalia of the 1990s where nobody was in charge. Statelessness would be more like what Thomas Hobbes described as the state nature. Besides, modern Somalia only qualified as stateless because the modern state failed after the traditional state had already been destroyed. The African community conscience and leadership were always comprehensive in dealing with issues of law and order and justice in traditional societies. The difference is in the methods. A state as Hegel rightly opines is the actualization of the ethical idea. This actualization is located in the community conscience of the society. Among the Igbo, this community is comprised of the living, the dead ancestors and the metaphysical forces constantly overlooking the society.

It is obvious that traditional African societies did in deed organize politically in many ways. Even among the larger nations (don't call them tribes) there were variations of who held power. For instance, among the Igbo, the Onitsha Igbo was a monarchy ruled by the Obi, whereas the rest of the Igbo nation was ruled by traditional democracy with significant deference to the elders. Yet there was one ubiquitous fact in African political philosophy, the heavy reliance on metaphysical sources in the management of communal power. Mass petition for divine intervention was in the nature of spontaneous mass protest. There were three major ways of enforcing communal power in traditional African polities namely: physical, moral and metaphysical power. There is a necessary unity of these three. Any disruptions in society upset everything and order must be restored. Those exercising power among the people must abide by these principles because if they managed to escape the people's censure, the ancestors and the divine powers would definitely hold them accountable. Elsewhere this author thus summed up the holistic nature of African life while describing the concept of beauty among the Igbo:
Every culture has its unique understanding and appreciation of the concept of the beautiful. As typical Africans, the Igbo have a culture that is pregnant with symbolism, where action is simply a rendition of the metaphysical, a world view that reflects a constant union of here and hereafter, and a systematic understanding of both the good and the beautiful. In Africa beauty is not in the eye of the beholder; it is in the eye of the community (B. Ma, Journal 1998).

The tragedy of today is that African societies were denied the natural evolution from their traditional values to contemporary states. In traditional Igbo society there were three essential qualities for leadership, namely: one with considerable means, one who spoke the truth with skill and a warrior or a man of courage. Of these three qualities, the two innate qualities of honor and courage were more critical than wealth acquisition in recommending someone for leadership. You did not need to be born in wealth to be given the chance to lead. In traditional Igbo society, similar to Machiavelli's *fortuna*, noble ancestry might give one a head start or initial access to leadership but it neither guaranteed the success of the leaders nor ensured the loyalty of the followers.

The traditional Igbo concept of justice resembles Rawls version of justice as fairness. The Igbo, for instance, say that they are allies of the just (*Ndi Igbo si na ha bu nwanne onye ozirila*). Justice is in the fact that what one sows is what one reaps (*Mkpuru onye kuru ka oga aghota*). It is in treating all people equally (*Emee onye ka emere ibe ya obi adi ya mma*). Justice is in being aware that providence protects the weak, the same way providence chases away flies for a tailless cow (*Ehi e nweghi odu chi ya na churu ya ijiji*). You don't seize the pygmy jerboa's bride because his penis is too small (*Anaghi ara nwunye nwambe n'ihi na utu ya di ntakiri*). Justice is letting the eagle perch and the hawk perch and the one that denies the other the right to perch should have fractured wings (*Egbe bere ugo bere nke si ibeya ebela nku kwaa ya*). He who wants to hurt the weak ends up hurting himself (*ochu nwa okuko nwe ada ma nwa okuko nwe oso*). Social responsibility and public accountability were expressed in the Igbo belief that a dog does not eat a bone hung around its neck (*nkita anaghi ata okpukpu anya wara ya n'olu*). This meant that one did not destroy what was placed under one's custody. Social equality was expressed in this rhetorical question which asks: Was the strong born to trample his peers to death? *(amuru onye ukwu si ya zogbuo ibe ya?)* Of course, to the Igbo, the answer was no. For them, real strength was found in the unity of the community (*umu nna wu ike or Igwe wu ike*). Life was live and let live *(biri ma mu biri)*. The idea of survival of the fittest was uncharacteristically African.

POLITICAL PARTICIPATION

With regard to *political participation,* traditional African politics was inclusive rather than exclusive. The Igbo say that if you excluded a brave or honorable man from vital conference you must do an encore (*agbawo dike izu agbaa ya mgba abuo*). You don't know the fetus that will be king (*amaghi afo ime ga wu eze*). Among the Igbo, no one person was greater than the community *(otu onye awughi nna m oha)*. Everyone was needed for success *(ukwu bia aka abia ekwuhee okpokoro)*. For the Igbo life was a communal endeavor as in all hands being on deck *(onye gbuwe achara onye gbuwe ma onye akpola ibe ya one ikoni)*. As Uchendu (1965) explained, the Igbo practiced direct democracy in which each village exercised autonomy in matter affecting it. They made important decision in open air meetings where all adult males participated with full right of self expression. They held public hearings and at the end of the open forum. They selected few representatives who would consult quietly, to return with a consensus verdict, which was would then be brought to the entire assemble for approval.

Among the Igbo political authority was quite diffused. For instance, the age grade was a common locus of political authority. According to Ottenberg (1965), among Afikpo Igbos, there are four age grade with distinctive functions. This comprised the young grade, made of young men mostly bachelors who acted like the police force, the junior grade married young men who administered the community; the middle grade that consisted of more mature men who engaged in legislative and adjudicatory duties and finally the oldest grade that played mostly advisory roles.

POLITICAL FUTURE OF AFRICA

On Africa's path to development lies a huge and impenetrable boulder. This stumbling block was put in place formally in Berlin in 1885 when Europeans arbitrarily carved up or **partitioned** the continent for themselves. They did this oblivious of the socio-cultural realities on the ground. In the nearly one century and fourteen years of this encounter, Africans have suffered untold hardships and atrocities many of them quite uncharacteristic of Africans. Whether it is the famine, civil wars, genocide, corruption, brutalization by police states, and ethno-religious violence, these are direct consequences of lumping people together by clueless foreigners who played God over the divergent peoples and cultures they found in Africa.

The truth is that millions of African lives have been sacrificed needlessly as a result of European greed and arrogance. It is now a moral imperative for the global community to require the same European powers that created this mess to supervise a judicious reordering of Africa, based on fundamental political freedoms. Europeans must wash their hands clean from the chaos they created in Africa by providing objective conditions for all willing African nations to regain the political rights they were robbed of in Berlin.

There are only two feasible ways forward, namely: violent revolutions and political altruism. The way of violent revolution would mean general uprisings throughout Africa to overthrow the status quo in these ill-conceived countries once the people come to the inevitable conclusion that there is no hope otherwise. It is not farfetched that as young Africans continue to experience unending frustration due to the political and economic violence they suffer in the hands of neocolonial agents who now lord it over them, they would rise to reclaim their lands and destinies. The spectacle would not pretty to behold. The sporadic crises that have been witnessed throughout the African continent in the last half century of pseudo-independence would simply pale in comparison to what is looming. It is so mind-boggling that since they inherited the current states at independence none of the ruling groups has shown sufficient interest in the welfare of the subjugated groups to allow them any chance to express their fundamental political rights, even in the midst of civil war, cruel maladministration or even pogroms and genocides. Most current African states are manned by bandits who would never willingly relinquish their colonially bestowed privileges. They have no interested in peace and stability in their respective countries if it meant losing their current privileges.

The peaceful alternative is the way of political altruism. This does not seem feasible. There is no local political will, to actualize this. Therefore, an international conference on Africa, like the one in Berlin in 1885, must be convened, to rearrange the political boundaries on the basis of popularly agreed referenda. Every group would be allowed to affirm or reject its current citizenship within the existing countries. If any group feels that it is getting a good deal from its current state it would simply opt to stay there. Otherwise, it should have the option to seek another form of existence. Political equality presupposes that no group no matter how big or small should be subjected to the perpetual rule by another. In all situations the global community in recognition of our common humanity must insist on all states putting forward to their peoples a constitution protecting their fundamental rights as a precondition for sovereignty in all multinational states throughout the world. This would be the real actualization of the United Nations Declaration on Human Rights. This suggests that the world must realize the untenable nature of the status quo in Africa and decide to change it. This can be changed through global co-operation and unity of purpose to restore what was destroyed in Africa by foreigners. The former colonial powers must place the interest of the masses of Africa over and above those of their surrogates now damaging these countries' prospects for political and economic development. The international community should establish a sanctions regime to monitor political rights across the globe, especially the rights of minorities. Like census, political referenda should be held among all vulnerable nationalities, at least, once every decade. This should be monitored by the international community to ensure continued protection of all citizens.

Making the people choose the country of their choice is the only way to a decent political future. When they are allowed to return to their deep-seated values, Africans would then according to Agbakoba (2004) return to the management of communal power based on moral coercive force. The Western style constitutions they borrowed cannot serve this purpose for Africa. This is because African communities do not share in the historical and cultural contexts out of which these Western institutions evolved. Instead, Africans must restore the principle of **total humiliation** that provided effective deterrence to egregious behaviors in the past. For instance, in the past, a criminal was made a public scorn much worse than the "A" for adultery label in Nathaniel Hawthorne's *Scarlet Letter*. In traditional Africa people avoided crime because it demeaned all members of their family and relatives. For instance, if any one was cut in the act of thievery the one shall have also placed the unenviable label on all his relatives as relatives of a thief. His brothers and sisters automatically become nothing but the brothers and sisters of the thief, the same goes for his spouse, parents, children et cetera. This ruthless condemnation of public crime and corruption was the reason traditional societies did not experience the public crimes now prevalent in modern African states.

The colonial intrusion left Africa with a legacy of **moral dualism**. For instance, in Igbo land, even today, if a woman steals a few cassava roots from her neighbor, she is ostracized and publicly disgraced as in the past, but if the same woman embezzled a billion dollars of government funds, she would become an idol of the same community. This shows there is no moral continuity between the traditional values and the new ethics of public office in modern African states. The fact is that the people continue to view the state as a renegade foreign imposition whose looting many seem to applaud. Until they can take possession of the state as the core or location of their ethical idea according to Hegel, the state can never do for Africans what it has done and is doing for people in other parts of the world. Unfortunately, they cannot take such possession until the peoples and the states become one, and their states' laws become intertwined with their traditional moral values.

CONCLUSION

In conclusion we must reiterate that the Igbo share with many other African cultures in varying degrees tenets of what many Western scholars erroneously describe as statelessness. The label of statelessness is a misnomer, since no society can be truly stateless without actually resembling state of nature. What is misconstrued as statelessness is the absence of elaborate structures and established bureaucracies that characterize other forms of government. The fact is that the Igbo political system had been described as republican with representative village assemblies comprising of the oldest members of the families or lineages. At the village levels extraordinary sessions were often convened for all adult members to make policies by way of consensus. The Igbo traditional political system is democratic nature. According to David Apter, the Igbo were instrumental segmental, which means progressivism and aggressive individualism, having neither king nor natural aristocracy, and they differ from others that are hierarchical, pyramidal and consummatory.

Like the Igbo, majority of traditional African societies were without kings. The local communities had heads, but such heads were never too powerful that the people could not control, and, if necessary, overthrow them. The leader was also the spiritual leader of the community. Hence moral actions were part of the political decision-making processes and outcomes. In all African societies, whatever the deity was, whether it was *Chukwu,* for the Igbo or any other traditionally accepted Supreme Being, His ruling was justice and fair-play with favor to all and malice towards none except the those whose hands were not clean. The leader was guided by the spirit of fair-play and was accountable to both the divine powers and the ancestors for all his actions. There was also the *vox populi vox dei,* that is, the voice of people is the voice of God, aspect of social control in traditional Africa in which case they posited that the public disgrace of a leader was worse than his execution *(mmevo nwa ogaranya ka ogbugbu ya).* In all, most traditional African cultures are communal and spiritual. They are cyclical in their cosmology, linking the activities of the living with those of dead ancestors and the supernatural in a complex moral relationship that eschews ruthlessness and extremism in human interactions.

SUMMARY

1. Political theory is the *raison d'etre* or what gives meaning to the practice of politics.

2. Prior to the advent of European imperialism, most of the nations of Africa who now share common statehood had very little or no interactions with one another. They had their cultural and political boundaries clearly defined by both language and geography.

3. As a result of European colonialism, nations of Africa now exist like strange bedfellows in the forced political unions in the so-called modern states.

4. Chinua Achebe is a Nigerian Igbo novelist, whose works have provided consistent political criticisms of modern African states, especially Nigeria. Inherent in Achebe criticisms of modern Nigeria is the postulation that the modern had failed because it was not connected with the past.

5. Pre-colonial Africa had many political systems and cultures. Like societies everywhere some were hierarchical and highly structured with established ruling groups and even ruling families. Others were less structured and more autonomous or non-cephalous.

6. The traditional Igbo political culture as explained in Kapoya (1998) was republican in nature. Henderson (1974) describes the Igbo as a culture with "king in every man."

7. In traditional Africa there was a very strong link between politics, morality and spirituality. The interwoven link between the political and the spiritual among the Igbo and Africans generally is reminiscent of theocracy under the Holy Roman Empire of medieval Europe and Islamic empires and monarchies around the world.

8. With regard to *political participation,* traditional African politics was inclusive rather than exclusive.

9. On Africa's path to development lies a huge and impenetrable boulder. This stumbling block was put in place formally in Berlin in 1885 when Europeans arbitrarily carved up or **partitioned** the continent for themselves.

10. The colonial intrusion left Africa with a legacy of **moral dualism**.

SECTION REVIEW

KEY TERMS

Artificial state
Colonialism
Communalism
Direct democracy
Multinational state
Nation
Nation-building
Nation-state
Neocolonialism
Partition
Total humiliation

CRITICAL THINKING

- Could traditional African political values have been relevant to the construction of modern African states?

- Is anything wrong with developing a people outside of their own heritage?

- Do modern African countries have to be big to deliver the political good to their people?

- Is anything wrong with imposing unity on numerous peoples and culture without their inputs?

- Are African societies similar enough to discard their differences?

- Can there be economic development without political development?

- Are Africans different from other cultures in terms of seeking political and economic wellbeing?

- How different is Africa from Europe in seeking political autonomy?

- Could Europe have tolerated something similar to the Berlin conference of 1885?

- Is it fair to expect Africans to accept boundaries arbitrarily drawn by Europeans?

- Are Africans inherently more corrupt than Europeans?

WORKS CITED

Achebe, C. The Trouble with Nigeria. Enugu: Fourth Dimension 1983.

  A Man of the People. London: Heinemann 1966.

  Arrow of God. London: London: Heinemann 1964.

  No Longer at Ease. London: Heinemann. 1960

  Things Fall Apart. London: Heinemann Publishers 1958.

Agbakoba, A.J.C. Traditional African Political Thought and the Crisis of Governance in Contemporary African Societies. *Journal for the study of religion and ideologies.* No. 7 Spring, 2004. p. 151

Apter, D. The Politics of Modernization (Chicago: University of Chicago Press, 1965). pp.1-42.

Henderson, R.N. The King in Every Man (New Haven: Yale University Press, 1972). p. 274.

Isichei, E. Igbo Worlds, (London: Macmillan Education Ltd, 1977) pp. 256 – 259

Ihejirika, C. The Communal nature of Igbo Aesthetics in DeLancey. "Cultural Studies/Cultural Wars: Review Essay." Guest Editor: Chieke Ihejirika. BMA: The   Sonia Sanchez Literary Review. 1.2 (Spring 1996) 30-42.

Khapoya, V. The African Experience. 2nd Edition. NJ: Prentice Hall 1998.

Okere, T. Chi bu Ndu: Ofufe Chukwu na Etiti ndi Igbo. Owerri: Assumpta Press 1997.

Okolo, M.S.C African Literature as Political Philosophy. Zed Books, 2007

Ottenberg, P. "Afikpo Ibo of Eastern Nigeria" in James L. Gibbs, Jr. ed., Peoples of Africa (New York: Holt, Rinehart & Winston. 1965.

Sieber, H. 1989. The Factual Basis of Ebo Landing Legend Retrieved March 2009 from http://www.biafraland.com/Igbo%20Landing,%20factual%20Basis.htm

Uchendu, V. The Igbo of Southeast Nigeria New York: Holt, Rinehart & Winston. 1965.

The Magna Carta
June 15, 1215

John, by the grace of God King of England, Lord of Ireland, Duke of Normandy and Aquitaine, and Count of Anjou, to his archbishops, bishops, abbots, earls, barons, justices, foresters, sheriffs, stewards, servants, and to all his officials and loyal subjects, greeting.

Know that before God, for the health of our soul and those of our ancestors and heirs, to the honour of God, the exaltation of the holy Church, and the better ordering of our kingdom, at the advice of our reverend fathers Stephen, archbishop of Canterbury, primate of all England, and cardinal of the holy Roman Church, Henry archbishop of Dublin, William bishop of London, Peter bishop of Winchester, Jocelin bishop of Bath and Glastonbury, Hugh bishop of Lincoln, Walter Bishop of Worcester, William bishop of Coventry, Benedict bishop of Rochester, Master Pandulf subdeacon and member of the papal household, Brother Aymeric master of the Knights of the Temple in England, William Marshal, earl of Pembroke, William earl of Salisbury, William earl of Warren, William earl of Arundel, Alan de Galloway constable of Scotland, Warin Fitz Gerald, Peter Fitz Herbert, Hubert de Burgh seneschal of Poitou, Hugh de Neville, Matthew Fitz Herbert, Thomas Basset, Alan Basset, Philip Daubeny, Robert de Roppeley, John Marshal, John Fitz Hugh, and other loyal subjects:

1. First, that we have granted to God, and by this present charter have confirmed for us and our heirs in perpetuity, that the English Church shall be free, and shall have its rights undiminished, and its liberties unimpaired. That we wish this so to be observed, appears from the fact that of our own free will, before the outbreak of the present dispute between us and our barons, we granted and confirmed by charter the freedom of the Church's elections - a right reckoned to be of the greatest necessity and importance to it - and caused this to be confirmed by Pope Innocent III. This freedom we shall observe ourselves, and desire to be observed in good faith by our heirs in perpetuity. We have also granted to all free men of our realm, for us and our heirs for ever, all the liberties written out below, to have and to keep for them and their heirs, of us and our heirs:

2. If any earl, baron, or other person that holds lands directly of the Crown, for military service, shall die, and at his death his heir shall be of full age and owe a `relief', the heir shall have his inheritance on payment of the ancient scale of `relief'. That is to say, the heir or heirs of an earl shall pay for the entire earl's barony, the heir or heirs of a knight l00s. at most for the entire knight's `fee', and any man that owes less shall pay less, in accordance with the ancient usage of `fees'

3. But if the heir of such a person is under age and a ward, when he comes of age he shall have his inheritance without `relief' or fine.

4. The guardian of the land of an heir who is under age shall take from it only reasonable revenues, customary dues, and feudal services. He shall do this without destruction or damage to men or property. If we have given the guardianship of the land to a sheriff, or to any person answerable to us for the revenues, and he commits destruction or damage,

we will exact compensation from him, and the land shall be entrusted to two worthy and prudent men of the same `fee', who shall be answerable to us for the revenues, or to the person to whom we have assigned them. If we have given or sold to anyone the guardianship of such land, and he causes destruction or damage, he shall lose the guardianship of it, and it shall be handed over to two worthy and prudent men of the same `fee', who shall be similarly answerable to us.

5. For so long as a guardian has guardianship of such land, he shall maintain the houses, parks, fish preserves, ponds, mills, and everything else pertaining to it, from the revenues of the land itself. When the heir comes of age, he shall restore the whole land to him, stocked with plough teams and such implements of husbandry as the season demands and the revenues from the land can reasonably bear.

6. Heirs may be given in marriage, but not to someone of lower social standing. Before a marriage takes place, it shall be' made known to the heir's next-of-kin.

7. At her husband's death, a widow may have her marriage portion and inheritance at once and without trouble. She shall pay nothing for her dower, marriage portion, or any inheritance that she and her husband held jointly on the day of his death. She may remain in her husband's house for forty days after his death, and within this period her dower shall be assigned to her.

8. No widow shall be compelled to marry, so long as she wishes to remain without a husband. But she must give security that she will not marry without royal consent, if she holds her lands of the Crown, or without the consent of whatever other lord she may hold them of.

9. Neither we nor our officials will seize any land or rent in payment of a debt, so long as the debtor has movable goods sufficient to discharge the debt. A debtor's sureties shall not be distrained upon so long as the debtor himself can discharge his debt. If, for lack of means, the debtor is unable to discharge his debt, his sureties shall be answerable for it. If they so desire, they may have the debtor's lands and rents until they have received satisfaction for the debt that they paid for him, unless the debtor can show that he has settled his obligations to them.

10. If anyone who has borrowed a sum of money from Jews dies before the debt has been repaid, his heir shall pay no interest on the debt for so long as he remains under age, irrespective of whom he holds his lands. If such a debt falls into the hands of the Crown, it will take nothing except the principal sum specified in the bond.

11. If a man dies owing money to Jews, his wife may have her dower and pay nothing towards the debt from it. If he leaves children that are under age, their needs may also be provided for on a scale appropriate to the size of his holding of lands. The debt is to be paid out of the residue, reserving the service due to his feudal lords. Debts owed to persons other than Jews are to be dealt with similarly.

12. No `scutage' or `aid' may be levied in our kingdom without its general consent, unless it is for the ransom of our person, to make our eldest son a knight, and (once) to marry

our eldest daughter. For these purposes only a reasonable `aid' may be levied. `Aids' from the city of London are to be treated similarly.

13. The city of London shall enjoy all its ancient liberties and free customs, both by land and by water. We also will and grant that all other cities, boroughs, towns, and ports shall enjoy all their liberties and free customs.

14. To obtain the general consent of the realm for the assessment of an `aid' - except in the three cases specified above - or a `scutage', we will cause the archbishops, bishops, abbots, earls, and greater barons to be summoned individually by letter. To those who hold lands directly of us we will cause a general summons to be issued, through the sheriffs and other officials, to come together on a fixed day (of which at least forty days notice shall be given) and at a fixed place. In all letters of summons, the cause of the summons will be stated. When a summons has been issued, the business appointed for the day shall go forward in accordance with the resolution of those present, even if not all those who were summoned have appeared.

15. In future we will allow no one to levy an `aid' from his free men, except to ransom his person, to make his eldest son a knight, and (once) to marry his eldest daughter. For these purposes only a reasonable `aid' may be levied.

16. No man shall be forced to perform more service for a knight's `fee', or other free holding of land, than is due from it.

17. Ordinary lawsuits shall not follow the royal court around, but shall be held in a fixed place.

18. Inquests of novel disseisin, mort d'ancestor, and darrein presentment shall be taken only in their proper county court. We ourselves, or in our absence abroad our chief justice, will send two justices to each county four times a year, and these justices, with four knights of the county elected by the county itself, shall hold the assizes in the county court, on the day and in the place where the court meets.

19. If any assizes cannot be taken on the day of the county court, as many knights and freeholders shall afterwards remain behind, of those who have attended the court, as will suffice for the administration of justice, having regard to the volume of business to be done.

20. For a trivial offence, a free man shall be fined only in proportion to the degree of his offence, and for a serious offence correspondingly, but not so heavily as to deprive him of his livelihood. In the same way, a merchant shall be spared his merchandise, and a husbandman the implements of his husbandry, if they fall upon the mercy of a royal court. None of these fines shall be imposed except by the assessment on oath of reputable men of the neighbourhood.

21. Earls and barons shall not be amerced save through their peers, and only according to the measure of the offence.

22. No clerk shall be amerced for his lay tenement ecept according to the manner of the other persons aforesaid; and not according to the amount of his ecclesiastical benefice.

23. Neither a town nor a man shall be forced to make bridges over the rivers, with the exception of those who, from of old and of right ought to do it.

24. No sheriff, constable, coroners, or other bailiffs of ours shall hold the pleas of our crown.

25. All counties, hundreds, wapentakes, and trithings – our demesne manors being exccepted – shall continue according to the old farms, without any increase at all.

26. If any one holding from us a lay fee shall die, and our sheriff or bailiff can show our letters patent containing our summons for the debt which the dead man owed to us, – our sheriff or bailiff may be allowed to attach and enroll the chattels of the dead man to the value of that debt, through view of lawful men; in such way, however, that nothing shall be removed thence until the debt is paid which was plainly owed to us. And the residue shall be left to the executors that they may carry out the will of the dead man. And if nothing is owed to us by him, all the chattels shall go to the use prescribed by the deceased, saving their reasonable portions to his wife and children.

27. If any freeman shall have died intestate his chattels shall be distributed through the hands of his near relatives and friends, by view of the church; saving to any one the debts which the dead man owed him.

28. No constable or other bailiff of ours shall take the corn or other chattels of any one except he straightway give money for them, or can be allowed a respite in that regard by the will of the seller.

29. No constable shall force any knight to pay money for castleward if he be willing to perform that ward in person, or – he for a reasonable cause not being able to perform it himself – through another proper man. And if we shall have led or sent him on a military expedition, he shall be quit of ward according to the amount of time during which, through us, he shall have been in military service.

30. No sheriff nor bailiff of ours, nor any one else, shall take the horses or carts of any freeman for transport, unless by the will of that freeman.

31. Neither we nor our bailiffs shall take another's wood for castles or for other private uses, unless by the will of him to whom the wood belongs.

32. We shall not hold the lands of those convicted of felony longer than a year and a day; and then the lands shall be restored to the lords of the fiefs.

33. Henceforth all the weirs in the Thames and Medway, and throughout all England, save on the sea-coast, shall be done away with entirely.

34. Henceforth the writ which is called Praecipe shall not be to served on any one for any holding so as to cause a free man to lose his court.

35. There shall be one measure of wine throughout our whole realm, and one measure of ale and one measure of corn – namely, the London quart; – and one width of dyed and russet and hauberk cloths – namely, two ells below the selvage. And with weights, moreover, it shall be as with measures.

36. Henceforth nothing shall be given or taken for a writ of inquest in a matter concerning life or limb; but it shall be conceded gratis, and shall not be denied.

37. If any one hold of us in fee-farm, or in socage, or in burkage, and hold land of another by military service, we shall not, by reason of that fee-farm, or socage, or burkage, have the wardship of his heir or of his land which is held in fee from another. Nor shall we have the wardship of that fee-farm, or socage, or burkage unless that fee-farm owe military service. We shall not, by reason of some petit-serjeanty which some one holds of us through the service of giving us knives or arrows or the like, have the wardship of his heir or of the land which he holds of another by military service.

38. No bailiff, on his own simple assertion, shall henceforth any one to his law, without producing faithful witnesses in evidence.

39. No freeman shall be taken, or imprisoned, or disseized, or outlawed, or exiled, or in any way harmed – nor will we go upon or send upon him – save by the lawful judgment of his peers or by the law of the land.

40. To none will we sell, to none deny or delay, right or justice.

41. All merchants may safely and securely go out of England, and come into England, and delay and pass through England, as well by land as by water, for the purpose of buying and selling, free from all evil taxes, subject to the ancient and right customs – save in time of war, and if they are of the land at war against us. And if such be found in our land at the beginning of the war, they shall be held, without harm to their bodies and goods, until it shall be known to us or our chief justice how the merchants of our land are to be treated who shall, at that time, be found in the land at war against us. And if ours shall be safe there, the others shall be safe in our land.

42. Henceforth any person, saving fealty to us, may go out of our realm and return to it, safely and securely, by land and by water, except perhaps for a brief period in time of war, for the common good of the realm. But prisoners and outlaws are excepted according to the law of the realm; also people of a land at war against us, and the merchants, with regard to whom shall be done as we have said.

43. If any one hold from any escheat – as from the honour of Walingford, Nottingham, Boloin, Lancaster, or the other escheats which are in our hands and are baronies – and shall die, his heir shall not give another relief, nor shall he perform for us other service than he would perform for a baron if that barony were in the hand of a baron; and we shall hold it in the same way in which the baron has held it.

44. Persons dwelling without the forest shall not henceforth come before the forest justices, through common summonses, unless they are impleaded or are the sponsors of some person or persons attached for matters concerning the forest.

45. We will not make men justices, constables, sheriffs, or bailiffs unless they are such as know the law of the realm, and are minded to observe it rightly.

46. All barons who have founded abbeys for which they have charters of the king of England, or ancient right of tenure, shall have, as they ought to have, their custody when vacant.

47. All forests constituted as such in our time shall straightway be annulled; and the same shall be done for river banks made into places of defence by us in our time.

48. All evil customs concerning forests and warrens, and concerning foresters and warreners, sheriffs and their servants, river banks and their guardians, shall straightway be inquired into each county, through twelve sworn knights from that county, and shall be eradicated by them, entirely, so that they shall never be renewed, within forty days after the inquest has been made; in such manner that we shall first know about them, or our justice if we be not in England.

49. We shall straightway return all hostages and charters which were delivered to us by Englishmen as a surety for peace or faithful service.

50. We shall entirey remove from their bailwicks the relatives of Gerard de Athyes, so that they shall henceforth have no bailwick in England: Engelard de Cygnes, Andrew Peter and Gyon de Chanceles, Gyon de Cygnes, Geoffrey de Martin and his brothers, Philip Mark and his brothers, and Geoffrey his nephew, and the whole following of them.

51. And straightway after peace is restored we shall remove from the realm all the foreign soldiers, crossbowmen, servants, hirelings, who may have come with horses and arms to the harm of the realm.

52. If any one shall have been disseized by us, or removed, without a legal sentence of his peers, from his lands, castles, liberties or lawful right, we shall straightway restore them to him. And if a dispute shall arise concerning this matter it shall be settled according to the judgment of the twenty-five barons who are mentioned below as sureties for the peace. But with regard to all those things of which any one was, by king Henry our father or king Richard our brother, disseized or dispossessed without legal judgment of his peers, which we have in our hand or which others hold, and for which we ought to give a guarantee: We shall have respite until the common term for crusaders. Except with regard to those concerning which a plea was moved, or an inquest made by our order, before we took the cross. But when we return from our pilgrimage, or if, by chance, we desist from our pilgrimage, we shall straightway then show full justice regarding them.

53. We shall have the same respite, moreover, and in the same manner, in the matter of showing justice with regard to forests to be annulled and forests to remain, which Henry our father or Richard our brother constituted; and in the matter of wardships of lands

which belong to the fee of another – wardships of which kind we have hitherto enjoyed by reason of the fee which some one held from us in military service; – and in the matter of abbeys founded in the fee of another than ourselves – in which the lord of the fee may say that he has jurisdiction. And when we return, or if we desist from our pilgrimage, we shall straightway exhibit full justice to those complaining with regard to these matters.

54. No one shall be taken or imprisoned on account of the appeal of a woman concerning the death of another than her husband.

55. All fines imposed by us unjustly and contrary to the law of the land, and all amerciaments made unjustly and contrary to the law of the land, shall be altogether remitted, or it shall be done with regard to them according to the judgment of the twenty five barons mentioned below as sureties for the peace, or according to the judgment of the majority of them together with the aforesaid Stephen archbishop of Canterbury, if he can be present, and with others whom he may wish to associate with himself for this purpose. And if he can not be present, the affair shall nevertheless proceed without him; in such way that, if one or more of the said twenty five barons shall be concerned in a similar complaint, they shall be removed as to this particular decision, and, in their place, for this purpose alone, others shall be subtituted who shall be chosen and sworn by the remainder of those twenty five.

56. If we have disseized or dispossessed Welshmen of their lands or liberties or other things without legal judgment of their peers, in England or in Wales, – they shall straightway be restored to them. And if a dispute shall arise concerning this, then action shall be taken upon it in the March through judgment of their peers- -concerning English holdings according to the law of England, concerning Welsh holdings according to the law of Wales, concerning holdings in the March according to the law of the March. The Welsh shall do likewise with regard to us and our subjects.

57. But with regard to all those things of which any one of the Welsh by king Henry our father or king Richard our brother, disseized or dispossessed without legal judgment of his peers, which we have in our hand or which others hold, and for which we ought to give a guarantee: we shall have respite until the common term for crusaders. Except with regard to those concerning which a plea was moved, or an inquest made by our order, before we took the cross. But when we return from our pilgrimage, or if, by chance, we desist from our pilgrimage, we shall straightway then show full justice regarding them, according to the laws of Wales and the aforesaid districts.

58. We shall straightway return the son of Llewelin and all the Welsh hostages, and the charters delivered to us as surety for the peace.

59. We shall act towards Alexander king of the Scots regarding the restoration of his sisters, and his hostages, and his liberties and his lawful right, as we shall act towards our other barons of England; unless it ought to be otherwise according to the charters which we hold from William, his father, the former king of the Scots. And this shall be done through judgment of his peers in our court.

60. Moreover all the subjects of our realm, clergy as well as laity, shall, as far as pertains to them, observe, with regard to their vassals, all these aforesaid customs and liberties which we have decreed shall, as far as pertains to us, be observed in our realm with regard to our own.

61. Inasmuch as, for the sake of God, and for the bettering of our realm, and for the more ready healing of the discord which has arisen between us and our barons, we have made all these aforesaid concessions, – wishing them to enjoy for ever entire and firm stability, we make and grant to them the following security: that the baron, namely, may elect at their pleaure twenty five barons from the realm, who ought, with all their strength, to observe, maintain and cause to be observed, the peace and privileges which we have granted to them and confirmed by this our present charter. In such wise, namely, that if we, or our justice, or our bailiffs, or any one of our servants shall have transgressed against any one in any respect, or shall have broken one of the articles of peace or security, and our transgression shall have been shown to four barons of the aforesaid twenty five: those four barons shall come to us, or, if we are abroad, to our justice, showing to us our error; and they shall ask us to cause that error to be amended without delay. And if we do not amend that error, or, we being abroad, if our justice do not amend it within a term of forty days from the time when it was shown to us or, we being abroad, to our justice: the aforesaid four barons shall refer the matter to the remainder of the twenty five barons, and those twenty five barons, with the whole land in common, shall distrain and oppress us in every way in their power, – namely, by taking our castles, lands and possessions, and in every other way that they can, until amends shall have been made according to their judnnent. Saving the persons of ourselves, our queen and our children. And when amends shall have been made they shall be in accord with us as they had been previously. And whoever of the land wishes to do so, shall swear that in carrying out all the aforesaid measures he will obey the mandates of the aforesaid twenty five barons, and that, with them, he will oppress us to the extent of his power. And, to any one who wishes to do so, we publicly and freely give permission to swear; and we will never prevent any one from swearing. Moreover, all those in the land who shall be unwilling, themselves and of their own accord, to swear to the twenty five barons as to distraining and oppressing us with them: such ones we shall make to wear by our mandate, as has been said. And if any one of the twenty five barons shall die, or leave the country, or in any other way be prevented from carrying out the aforesaid measures, – the remainder of the aforesaid twenty five barons shall choose another in his place, according to their judgment, who shall be sworn in the same way as the others. Moreover, in all things entrusted to those twenty five barons to be carried out, if those twenty five shall be present and chance to disagree among themselves with regard to some matter, or if some of them, having been summoned, shall be unwilling or unable to be present: that which the majority of those present shall decide or decree shall be considered binding and valid, just as if all the twenty five had consented to it. And the aforesaid twenty five shall swear that they will faithfully observe all the foregoing, and will caue them be observed to the extent of their power. And we shall obtain nothing from any one, either through ourselves or through another, by which any of those concessions and liberties may be revoked or diminished. And if any such thing shall have been obtained, it shall be vain and invalid, and we shall never make use of it either through ourselves or through another.

62. And we have fully remitted to all, and pardoned, all the ill- will, anger and rancour which have arisen between us and our subjects, clergy and laity, from the time of the struggle. Moreover have fully remitted to all, clergy and laity, and – as far as pertains to

us – have pardoned fully all the transgressions committed, on the occasion of that same struggle, from Easter of the sixteenth year of our reign until the re-establishment of peace. In witness of which, more-over, we have caused to be drawn up for them letters patent of lord Stephen, archbishop of Canterbury, lord Henry, archbishop of Dubland the aforesaid bishops and master Pandulf, regarding that surety and the aforesaid concessions.

63. Wherefore we will and firmly decree that the English church shall be free, and that the subjects of our realm shall have and hold all the aforesaid liberties, rights and concessions, duly and in peace, freely and quietly, fully and entirely, for themselves and their heirs from us and our heirs, in all matters and in all places, forever, as has been said. Moreover it has been sworn, on our part as well as on the part of the barons, that all these above mentioned provisions shall observed with good faith and without evil intent. The witnesses being the above mentioned and many others. Given through our hand, in the plain called Runnymede between Windsor and Stanes, on the fifteenth day of June, in the seventeenth year of our reign.

The Declaration of Independence
July 4, 1776

When in the Course of human events, it becomes necessary for one people to dissolve the political bands which have connected them with another, and to assume among the powers of the earth, the separate and equal station to which the Laws of Nature and of Nature's God entitle them, a decent respect to the opinions of mankind requires that they should declare the causes which impel them to the separation.

We hold these truths to be self-evident, that all men are created equal, that they are endowed by their Creator with certain unalienable Rights, that among these are Life, Liberty and the pursuit of Happiness. – That to secure these rights, Governments are instituted among Men, deriving their just powers from the consent of the governed, – That whenever any Form of Government becomes destructive of these ends, it is the Right of the People to alter or to abolish it, and to institute new Government, laying its foundation on such principles and organizing its powers in such form, as to them shall seem most likely to effect their Safety and Happiness. Prudence, indeed, will dictate that Governments long established should not be changed for light and transient causes; and accordingly all experience hath shewn, that mankind are more disposed to suffer, while evils are sufferable, than to right themselves by abolishing the forms to which they are accustomed. But when a long train of abuses and usurpations, pursuing invariably the same Object evinces a design to reduce them under absolute Despotism, it is their right, it is their duty, to throw off such Government, and to provide new Guards for their future security. – Such has been the patient sufferance of these Colonies; and such is now the necessity which constrains them to alter their former Systems of Government. The history of the present King of Great Britain [George III] is a history of repeated injuries and usurpations, all having in direct object the establishment of an absolute Tyranny over these States. To prove this, let Facts be submitted to a candid world.

He has refused his Assent to Laws, the most wholesome and necessary for the public good.

He has forbidden his Governors to pass Laws of immediate and pressing importance, unless suspended in their operation till his Assent should be obtained; and when so suspended, he has utterly neglected to attend to them.

He has refused to pass other Laws for the accommodation of large districts of people, unless those people would relinquish the right of Representation in the Legislature, a right inestimable to them and formidable to tyrants only.

He has called together legislative bodies at places unusual, uncomfortable, and distant from the depository of their public Records, for the sole purpose of fatiguing them into compliance with his measures.

He has dissolved Representative Houses repeatedly, for opposing with manly firmness his invasions on the rights of the people.

He has refused for a long time, after such dissolutions, to cause others to be elected; whereby the Legislative powers, incapable of Annihilation, have returned to the People at large for their exercise; the State remaining in the mean time exposed to all the dangers of invasion from without, and convulsions within.

He has endeavoured to prevent the population of these States; for that purpose obstructing the Laws for Naturalization of Foreigners; refusing to pass others to encourage their migrations hither, and raising the conditions of new Appropriations of Lands.

He has obstructed the Administration of Justice, by refusing his Assent to Laws for establishing Judiciary powers.

He has made Judges dependent on his Will alone, for the tenure of their offices, and the amount and payment of their salaries.

He has erected a multitude of New Offices, and sent hither swarms of Officers to harass our people, and eat out their substance.

He has kept among us, in times of peace, Standing Armies without the consent of our legislatures.

He has affected to render the Military independent of and superior to the Civil power.

He has combined with others to subject us to a jurisdiction foreign to our constitution and unacknowledged by our laws; giving his Assent to their Acts of pretended Legislation:

For Quartering large bodies of armed troops among us:

For protecting them, by a mock Trial, from punishment for any Murders which they should commit on the Inhabitants of these States:

For cutting off our Trade with all parts of the world:

For imposing Taxes on us without our Consent:

For depriving us, in many cases, of the benefits of Trial by Jury:

For transporting us beyond Seas to be tried for pretended offences:

For abolishing the free System of English Laws in a neighbouring Province, establishing therein an Arbitrary government, and enlarging its Boundaries so as to render it at once an example and fit instrument for introducing the same absolute rule into these Colonies: For taking away our Charters, abolishing our most valuable Laws, and altering fundamentally the Forms of our Governments:

For suspending our own Legislatures, and declaring themselves invested with power to legislate for us in all cases whatsoever.

He has abdicated Government here, by declaring us out of his Protection and waging War against us.

He has plundered our seas, ravaged our Coasts, burnt our towns, and destroyed the lives of our people.

He is at this time transporting large Armies of foreign Mercenaries to compleat the works of death, desolation and tyranny, already begun with circumstances of Cruelty and perfidy scarcely paralleled in the most barbarous ages, and totally unworthy the Head of a civilized nation.

He has constrained our fellow Citizens taken Captive on the high Seas to bear Arms against their Country, to become the executioners of their friends and Brethren, or to fall themselves by their Hands.

He has excited domestic insurrections amongst us, and has endeavoured to bring on the inhabitants of our frontiers, the merciless Indian Savages, whose known rule of warfare, is an undistinguished destruction of all ages, sexes and conditions.

In every stage of these Oppressions We have Petitioned for Redress in the most humble terms: Our repeated Petitions have been answered only by repeated injury. A Prince whose character is thus marked by every act which may define a Tyrant, is unfit to be the ruler of a free people.

Nor have We been wanting in attentions to our British brethren. We have warned them from time to time of attempts by their legislature to extend an unwarrantable jurisdiction over us. We have reminded them of the circumstances of our emigration and settlement here. We have appealed to their native justice and magnanimity, and we have conjured them by the ties of our common kindred to disavow these usurpations, which, would inevitably interrupt our connections and correspondence. They too have been deaf to the voice of justice and of consanguinity. We must, therefore, acquiesce in the necessity, which denounces our Separation, and hold them, as we hold the rest of mankind, Enemies in War, in Peace Friends.

We, therefore, the Representatives of the united States of America, in General Congress, Assembled, appealing to the Supreme Judge of the world for the rectitude of our intentions, do, in the Name, and by the Authority of the good People of these Colonies, solemnly publish and declare, That these United Colonies are, and of Right ought to be Free and Independent States; that they are Absolved from all Allegiance to the British Crown, and that all political connection between them and the State of Great Britain, is and ought to be totally dissolved; and that as Free and Independent States, they have full Power to levy War, conclude Peace, contract Alliances, establish Commerce, and to do all other Acts and Things which Independent States may of right do. And for the support of this Declaration, with a firm reliance on the protection of divine Providence, we mutually pledge to each other our Lives, our Fortunes and our sacred Honor.

The signers of the Declaration represented the new states as follows:

New Hampshire
Josiah Bartlett, William Whipple, Matthew Thornton

Massachusetts
John Hancock, Samuel Adams, John Adams, Robert Treat Paine, Elbridge Gerry

Rhode Island
Stephen Hopkins, William Ellery

Connecticut
Roger Sherman, Samuel Huntington, William Williams, Oliver Wolcott

New York
William Floyd, Philip Livingston, Francis Lewis, Lewis Morris

New Jersey
Richard Stockton, John Witherspoon, Francis Hopkinson, John Hart, Abraham Clark

Pennsylvania
Robert Morris, Benjamin Rush, Benjamin Franklin, John Morton, George Clymer, James Smith, George Taylor, James Wilson, George Ross

Delaware
Caesar Rodney, George Read, Thomas McKean

Maryland
Samuel Chase, William Paca, Thomas Stone, Charles Carroll of Carrollton

Virginia
George Wythe, Richard Henry Lee, Thomas Jefferson, Benjamin Harrison, Thomas Nelson, Jr., Francis Lightfoot Lee, Carter Braxton

North Carolina
William Hooper, Joseph Hewes, John Penn

South Carolina
Edward Rutledge, Thomas Heyward, Jr., Thomas Lynch, Jr., Arthur Middleton

Georgia
Button Gwinnett, Lyman Hall, George Walton

The Constitution of the United States of America
September 17, 1787

Preamble

We the People of the United States, in Order to form a more perfect Union, establish Justice, insure domestic Tranquility, provide for the common defense, promote the general Welfare, and secure the Blessings of Liberty to ourselves and our Posterity, do ordain and establish this Constitution for the United States of America.

Article I - The Legislative Branch

Section 1 - The Legislature

All legislative Powers herein granted shall be vested in a Congress of the United States, which shall consist of a Senate and House of Representatives.

Section 2 - The House

The House of Representatives shall be composed of Members chosen every second Year by the People of the several States, and the Electors in each State shall have the Qualifications requisite for Electors of the most numerous Branch of the State Legislature.

No Person shall be a Representative who shall not have attained to the Age of twenty five Years, and been seven Years a Citizen of the United States, and who shall not, when elected, be an Inhabitant of that State in which he shall be chosen.

Representatives and direct Taxes shall be apportioned among the several States which may be included within this Union, according to their respective Numbers, which shall be determined by adding to the whole Number of free Persons, including those bound to Service for a Term of Years, and excluding Indians not taxed, three fifths of all other Persons. The actual Enumeration shall be made within three Years after the first Meeting of the Congress of the United States, and within every subsequent Term of ten Years, in such Manner as they shall by Law direct. The Number of Representatives shall not exceed one for every thirty Thousand, but each State shall have at Least one Representative; and until such enumeration shall be made, the State of New Hampshire shall be entitled to chuse three, Massachusetts eight, Rhode Island and Providence Plantations one, Connecticut five, New York six, New Jersey four, Pennsylvania eight, Delaware one, Maryland six, Virginia ten, North Carolina five, South Carolina five and Georgia three.

When vacancies happen in the Representation from any State, the Executive Authority thereof shall issue Writs of Election to fill such Vacancies.

The House of Representatives shall chuse their Speaker and other Officers; and shall have the sole Power of Impeachment.

Section 3 - The Senate

The Senate of the United States shall be composed of two Senators from each State, chosen by the Legislature thereof, for six Years; and each Senator shall have one Vote.

Immediately after they shall be assembled in Consequence of the first Election, they shall be divided as equally as may be into three Classes. The Seats of the Senators of the first Class shall be vacated at the Expiration of the second Year, of the second Class at the Expiration of the fourth Year, and of the third Class at the Expiration of the sixth Year, so that one third may be chosen every second Year; and if Vacancies happen by Resignation, or otherwise, during the Recess of the Legislature of any State, the Executive thereof may make temporary Appointments until the next Meeting of the Legislature, which shall then fill such Vacancies.

No person shall be a Senator who shall not have attained to the Age of thirty Years, and been nine Years a Citizen of the United States, and who shall not, when elected, be an Inhabitant of that State for which he shall be chosen.

The Vice President of the United States shall be President of the Senate, but shall have no Vote, unless they be equally divided.

The Senate shall chuse their other Officers, and also a President pro tempore, in the absence of the Vice President, or when he shall exercise the Office of President of the United States.

The Senate shall have the sole Power to try all Impeachments. When sitting for that Purpose, they shall be on Oath or Affirmation. When the President of the United States is tried, the Chief Justice shall preside: And no Person shall be convicted without the Concurrence of two thirds of the Members present.

Judgment in Cases of Impeachment shall not extend further than to removal from Office, and disqualification to hold and enjoy any Office of honor, Trust or Profit under the United States: but the Party convicted shall nevertheless be liable and subject to Indictment, Trial, Judgment and Punishment, according to Law.

Section 4 - Elections, Meetings

The Times, Places and Manner of holding Elections for Senators and Representatives, shall be prescribed in each State by the Legislature thereof; but the Congress may at any time by Law make or alter such Regulations, except as to the Place of Chusing Senators.

The Congress shall assemble at least once in every Year, and such Meeting shall be on the first Monday in December, unless they shall by Law appoint a different Day.

Section 5 - Membership, Rules, Journals, Adjournment

Each House shall be the Judge of the Elections, Returns and Qualifications of its own Members, and a Majority of each shall constitute a Quorum to do Business; but a smaller number may adjourn from day to day, and may be authorized to compel the Attendance of absent Members, in such Manner, and under such Penalties as each House may provide.

Each House may determine the Rules of its Proceedings, punish its Members for disorderly Behavior, and, with the Concurrence of two-thirds, expel a Member.

Each House shall keep a Journal of its Proceedings, and from time to time publish the same, excepting such Parts as may in their Judgment require Secrecy; and the Yeas and Nays of the Members of either House on any question shall, at the Desire of one fifth of those Present, be entered on the Journal.

Neither House, during the Session of Congress, shall, without the Consent of the other, adjourn for more than three days, nor to any other Place than that in which the two Houses shall be sitting.

Section 6 - Compensation

The Senators and Representatives shall receive a Compensation for their Services, to be ascertained by Law, and paid out of the Treasury of the United States. They shall in all Cases, except Treason, Felony and Breach of the Peace, be privileged from Arrest during their Attendance at the Session of their respective Houses, and in going to and returning from the same; and for any Speech or Debate in either House, they shall not be questioned in any other Place.

No Senator or Representative shall, during the Time for which he was elected, be appointed to any civil Office under the Authority of the United States which shall have been created, or the Emoluments whereof shall have been increased during such time; and no Person holding any Office under the United States, shall be a Member of either House during his Continuance in Office.

Section 7 - Revenue Bills, Legislative Process, Presidential Veto

All bills for raising Revenue shall originate in the House of Representatives; but the Senate may propose or concur with Amendments as on other Bills.

Every Bill which shall have passed the House of Representatives and the Senate, shall, before it become a Law, be presented to the President of the United States; If he approve he shall sign it, but if not he shall return it, with his Objections to that House in which it shall have originated, who shall enter the Objections at large on their Journal, and proceed to reconsider it. If after such Reconsideration two thirds of that House shall agree to pass the Bill, it shall be sent, together with the Objections, to the other House, by which it shall likewise be reconsidered, and if approved by two thirds of that House, it shall become a Law. But in all such Cases the Votes of both Houses shall be determined by Yeas and Nays, and the Names of the Persons voting for and against the Bill shall be entered on the Journal of each House respectively. If any Bill shall not be returned by the President within ten Days (Sundays excepted) after it shall have been presented to him, the Same shall be a Law, in like Manner as if he had signed it, unless the Congress by their Adjournment prevent its Return, in which Case it shall not be a Law.

Every Order, Resolution, or Vote to which the Concurrence of the Senate and House of Representatives may be necessary (except on a question of Adjournment) shall be presented to the President of the United States; and before the Same shall take Effect, shall be approved by him, or being disapproved by him, shall be repassed by two thirds of the Senate and House of Representatives, according to the Rules and Limitations prescribed in the Case of a Bill.

Section 8 - Powers of Congress

The Congress shall have Power To lay and collect Taxes, Duties, Imposts and Excises, to pay the Debts and provide for the common Defence and general Welfare of the United States; but all Duties, Imposts and Excises shall be uniform throughout the United States;

To borrow money on the credit of the United States;

To regulate Commerce with foreign Nations, and among the several States, and with the Indian Tribes;

To establish an uniform Rule of Naturalization, and uniform Laws on the subject of Bankruptcies throughout the United States;

To coin Money, regulate the Value thereof, and of foreign Coin, and fix the Standard of Weights and Measures;

To provide for the Punishment of counterfeiting the Securities and current Coin of the United States;

To establish Post Offices and Post Roads;

To promote the Progress of Science and useful Arts, by securing for limited Times to Authors and Inventors the exclusive Right to their respective Writings and Discoveries;

To constitute Tribunals inferior to the supreme Court;

To define and punish Piracies and Felonies committed on the high Seas, and Offenses against the Law of Nations;

To declare War, grant Letters of Marque and Reprisal, and make Rules concerning Captures on Land and Water;

To raise and support Armies, but no Appropriation of Money to that Use shall be for a longer Term than two Years;

To provide and maintain a Navy;

To make Rules for the Government and Regulation of the land and naval Forces;

To provide for calling forth the Militia to execute the Laws of the Union, suppress Insurrections and repel Invasions;

To provide for organizing, arming, and disciplining the Militia, and for governing such Part of them as may be employed in the Service of the United States, reserving to the States respectively, the Appointment of the Officers, and the Authority of training the Militia according to the discipline prescribed by Congress;

To exercise exclusive Legislation in all Cases whatsoever, over such District (not exceeding ten Miles square) as may, by Cession of particular States, and the acceptance of Congress, become the Seat of the Government of the United States, and to exercise like Authority over all Places purchased by the Consent of the Legislature of the State in which the Same shall be, for the Erection of Forts, Magazines, Arsenals, dock-Yards, and other needful Buildings; And

To make all Laws which shall be necessary and proper for carrying into Execution the foregoing Powers, and all other Powers vested by this Constitution in the Government of the United States, or in any Department or Officer thereof.

Section 9 - Limits on Congress

The Migration or Importation of such Persons as any of the States now existing shall think proper to admit, shall not be prohibited by the Congress prior to the Year one thousand eight hundred and eight, but a tax or duty may be imposed on such Importation, not exceeding ten dollars for each Person.

The privilege of the Writ of Habeas Corpus shall not be suspended, unless when in Cases of Rebellion or Invasion the public Safety may require it.

No Bill of Attainder or ex post facto Law shall be passed.

No capitation, or other direct, Tax shall be laid, unless in Proportion to the Census or Enumeration herein before directed to be taken.

No Tax or Duty shall be laid on Articles exported from any State.

No Preference shall be given by any Regulation of Commerce or Revenue to the Ports of one State over those of another: nor shall Vessels bound to, or from, one State, be obliged to enter, clear, or pay Duties in another.

No Money shall be drawn from the Treasury, but in Consequence of Appropriations made by Law; and a regular Statement and Account of the Receipts and Expenditures of all public Money shall be published from time to time.

No Title of Nobility shall be granted by the United States: And no Person holding any Office of Profit or Trust under them, shall, without the Consent of the Congress, accept of any present, Emolument, Office, or Title, of any kind whatever, from any King, Prince or foreign State.

Section 10 - Powers prohibited of States

No State shall enter into any Treaty, Alliance, or Confederation; grant Letters of Marque and Reprisal; coin Money; emit Bills of Credit; make any Thing but gold and silver Coin a Tender in Payment of Debts; pass any Bill of Attainder, ex post facto Law, or Law impairing the Obligation of Contracts, or grant any Title of Nobility.

No State shall, without the Consent of the Congress, lay any Imposts or Duties on Imports or Exports, except what may be absolutely necessary for executing it's inspection Laws: and the net Produce of all Duties and Imposts, laid by any State on Imports or Exports, shall be for the Use of the Treasury of the United States; and all such Laws shall be subject to the Revision and Controul of the Congress.

No State shall, without the Consent of Congress, lay any duty of Tonnage, keep Troops, or Ships of War in time of Peace, enter into any Agreement or Compact with another State, or with a foreign Power, or engage in War, unless actually invaded, or in such imminent Danger as will not admit of delay.

Article II - The Executive Branch

Section 1 - The President

The executive Power shall be vested in a President of the United States of America. He shall hold his Office during the Term of four Years, and, together with the Vice-President chosen for the same Term, be elected, as follows:

Each State shall appoint, in such Manner as the Legislature thereof may direct, a Number of Electors, equal to the whole Number of Senators and Representatives to which the State may be entitled in the Congress: but no Senator or Representative, or Person holding an Office of Trust or Profit under the United States, shall be appointed an Elector.

The Electors shall meet in their respective States, and vote by Ballot for two persons, of whom one at least shall not lie an Inhabitant of the same State with themselves. And they shall make a List of all the Persons voted for, and of the Number of Votes for each; which List they shall sign and certify, and transmit sealed to the Seat of the Government of the United States, directed to the President of the Senate. The President of the Senate shall, in the Presence of the Senate and House of Representatives, open all the Certificates, and the Votes shall then be counted. The Person having the greatest Number of Votes shall be the President, if such Number be a Majority of the whole Number of Electors appointed; and if there be more than one who have such Majority, and have an equal Number of Votes, then the House of Representatives shall immediately chuse by Ballot one of them for President; and if no Person have a Majority, then from the five highest on the List the said House shall in like Manner chuse the President. But in chusing the President, the Votes shall be taken by States, the Representation from each State having one Vote; a quorum for this Purpose shall consist of a Member or Members from two-thirds of the States, and a Majority of all the States shall be necessary to a Choice. In every Case, after the Choice of the President, the Person having the greatest Number of Votes of the Electors shall be the Vice President. But if there should remain two or more who have equal Votes, the Senate shall chuse from them by Ballot the Vice-President.

The Congress may determine the Time of chusing the Electors, and the Day on which they shall give their Votes; which Day shall be the same throughout the United States.

No person except a natural born Citizen, or a Citizen of the United States, at the time of the Adoption of this Constitution, shall be eligible to the Office of President; neither shall any Person be eligible to that Office who shall not have attained to the Age of thirty-five Years, and been fourteen Years a Resident within the United States. In Case of the Removal of the President from Office, or of his Death, Resignation, or Inability to discharge the Powers and Duties of the said Office, the same shall devolve on the Vice President, and the Congress may by Law provide for the Case of Removal, Death, Resignation or Inability, both of the President and Vice President, declaring what Officer shall then act as President, and such Officer shall act accordingly, until the Disability be removed, or a President shall be elected.

The President shall, at stated Times, receive for his Services, a Compensation, which shall neither be increased nor diminished during the Period for which he shall have been elected, and he shall not receive within that Period any other Emolument from the United States, or any of them.

Before he enter on the Execution of his Office, he shall take the following Oath or Affirmation:

"I do solemnly swear (or affirm) that I will faithfully execute the Office of President of the United States, and will to the best of my Ability, preserve, protect and defend the Constitution of the United States."

Section 2 - Civilian Power over Military, Cabinet, Pardon Power, Appointments

The President shall be Commander in Chief of the Army and Navy of the United States, and of the Militia of the several States, when called into the actual Service of the United States; he may require the Opinion, in writing, of the principal Officer in each of the executive Departments, upon any subject relating to the Duties of their respective

Offices, and he shall have Power to Grant Reprieves and Pardons for Offenses against the United States, except in Cases of Impeachment.

He shall have Power, by and with the Advice and Consent of the Senate, to make Treaties, provided two thirds of the Senators present concur; and he shall nominate, and by and with the Advice and Consent of the Senate, shall appoint Ambassadors, other public Ministers and Consuls, Judges of the supreme Court, and all other Officers of the United States, whose Appointments are not herein otherwise provided for, and which shall be established by Law: but the Congress may by Law vest the Appointment of such inferior Officers, as they think proper, in the President alone, in the Courts of Law, or in the Heads of Departments.

The President shall have Power to fill up all Vacancies that may happen during the Recess of the Senate, by granting Commissions which shall expire at the End of their next Session.

Section 3 - State of the Union, Convening Congress

He shall from time to time give to the Congress Information of the State of the Union, and recommend to their Consideration such Measures as he shall judge necessary and expedient; he may, on extraordinary Occasions, convene both Houses, or either of them, and in Case of Disagreement between them, with Respect to the Time of Adjournment, he may adjourn them to such Time as he shall think proper; he shall receive Ambassadors and other public Ministers; he shall take Care that the Laws be faithfully executed, and shall Commission all the Officers of the United States.

Section 4 - Disqualification

The President, Vice President and all civil Officers of the United States, shall be removed from Office on Impeachment for, and Conviction of, Treason, Bribery, or other high Crimes and Misdemeanors.

Article III - The Judicial Branch

Section 1 - Judicial powers

The judicial Power of the United States, shall be vested in one supreme Court, and in such inferior Courts as the Congress may from time to time ordain and establish. The Judges, both of the supreme and inferior Courts, shall hold their Offices during good Behavior, and shall, at stated Times, receive for their Services a Compensation which shall not be diminished during their Continuance in Office.

Section 2 - Trial by Jury, Original Jurisdiction, Jury Trials

The judicial Power shall extend to all Cases, in Law and Equity, arising under this Constitution, the Laws of the United States, and Treaties made, or which shall be made, under their Authority; to all Cases affecting Ambassadors, other public Ministers and Consuls; to all Cases of admiralty and maritime Jurisdiction; to Controversies to which the United States shall be a Party; to Controversies between two or more States; between a State and Citizens of another State; between Citizens of different States; between Citizens of the same State claiming Lands under Grants of different States, and between a State, or the Citizens thereof, and foreign States, Citizens or Subjects.

In all Cases affecting Ambassadors, other public Ministers and Consuls, and those in which a State shall be Party, the supreme Court shall have original Jurisdiction. In all the other Cases before mentioned, the supreme Court shall have appellate Jurisdiction, both as to Law and Fact, with such Exceptions, and under such Regulations as the Congress shall make.

The Trial of all Crimes, except in Cases of Impeachment, shall be by Jury; and such Trial shall be held in the State where the said Crimes shall have been committed; but when not committed within any State, the Trial shall be at such Place or Places as the Congress may by Law have directed.

Section 3 - Treason

Treason against the United States, shall consist only in levying War against them, or in adhering to their Enemies, giving them Aid and Comfort. No Person shall be convicted of Treason unless on the Testimony of two Witnesses to the same overt Act, or on Confession in open Court.

The Congress shall have power to declare the Punishment of Treason, but no Attainder of Treason shall work Corruption of Blood, or Forfeiture except during the Life of the Person attainted.

Article IV - The States

Section 1 - Each State to Honor all others

Full Faith and Credit shall be given in each State to the public Acts, Records, and judicial Proceedings of every other State. And the Congress may by general Laws prescribe the Manner in which such Acts, Records and Proceedings shall be proved, and the Effect thereof.

Section 2 - State citizens, Extradition

The Citizens of each State shall be entitled to all Privileges and Immunities of Citizens in the several States.

A Person charged in any State with Treason, Felony, or other Crime, who shall flee from Justice, and be found in another State, shall on demand of the executive Authority of the State from which he fled, be delivered up, to be removed to the State having Jurisdiction of the Crime.

No Person held to Service or Labour in one State, under the Laws thereof, escaping into another, shall, in Consequence of any Law or Regulation therein, be discharged from such Service or Labour, But shall be delivered up on Claim of the Party to whom such Service or Labour may be due.

Section 3 - New States

New States may be admitted by the Congress into this Union; but no new States shall be formed or erected within the Jurisdiction of any other State; nor any State be formed by the Junction of two or more States, or parts of States, without the Consent of the Legislatures of the States concerned as well as of the Congress.

The Congress shall have Power to dispose of and make all needful Rules and Regulations respecting the Territory or other Property belonging to the United States; and nothing in this Constitution shall be so construed as to Prejudice any Claims of the United States, or of any particular State.

Section 4 - Republican government

The United States shall guarantee to every State in this Union a Republican Form of Government, and shall protect each of them against Invasion; and on Application of the Legislature, or of the Executive (when the Legislature cannot be convened) against domestic Violence.

Article V - Amendment

The Congress, whenever two thirds of both Houses shall deem it necessary, shall propose Amendments to this Constitution, or, on the Application of the Legislatures of two thirds of the several States, shall call a Convention for proposing Amendments, which, in either Case, shall be valid to all Intents and Purposes, as part of this Constitution, when ratified by the Legislatures of three fourths of the several States, or by Conventions in three fourths thereof, as the one or the other Mode of Ratification may be proposed by the Congress; Provided that no Amendment which may be made prior to the Year One thousand eight hundred and eight shall in any Manner affect the first and fourth Clauses in the Ninth Section of the first Article; and that no State, without its Consent, shall be deprived of its equal Suffrage in the Senate.

Article VI - Debts, Supremacy, Oaths

All Debts contracted and Engagements entered into, before the Adoption of this Constitution, shall be as valid against the United States under this Constitution, as under the Confederation.

This Constitution, and the Laws of the United States which shall be made in Pursuance thereof; and all Treaties made, or which shall be made, under the Authority of the United States, shall be the supreme Law of the Land; and the Judges in every State shall be bound thereby, any Thing in the Constitution or Laws of any State to the Contrary notwithstanding.

The Senators and Representatives before mentioned, and the Members of the several State Legislatures, and all executive and judicial Officers, both of the United States and of the several States, shall be bound by Oath or Affirmation, to support this Constitution; but no religious Test shall ever be required as a Qualification to any Office or public Trust under the United States.

Article VII - Ratification Documents

The Amendments

The following are the Amendments to the Constitution. The first ten Amendments collectively are commonly known as the Bill of Rights.

Amendment 1 - Freedom of Religion, Press, Expression. Ratified 12/15/1791.

Congress shall make no law respecting an establishment of religion, or prohibiting the free exercise thereof; or abridging the freedom of speech, or of the press; or the right of the people peaceably to assemble, and to petition the Government for a redress of grievances.

Amendment 2 - Right to Bear Arms. Ratified 12/15/1791.

A well regulated Militia, being necessary to the security of a free State, the right of the people to keep and bear Arms, shall not be infringed.

Amendment 3 - Quartering of Soldiers. Ratified 12/15/1791.

No Soldier shall, in time of peace be quartered in any house, without the consent of the Owner, nor in time of war, but in a manner to be prescribed by law.

Amendment 4 - Search and Seizure. Ratified 12/15/1791.

The right of the people to be secure in their persons, houses, papers, and effects, against unreasonable searches and seizures, shall not be violated, and no Warrants shall issue, but upon probable cause, supported by Oath or affirmation, and particularly describing the place to be searched, and the persons or things to be seized.

Amendment 5 - Trial and Punishment, Compensation for Takings. Ratified 12/15/1791.

No person shall be held to answer for a capital, or otherwise infamous crime, unless on a presentment or indictment of a Grand Jury, except in cases arising in the land or naval forces, or in the Militia, when in actual service in time of War or public danger; nor shall any person be subject for the same offense to be twice put in jeopardy of life or limb; nor shall be compelled in any criminal case to be a witness against himself, nor be deprived of life, liberty, or property, without due process of law; nor shall private property be taken for public use, without just compensation.

Amendment 6 - Right to Speedy Trial, Confrontation of Witnesses. Ratified 12/15/1791.

In all criminal prosecutions, the accused shall enjoy the right to a speedy and public trial, by an impartial jury of the State and district wherein the crime shall have been committed, which district shall have been previously ascertained by law, and to be informed of the nature and cause of the accusation; to be confronted with the witnesses against him; to have compulsory process for obtaining witnesses in his favor, and to have the Assistance of Counsel for his defence.

Amendment 7 - Trial by Jury in Civil Cases. Ratified 12/15/1791.

In Suits at common law, where the value in controversy shall exceed twenty dollars, the right of trial by jury shall be preserved, and no fact tried by a jury, shall be otherwise re-examined in any Court of the United States, than according to the rules of the common law.

Amendment 8 - Cruel and Unusual Punishment. Ratified 12/15/1791.

Excessive bail shall not be required, nor excessive fines imposed, nor cruel and unusual punishments inflicted.

Amendment 9 - Construction of Constitution. Ratified 12/15/1791.

The enumeration in the Constitution, of certain rights, shall not be construed to deny or disparage others retained by the people.

Amendment 10 - Powers of the States and People. Ratified 12/15/1791.

The powers not delegated to the United States by the Constitution, nor prohibited by it to the States, are reserved to the States respectively, or to the people.

Amendment 11 - Judicial Limits. Ratified 2/7/1795.

The Judicial power of the United States shall not be construed to extend to any suit in law or equity, commenced or prosecuted against one of the United States by Citizens of another State, or by Citizens or Subjects of any Foreign State.

Amendment 12 - Choosing the President, Vice-President. Ratified 6/15/1804.

The Electors shall meet in their respective states, and vote by ballot for President and Vice-President, one of whom, at least, shall not be an inhabitant of the same state with themselves; they shall name in their ballots the person voted for as President, and in distinct ballots the person voted for as Vice-President, and they shall make distinct lists of all persons voted for as President, and of all persons voted for as Vice-President and of the number of votes for each, which lists they shall sign and certify, and transmit sealed to the seat of the government of the United States, directed to the President of the Senate;

The President of the Senate shall, in the presence of the Senate and House of Representatives, open all the certificates and the votes shall then be counted;

The person having the greatest Number of votes for President, shall be the President, if such number be a majority of the whole number of Electors appointed; and if no person have such majority, then from the persons having the highest numbers not exceeding three on the list of those voted for as President, the House of Representatives shall choose immediately, by ballot, the President. But in choosing the President, the votes shall be taken by states, the representation from each state having one vote; a quorum for this purpose shall consist of a member or members from two-thirds of the states, and a majority of all the states shall be necessary to a choice. And if the House of Representatives shall not choose a President whenever the right of choice shall devolve upon them, before the fourth day of March next following, then the Vice-President shall act as President, as in the case of the death or other constitutional disability of the President.

The person having the greatest number of votes as Vice-President, shall be the Vice-President, if such number be a majority of the whole number of Electors appointed, and if no person have a majority, then from the two highest numbers on the list, the Senate shall choose the Vice-President; a quorum for the purpose shall consist of two-thirds of the whole number of Senators, and a majority of the whole number shall be necessary to a choice. But no person constitutionally ineligible to the office of President shall be eligible to that of Vice-President of the United States.

Amendment 13 - Slavery Abolished. Ratified 12/6/1865.

1. Neither slavery nor involuntary servitude, except as a punishment for crime whereof the party shall have been duly convicted, shall exist within the United States, or any place subject to their jurisdiction.

2. Congress shall have power to enforce this article by appropriate legislation.

Amendment 14 - Citizenship Rights. Ratified 7/9/1868.

1. All persons born or naturalized in the United States, and subject to the jurisdiction thereof, are citizens of the United States and of the State wherein they reside. No State shall make or enforce any law which shall abridge the privileges or immunities of citizens of the United States; nor shall any State deprive any person of life, liberty, or property, without due process of law; nor deny to any person within its jurisdiction the equal protection of the laws.

2. Representatives shall be apportioned among the several States according to their respective numbers, counting the whole number of persons in each State, excluding Indians not taxed. But when the right to vote at any election for the choice of electors for President and Vice-President of the United States, Representatives in Congress, the Executive and Judicial officers of a State, or the members of the Legislature thereof, is denied to any of the male inhabitants of such State, being twenty-one years of age, and citizens of the United States, or in any way abridged, except for participation in rebellion, or other crime, the basis of representation therein shall be reduced in the proportion which the number of such male citizens shall bear to the whole number of male citizens twenty-one years of age in such State.

3. No person shall be a Senator or Representative in Congress, or elector of President and Vice-President, or hold any office, civil or military, under the United States, or under any State, who, having previously taken an oath, as a member of Congress, or as an officer of the United States, or as a member of any State legislature, or as an executive or judicial officer of any State, to support the Constitution of the United States, shall have engaged in insurrection or rebellion against the same, or given aid or comfort to the enemies thereof. But Congress may by a vote of two-thirds of each House, remove such disability.

4. The validity of the public debt of the United States, authorized by law, including debts incurred for payment of pensions and bounties for services in suppressing insurrection or rebellion, shall not be questioned. But neither the United States nor any State shall assume or pay any debt or obligation incurred in aid of insurrection or rebellion against the United States, or any claim for the loss or emancipation of any slave; but all such debts, obligations and claims shall be held illegal and void.

5. The Congress shall have power to enforce, by appropriate legislation, the provisions of this article.

Amendment 15 - Race No Bar to Vote. Ratified 2/3/1870.

1. The right of citizens of the United States to vote shall not be denied or abridged by the United States or by any State on account of race, color, or previous condition of servitude.

2. The Congress shall have power to enforce this article by appropriate legislation.

Amendment 16 - Status of Income Tax Clarified. Ratified 2/3/1913.

The Congress shall have power to lay and collect taxes on incomes, from whatever source derived, without apportionment among the several States, and without regard to any census or enumeration.

Amendment 17 - Senators Elected by Popular Vote. Ratified 4/8/1913.

The Senate of the United States shall be composed of two Senators from each State, elected by the people thereof, for six years; and each Senator shall have one vote. The electors in each State shall have the qualifications requisite for electors of the most numerous branch of the State legislatures.

When vacancies happen in the representation of any State in the Senate, the executive authority of such State shall issue writs of election to fill such vacancies: Provided, That the legislature of any State may empower the executive thereof to make temporary appointments until the people fill the vacancies by election as the legislature may direct.

This amendment shall not be so construed as to affect the election or term of any Senator chosen before it becomes valid as part of the Constitution.

Amendment 18 - Liquor Abolished. Ratified 1/16/1919.

1. After one year from the ratification of this article the manufacture, sale, or transportation of intoxicating liquors within, the importation thereof into, or the exportation thereof from the United States and all territory subject to the jurisdiction thereof for beverage purposes is hereby prohibited.

2. The Congress and the several States shall have concurrent power to enforce this article by appropriate legislation.

3. This article shall be inoperative unless it shall have been ratified as an amendment to the Constitution by the legislatures of the several States, as provided in the Constitution, within seven years from the date of the submission hereof to the States by the Congress.

Amendment 19 - Women's Suffrage. Ratified 8/18/1920.

The right of citizens of the United States to vote shall not be denied or abridged by the United States or by any State on account of sex.

Congress shall have power to enforce this article by appropriate legislation.

Amendment 20 - Presidential, Congressional Terms. Ratified 1/23/1933.

1. The terms of the President and Vice President shall end at noon on the 20th day of January, and the terms of Senators and Representatives at noon on the 3d day of January, of the years in which such terms would have ended if this article had not been ratified; and the terms of their successors shall then begin.

2. The Congress shall assemble at least once in every year, and such meeting shall begin at noon on the 3d day of January, unless they shall by law appoint a different day.

3. If, at the time fixed for the beginning of the term of the President, the President elect shall have died, the Vice President elect shall become President. If a President shall not have been chosen before the time fixed for the beginning of his term, or if the President elect shall have failed to qualify, then the Vice President elect shall act as President until a President shall have qualified; and the Congress may by law provide for the case wherein neither a President elect nor a Vice President elect shall have qualified, declaring who shall then act as President, or the manner in which one who is to act shall be selected, and such person shall act accordingly until a President or Vice President shall have qualified.

4. The Congress may by law provide for the case of the death of any of the persons from whom the House of Representatives may choose a President whenever the right of choice shall have devolved upon them, and for the case of the death of any of the persons from whom the Senate may choose a Vice President whenever the right of choice shall have devolved upon them.

5. Sections 1 and 2 shall take effect on the 15th day of October following the ratification of this article.

6. This article shall be inoperative unless it shall have been ratified as an amendment to the Constitution by the legislatures of three-fourths of the several States within seven years from the date of its submission.

Amendment 21 - Amendment 18 Repealed. Ratified 12/5/1933.

1. The eighteenth article of amendment to the Constitution of the United States is hereby repealed.

2. The transportation or importation into any State, Territory, or possession of the United States for delivery or use therein of intoxicating liquors, in violation of the laws thereof, is hereby prohibited.

3. The article shall be inoperative unless it shall have been ratified as an amendment to the Constitution by conventions in the several States, as provided in the Constitution, within seven years from the date of the submission hereof to the States by the Congress.

Amendment 22 - Presidential Term Limits. Ratified 2/27/1951.

1. No person shall be elected to the office of the President more than twice, and no person who has held the office of President, or acted as President, for more than two years of a

term to which some other person was elected President shall be elected to the office of the President more than once. But this Article shall not apply to any person holding the office of President, when this Article was proposed by the Congress, and shall not prevent any person who may be holding the office of President, or acting as President, during the term within which this Article becomes operative from holding the office of President or acting as President during the remainder of such term.

2. This article shall be inoperative unless it shall have been ratified as an amendment to the Constitution by the legislatures of three-fourths of the several States within seven years from the date of its submission to the States by the Congress.

Amendment 23 - Presidential Vote for District of Columbia. Ratified 3/29/1961.

1. The District constituting the seat of Government of the United States shall appoint in such manner as the Congress may direct: A number of electors of President and Vice President equal to the whole number of Senators and Representatives in Congress to which the District would be entitled if it were a State, but in no event more than the least populous State; they shall be in addition to those appointed by the States, but they shall be considered, for the purposes of the election of President and Vice President, to be electors appointed by a State; and they shall meet in the District and perform such duties as provided by the twelfth article of amendment.

2. The Congress shall have power to enforce this article by appropriate legislation.

Amendment 24 - Poll Tax Barred. Ratified 1/23/1964.

1. The right of citizens of the United States to vote in any primary or other election for President or Vice President, for electors for President or Vice President, or for Senator or Representative in Congress, shall not be denied or abridged by the United States or any State by reason of failure to pay any poll tax or other tax.

2. The Congress shall have power to enforce this article by appropriate legislation.

Amendment 25 - Presidential Disability and Succession. Ratified 2/10/1967.

1. In case of the removal of the President from office or of his death or resignation, the Vice President shall become President.

2. Whenever there is a vacancy in the office of the Vice President, the President shall nominate a Vice President who shall take office upon confirmation by a majority vote of both Houses of Congress.

3. Whenever the President transmits to the President pro tempore of the Senate and the Speaker of the House of Representatives his written declaration that he is unable to discharge the powers and duties of his office, and until he transmits to them a written declaration to the contrary, such powers and duties shall be discharged by the Vice President as Acting President.

4. Whenever the Vice President and a majority of either the principal officers of the executive departments or of such other body as Congress may by law provide, transmit to the President pro tempore of the Senate and the Speaker of the House of Representatives their written declaration that the President is unable to discharge the powers and duties of his office, the Vice President shall immediately assume the powers and duties of the office as Acting President.

Thereafter, when the President transmits to the President pro tempore of the Senate and the Speaker of the House of Representatives his written declaration that no inability exists, he shall resume the powers and duties of his office unless the Vice President and a majority of either the principal officers of the executive department or of such other body as Congress may by law provide, transmit within four days to the President pro tempore of the Senate and the Speaker of the House of Representatives their written declaration that the President is unable to discharge the powers and duties of his office. Thereupon Congress shall decide the issue, assembling within forty eight hours for that purpose if not in session. If the Congress, within twenty one days after receipt of the latter written declaration, or, if Congress is not in session, within twenty one days after Congress is required to assemble, determines by two thirds vote of both Houses that the President is unable to discharge the powers and duties of his office, the Vice President shall continue to discharge the same as Acting President; otherwise, the President shall resume the powers and duties of his office.

Amendment 26 - Voting Age Set to 18 Years. Ratified 7/1/1971.

1. The right of citizens of the United States, who are eighteen years of age or older, to vote shall not be denied or abridged by the United States or by any State on account of age.

2. The Congress shall have power to enforce this article by appropriate legislation.

Amendment 27 - Limiting Congressional Pay Increases. Ratified 5/7/1992.

No law, varying the compensation for the services of the Senators and Representatives, shall take effect, until an election of Representatives shall have intervened.

The Gettysburg Address
Gettysburg, Pennsylvania, November 19, 1863

On June 1, 1865, Senator Charles Sumner commented on what is now considered the most famous speech by President Abraham Lincoln. In his eulogy on the slain president, he called it a "monumental act." He said Lincoln was mistaken that "the world will little note, nor long remember what we say here." Rather, the Bostonian remarked, "The world noted at once what he said, and will never cease to remember it. The battle itself was less important than the speech."

Four score and seven years ago our fathers brought forth on this continent, a new nation, conceived in Liberty, and dedicated to the proposition that all men are created equal.

Now we are engaged in a great civil war, testing whether that nation, or any nation so conceived and so dedicated, can long endure. We are met on a great battle-field of that war. We have come to dedicate a portion of that field, as a final resting place for those who here gave their lives that that nation might live. It is altogether fitting and proper that we should do this.

But, in a larger sense, we can not dedicate – we can not consecrate – we can not hallow – this ground. The brave men, living and dead, who struggled here, have consecrated it, far above our poor power to add or detract. The world will little note, nor long remember what we say here, but it can never forget what they did here. It is for us the living, rather, to be dedicated here to the unfinished work which they who fought here have thus far so nobly advanced. It is rather for us to be here dedicated to the great task remaining before us – that from these honored dead we take increased devotion to that cause for which they gave the last full measure of devotion – that we here highly resolve that these dead shall not have died in vain – that this nation, under God, shall have a new birth of freedom – and that government of the people, by the people, for the people, shall not perish from the earth.

GLOSSARY

A priori – In philosophy, a term used to denote the kind of knowledge derived from intellect or reason as contrasted with that which comes from sense experience, called a posteriori.

Abolitionist – a supporter of Abolitionism, which was a movement to end the slave trade and emancipate slaves in Western Europe and the Americas. The slave system aroused little protest until the 18th century, when rationalist thinkers of the Enlightenment criticized it for violating the rights of man, and Christian religious groups, especially in the United States, condemned it as un-Christian.

Academy – A garden in ancient Greece where Plato taught his students. Subsequent followers of Plato were referred to as academics.

Acquired Sovereignty – The condition of rule whereby the ruling body is in power simply because it has conquered the state.

Allegory of the Cave – A story told by Socrates in Plato's Republic illustrating how the ignorant are blinded when confronted by the light of the truth.

Andalusia – was the Arabic name given to those parts of the Iberian Peninsula governed by Arab Muslims, at various times in the period between 711 and 1492. Today it is an autonomous region of southern Spain bordered by the Mediterranean Sea and the Atlantic Ocean. It contains the historic cities of Seville, Granada, and Cadiz and many examples of Moorish architecture.

Anti-formalism – A political theory that says real change can only be achieved by overthrowing the existing political system.

Amoral – Without moral standards: not caring about good behavior or morals

Andalusia or Al-Andalus, – an Arabic name given to the parts of Iberian Peninsula governed by Arab Muslims in the period between 711 and 1492 AD.

Apologist – somebody who defends a doctrine or ideology. Eastern Orthodox and Catholic Christian faiths are especially rich in great apologists, for example, St. Augustine of Hippo, Basil the Great, Zviad Gamsakhurdia and Ilia Chavchavadze.

Aristocracy – Form of government in which the sovereign power is vested in a small number of citizens who are theoretically the best qualified to rule.

Artificial State – A creation based on such a "fictitious nation." The nations living on its territory have not evolved into subnations of a new encompassing nation

Ashari – A school of early Muslim speculative theology founded by the theologian Abu al-Hasan al-Ash'ari. It was instrumental in drastically changing the direction of Islamic theology, separating its development radically from that of theology in the Christian world.

Atypical – unusual or unconventional.

Authoritarian Depoliticization – Keeping the populace poor and destitute so they will not have enough strength to unite and revolt against the ruler, and so they will not participate in politics.

Benjamin Franklin – one of the founding fathers of the United States. He was one of the most progressive thinkers of the 18th century. He was a pragmatic idealist, philosopher, writer, entrepreneur, political activist and a devout public servant.

Biblical Scholar – Someone who is well-versed in and studies the bible regularly.

Browder v. Gayle – (1956) A case heard before the U.S. District Court for the Middle District of Alabama regarding Montgomery bus segregation laws. It was the US District Court's ruling in this case that ended segregation on Montgomery public buses.

Canonize – In the Eastern Orthodox and Roman Catholic Church, to declare someone a saint.

Cappadocia – ancient state of Cappadocians, who are the people of proto-Georgian origin. Cappadocia falls in modern day central Turkey. Cappadocians are famous for their devotion to Orthodox Christian Theology and Mysticism. St. Basil the Great, Gregory of Nyssa, Gregory Nazianzus and many other most influential Orthodox Theologians were Cappadocians. They are collectively known as Cappadocian Fathers.

Cartesian doubt – A type of philosophical skepticism associated with Rene Descartes. It is used primarily as a route to certain knowledge. The methodology dictates that one disbelieves everything until an infallible point is reached. Descartes was extremely skeptical over sense perception.

Caucasia – Mountainous region separating Eastern Europe from Asia. Southern Caucasus was historically inhabited by Georgians, but due to decline of Georgia's political power and increase of Russian and Iranian influences now is home to Georgia, Azerbaijan and Armenia. Northern Caucasus is inhabited by the people of proto-Georgian languages, such as Chechnyans and Ingushetians, by the people of proto-Scythian and Proto-Sarmatian origin, such as Adygeans, North Osetians, Alanians, etc. now in Russian Federation.

Causation – The fact that something causes an effect, or the action of causing an effect.

Child Collectives – collectives for children in the Soviet Union.

Christian Humanist – a devotee to Christian Humanism, which is a philosophical union of Christian religion and humanist principles.

Christology – the field of study within Christian theology which is primarily concerned with the nature and person of Jesus Christ.

Civil Activist – a devotee to civil activism, which is a form of activism directed to bringing about social or political change.

Civil disobedience – a political strategy made prominent by the Civil Right Movement of the 1950s and 1960s in the United States, requiring non-violent boycotts of unjust racial laws.

Civil Liberties – Political and social concepts referring to guarantees of freedom, justice, and equality that a state may make to its citizens.

Civil Rights Movement – in the United States the term refers to a set of noted events and reform movements in that country aimed at abolishing public and private acts of racial discrimination and racism against African Americans between 1954 to 1968, particularly in the southern United States. It is sometimes referred to as the Second Reconstruction era.

Colonialism – The extension of a nation's sovereignty over territory beyond its borders by the establishment of either settler or exploitation colonies in which indigenous populations are directly ruled, displaced, or exterminated. Colonizing nations generally dominate the resources, labor, and markets of the colonial territory, and may also impose socio-cultural, religious, and linguistic structures on the indigenous population

Cognitive Dissonance – An uncomfortable feeling caused by holding two contradictory ideas simultaneously. It normally occurs when a person perceives a logical inconsistency among his or her cognitions.

Cold War – Term used to describe the post-World War II struggle between the United States and its allies and the Union of Soviet Socialist Republics (USSR) and its allies.

Communalism – Modern term that describes a broad range of intricate relationships in society especially in traditional Africa, centered on the supremacy of the community. Here the individual always remains conscious of his relevance and acceptability to his community. This is very different from communism.

Confucianism – The teachings of Confucius or his followers, emphasizing self-control, adherence to a social hierarchy, and social and political order. Cornerstone of Confucian dogmas is social responsibility, rather than personal spiritualism.

Consensual democracy – a variant of democracy akin to traditional Igbo society where decisions reached via the consensus of all adult males assembled in the village or community arenas.

Constitutional Republic – A state where the head of state and other officials are elected as representatives of the people, and must govern according to existing constitutional law that limits the government's power over citizens.

Corporeal – Concerning the physical body: relating to or involving the physical body rather than the mind or spirit

Corrective Justice – This idea is centered on numerical equality in transactions both voluntary (e.g. contracts) and involuntary (e.g. crime); one good is distributed to one person.

Corrective Labor Camps – Imperial Russia operated a system of remote Siberian forced labor camps as a part of its regular judicial system, called Katorga. The Soviet Union took over the already extensive Katorga system and expanded it immensely, eventually organizing the Gulag to run the camps.

Correlation – The degree to which two or more variables are related and change together.

David Hume – A Scottish philosopher and avid supporter of empiricism.

Decentralized Government – Rule that is divided between many subsidiary branches of government rather than being held by one strong central power.

Demagogic – Machiavellian despot or ruthless tyrant.

Democracy – Political system in which the people of a country rule through any form of government they choose to establish. Greek term meaning "rule by the people."

Deontology – Logic of moral obligation: the study of what is morally obligatory, permissible, right, or wrong.

Determinism – Philosophical doctrine holding that every event, mental as well as physical, has a cause, and that, the cause being given, the event follows invariably.

Diaphonia – Greek term referring to a variety of perspectives on a given issue.

Direct Democracy – A form of democracy and theory of civics wherein sovereignty is lodged in the assembly of all citizens who choose to participate. Depending on the particular system, this assembly might pass executive motions, make laws, elect and dismiss officials and conduct trials.

Distributive Justice – Concerns what is just or right with respect to the allocation of goods in a society.

Divine Right of Kings – A political and religious doctrine of royal absolutism. It asserts that a monarch is subject to no earthly authority, deriving his right to rule directly from the will of God.

Dominican Order – Catholic religious order, founded by Saint Dominic in the early 13th century in France.

Economic Models – A theoretical construct that represents economic processes by a set of variables and a set of logical and/or quantitative relationships between them. The economic model is a simplified framework designed to illustrate complex processes, often but not always using mathematical techniques.

Efficient Cause – In Aristotle's four causes of government, the legislators serve the role of putting the laws into writing.

Empiricism – A doctrine that affirms that all knowledge is based on experience, and denies the possibility of spontaneous ideas or a priori thought.

Enlightenment – The concept refers mainly to the European intellectual movement known as the Age of Enlightenment, also called the Age of Reason referring to philosophical developments related to scientific rationality in the 17th and 18th centuries. The time period was marked by a strong faith in reason and usually a rejection of institutionalized religion.

Environmentalist – somebody involved in issues relating to the protection of the natural world. In modern world it is especially a member of a political group campaigning against the perceived harmful effects of industrialized societies

Epicureans – Followers of Epicurus who believe pleasure is the only good one should strive toward.

Equity – Actions, treatment of others, or a general condition characterized by justice, fairness, and impartiality.

Etiquette – a code of behavior that delineates expectations for social behavior according to contemporary conventional norms within a society, social class, or group. The French word étiquette, signifying ticket (of admission, etc.) first appeared in English around 1750.

Eudaimonia – Greek term referring to overall happiness and fulfillment.

Eusebius – He is often referred to as the Father of Church History because of his work in recording the history of the early Christian church

Exegesis – a critical explanation or interpretation of a text, especially a religious text.

Evil Empire – this is a phrase applied to Russia (back then known as the Soviet Union) by the U.S. President, Ronald Reagan and American conservatives, who took an aggressive, hard-line stance against the USSR.

Fanaticism – Holding extreme or irrational enthusiasms or beliefs, especially in religion or politics.

Fascism – a radical extreme right-wing authoritarian nationalist political principle belief e.g. Nazism.

Final Cause – In Aristotle's four causes of government, the end result which is a good and effective government.

Five Good Emperors – A term that refers to five consecutive emperors of the Roman Empire who represented a line of virtuous and just rule – Nerva, Trajan, Hadrian, Antoninus Pius, and Marcus Aurelius. The term was coined by the political philosopher Niccolò Machiavelli.

Formal Cause – In Aristotle's four causes of government, a constitution should serve the purpose of putting all laws and the structure of the regime into writing.

Fortuna – Fortune.

Free Market – Market that is free of government intervention and regulation, besides the minimal function of maintaining the legal system and protecting property rights.

Freedom of Choice – freedom to exercise one's will. Freedom of choice entails that all men are created equal as all men are able to reason, which, in turn, entitles them to freedom of choice.

G.K. Chesterton – An influential English writer of the early 20th century who is well known for his reasoned apologetics and witty paradoxes.

General will – A key concept in Rousseau's theory of government by which an individual will concede their individual will for the will of the majority.

Georgia – a transcontinental country in the Caucasus region located at the dividing line of Europe and Asia. The territory of modern-day Georgia has been continuously inhabited since the early Stone Age. Georgia has its own alphabet and indigenous language. The country is predominantly Orthodox Christian. Georgia was first introduced to Christianity by the Apostles Andrew and Simon. List of notable Georgians includes a great theologian St. Basil the Great, philosophers, such as Shota Rustaveli, Davit Guramishvili and Ilia Chavchavadze. Today Georgia is a democratic state. It is a close U.S. ally on the war against terrorism – Georgia contributes more troops than any other nation to the U.S. and British led coalition forces in Iraq and Afghanistan. For the past two centuries Georgians have greatly suffered from imperialism of its neighboring Russia. Encroachment on Georgia's freedom and brutal interventions have been numerously carried out first by the old Russian Empire and its Tsars, then under an umbrella of the Soviet Union and lately by Russian Federation. Most recently, in August of 2008, Russia commenced a full-fledged conquest against the sovereign Georgia during which Russian forces and paramilitaries conducted ethnic cleansing of Georgians.

Ghandian Thought – political philosophy of Mohandas Ghandi which included a policy of civil disobedience and nonviolence.

Globalization – The process of transformation of local or regional phenomena into global ones. It can be described as a process by which the people of the world are unified into a single society and function together.

Golden Fleece – In Greek Mythology, the fleece of the winged ram Chrysomallo. It figures in the tale of Jason and his band of Argonauts, who set out to Colchi, an ancient Georgian state, on a quest for the fleece in order to place Jason rightfully on the throne of Iolcus in Thessaly. Golden Fleece is an allegory; it is a symbol of mystical wisdom, similar to a Holy Grail, the Philosopher's Stone, etc.

Golden mean – In Aristotle's conception of goodness, virtue consists of finding a middle ground between two vices (e.g. bravery is the mean between cowardice and rashness).

Grammarian – a grammar expert; somebody who is skilled in grammar; a writer on grammar, especially one who espouses prescriptive rules

Greco-Roman – belonging to Greece and Roman legacy, traditions or heritage, commonly known as Western.

Guang Zhong – Famous political philosopher and the prime minister of the state of Qi.

Hadith – Oral traditions relating to the words and deeds of the Islamic prophet Muhammad. Hadith collections are regarded as important tools for determining the Sunnah, or Muslim way of life, by all traditional schools of jurisprudence.

Harm principle – A central part of Mill's theory on liberty stating that no one's actions should be hindered unless they directly affect someone else adversely.

Hebrew – a Jew or the predominant Jewish language of the Jewish people today. The word "Hebrew" interpreted means the "one who passes over and beyond" – the one who can look over and beyond pleasures, the one who is temperate.

Hedonism – a school which argues that pleasure is the only intrinsic good.

Hellenistic – Term referring to Greek influence in the ancient world.

Hermaneutics – the study of interpretation theory, and can be either the art of interpretation, or the theory and practice of interpretation. Traditional Hermeneutics, which includes Biblical Hermeneutics, refers to the study of the interpretation of written texts, especially allegorical and mystical texts in the areas of literature, religion and law.

Historical Precedent – An action or decision that can be used subsequently as an example for a similar decision or to justify a similar action.

Holocaust – from the Greek "holókaustos": hólos, "whole" and kaustós, "burnt", a systematic state-sponsored extermination of about six million Jews by Nazi Germany.

Holy Roman Empire – A union of territories in Central Europe during the Middle Ages and the Early Modern period under a Holy Roman Emperor.

Homo faber – man as making or creating animal.

Homo Homine Lupus – A central concept of Hobbes' state of nature meaning "a man to a man is like a wolf."

Homo laborans – man as a working animal.

Human Rights – Rights and freedoms to which all humans are entitled by reason of being a human.

Humans qua humans – humans as humans.

Hundred Schools of Thought – Philosophers and schools that had flourished from 770 to 221 BC, an era of great cultural and intellectual expansion in China. It is also known as the Golden Age of Chinese philosophy because various thoughts and ideas were developed and discussed freely.

Hylomorphic – Term referring to a philosophy which takes under consideration both matter and form as opposed to anthromorphic which only considers form.

Hymnographer – One who writes a religious hymn or a prayer.

Iberia – Ancient region in the Caucasus, roughly equivalent to present-day eastern Georgia. Iberia also refers to the peninsula, where today's Spain and Portugal are located, because, before arrival of Greek tribes from Asia, Mediterranean Europe was inhabited by proto Iberian, proto Georgian people, such as Colchis, Cappadocians, Mushkis, Basques, etc.

Igbo (Ibo) – One of the three main nationalities in Nigeria, native mainly in South-Eastern Nigeria.

Imperialism – The practice of extending the power, control or rule by one country over areas outside its borders.

Inclusion – political philosophy of fighting for one's rights through an already established political system.

Institutional Sovereignty – A type of sovereignty whereby a group of people commonly agree to be ruled by a government.

Irony – Humor based on using words to suggest the opposite of their literal meaning.

Islam – A monotheistic, Abrahamic religion originating with the teachings of the Islamic prophet Muhammad, a 7th century Arab religious and political figure. The word Islam means "submission", or the total surrender of oneself to God.

Jami – a basic commentary, simplified overview, usually of the Koran.

Jesuit – A member of the Society of Jesus, a Roman Catholic religious order engaged in missionary and educational work worldwide. The order was founded by Saint Ignatius Loyola in 1534 with the objective of defending Catholicism against the Reformation.

Jim Crow Laws – A series of state and local laws passed between 1876-1965 which made it mandatory for segregation of blacks in public places.

John F. Kennedy – the 35th President of the United States, serving from 1961 until his assassination in 1963. He is one of the most popular and iconic presidents in the U.S. history.

Josephus – also known as Yosef Ben Matityahu (Joseph son of Matthias) and Titus Flavius Josephus was a first-century Jewish historian and hagiographer of priestly and royal ancestry who recorded first century Jewish history, such as the First Jewish-Roman War which resulted in the Destruction of Jerusalem in 70 AD. He has been credited by many as recording some of the earliest history of Jesus Christ outside of the gospels.

Judaism – the religion of Jewish people.

Just War Theory – A doctrine concerning the ethics of war.

Labor Commune – a commune of collective, usually forced, labor in the Soviet Union.

Laissez faire – French term meaning "let alone." Economic policy advocated by Adam Smith, which entails minimal government regulations and increased freedom for capitalists.

Leviathan – The title of Hobbes' famous treatise on government named from a mythical creature in the Book of Job in the Bible.

Litigation – Court proceedings.

Lobotomy – a neurosurgical procedure, a form of psychosurgery, also known as a leukotomy or leucotomy. It consists of cutting the connections to and from the prefrontal cortex, the anterior part of the frontal lobes of the brain.

Lyceum – The name of the place where Aristotle taught his students.

Macrocosm – A comparison that is made assuming that a definitive pattern exists on all levels from the largest to the smallest.

Magnus Opus – The greatest work by a given writer.

Malcolm X – A controversial African-American Muslim minister, public speaker, and human rights activist. He was noted as both a courageous advocate for the rights of African Americans, and a preacher of black supremacy.

Maliki Law – One of the four schools of Fiqh or religious law within Sunni Islam. It is the third-largest of the four schools, followed by approximately 15% of Muslims, mostly in North Africa and West Africa.

Manifestos – A public declaration of principles and intentions.

Maoism – A variation of Marxism, named after Chinese Communist leader Mao Zedong by which the exploitation of the population at large is preached.

Maqasid – The Arabic word for goals or purposes. In Islamic context, it can refer to the purposes of Islamic faith.

March on Washington for Jobs and Freedom – A political rally in support of civil and economic rights for African-Americans that took place in Washington, D.C. on Wednesday, August 28, 1963. Martin Luther King, Jr. delivered his historic "I Have a Dream" speech advocating racial harmony at the Lincoln Memorial during the march.

Marcus Varro – A Roman scholar and writer who chronicled the history of ancient Rome.

Marketplace of Ideas – A rationale for freedom of expression based on an analogy to the economic concept of a free market. The "marketplace of ideas" belief holds that the truth or the best policy arises out of the competition of widely various ideas in free, transparent public discourse, an important part of liberal democracy.

Martin Luther King – an American clergyman, activist and prominent leader in the African-American civil rights movement. His main legacy was to secure progress on civil rights in the United States and he is frequently referenced as a human rights symbol today.

Martyr – One who dies for a cause to improve humanity.

Material cause – In Aristotle's four causes, it includes the citizens, non-citizens and all of a country's resources.

Materialism – The philosophical theory that physical matter is the only reality and that psychological states such as emotions, reason, thought, and desire will eventually be explained as physical functions.

Merit-incentive correlation – cause-and-effect relationship of incentives with merits or rewards usually found in capitalist countries.

Metaphor of the Lion and the Fox – A central part of Machiavelli's political theory. He explains that a ruler must be able to scare subjects like a lion and outsmart them like a fox.

Modern Liberalism – A political ideology stating that all social and political institutions should serve the purpose of ensuring an individual's rights.

Modus Vivendi – Latin, meaning condition of living together.

Mohandas Gandhi – A major political and spiritual leader of India and the Indian independence movement. He was the pioneer of satyagraha – resistance to tyranny through mass civil disobedience, firmly founded upon ahimsa or total non-violence – which led India to independence and inspired movements for civil rights and freedom across the world. He is commonly known around the world as Mahatma Gandhi.
Multinational State – A State comprised of multiple ethnicities.

Mysticism – The belief that personal communication or union with the divine is achieved through intuition, faith, ecstasy, or sudden insight rather than through rational thought.

Nation – A cultural and social community. Members of a "nation" share a common identity, and usually a common origin, in the sense of history, ancestry, parentage or descent.

Nation Building – The process of constructing or structuring a national identity using the power of the state. This process aims at the unification of the people or peoples within the state so that it remains politically stable and viable in the long run.

Nation-State – A certain form of state that derives its legitimacy from serving as a sovereign entity for a nation as a sovereign territorial unit.

Naturalist – One who studies natural history, which is the scientific research of plants or animals.

Natural Law – Theory of law which suggests that law has its origin in nature and is therefore valid everywhere. Natural Law is present in a human by means of conscience and reason.

Natural Liberties – An important term in social contract theory. Natural liberties are the freedoms which man has prior to entering into a social contract.

Nazi Germany or the Third Reich – is the common name for the country of Germany under Adolf Hitler and his National Socialist Workers' Party (NSDAP) from 1933 to 1945.

Nelson Mandela – was the first President of South Africa to be elected in a fully representative democratic election, serving in the office from 1994–1999. Before his presidency, Mandela was an anti-apartheid activist, and the leader of the African National Congress's armed wing Umkhonto we Sizwe. The South African courts convicted him on charges of sabotage, as well as other crimes committed while he led the movement against apartheid. In accordance with his conviction, Mandela served 27 years in prison. Mandela has received more than one hundred awards over four decades, most notably the Nobel Peace Prize in 1993.

Neocolonialism – A term used by post-colonial critics of developed countries' involvement in the developing world. Critics of neocolonialism argue that existing or past international economic arrangements created by former colonial powers were or are used to maintain control of their former colonies and dependencies after the colonial independence movements of the post World War II period.

Neo-Platonists – People who wanted to preserve the teachings of Plato but were unique enough in their philosophies to be distinguished.

New Englander – A region of the United States located in the northeastern corner of the country, bounded by the Atlantic Ocean, Canada and New York State, and consisting of the modern states of Maine, New Hampshire, Vermont, Massachusetts, Rhode Island, and Connecticut. It is one of the earliest English settlements in the New World, which originally consisted of English Pilgrims fleeing religious persecution in Europe. New England has been known for its excellent schools of higher education, such as Yale and Harvard, and among its inhabitants, known as Yankees, one may find many notable thinkers in the US history, such as Henry David Thoreau, Ralph Waldo Emerson, Nathaniel Hawthorne and others.

Nobel Peace Prize – A prize named after Swedish scientist Alfred Nobel which is given to someone who promotes peace between nations and strives towards ending world conflicts.

Noble Savage – Key term in Rousseau's political thought which lauds man's condition in the state of nature.

Old World – The part of the world, consisting of Europe, Asia, and Africa, that was known to Europeans before Columbus made his first voyage to the Americas.

Oligarchy – A form of government where political power effectively rests with a small elite segment of society distinguished by royalty, wealth, family, military powers or occult spiritual hegemony.

Oracle of Delphi – The best-known oracle at the sanctuary that became dedicated to Apollo during the classical period. Oracle of Delphi gave birth to the idea of Sophrosyne.

Original position – that primeval moment, according John Rawls, when the parameters for a just society are set.

Otium Cum Dignitate – Latin term meaning "peace with dignity."

Paradox – Statement or proposition that contradicts itself.

Par excellence – something at its best or best example of something.

Partition – To divide up a piece of land into separate portions.

Paternalism – A style of government in which the desire to help, advise, and protect may neglect individual choice and personal responsibility.

Pater Patriae – a Latin honorific meaning "Father of the Country". This honorific title was first awarded to Cicero. In modern times, the title was awarded to Prince Ilia Chavchavadze, later sanctified as St. Ilia the Righteous of Georgia.

Patron Saint – A saint who is regarded as the intercessor and advocate in heaven of a nation, place, craft, activity, class, or person.

Peripatetic – A follower of Aristotle's school of thought.

Philosopher King – The optimal ruler in Plato's Republic. A ruler must be both a thinker and someone who has practical ability and authority.

Plotinus – A major philosopher of the ancient world who is widely considered the founder of Neoplatonism.

Polis – A Greek city-state.

Political Animal – A famous characterization by Aristotle used to show that humans are naturally social creatures.

Political Economy – The term for studying production, buying and selling, and their relations with law, custom, and government.

Political Realism – A theory of international relations declaring that states are primarily motivated by the desire for military and economic power or security, rather than ideals or ethics. This term is often synonymous with power politics.

Poll Tax – A tax charged at a polling station with the goal of deterring certain people from voting.

Polymath – A person who knows much about many different things.

Polytheist –Someone who believes in more than one God.

Pragmatic Anachronism – An error in chronology, which is not an error in a holistic sense.

Pragmatic Idealist – An idealist who maintains a certain degree of practicality in their thoughts so they do not become irrational.

Pre-Christian Mysticism – a system of pre-Christian religious beliefs and spiritual practices that people followed to achieve personal communication or union with the divine, especially among early proto-Georgian people, such as Torjans, Iberians, Amazons, Mushkis, Iberians and Colchis, and proto-Greek people, such as described in "Iliad" by Homer.

Proletariat – A laborer in Karl Marx's theory of political economy.

Prometheus – also known as Amirani. Name "Prometheus" means "forethought" in Greek. In pre-Christian Georgian and Greek mythologies Prometheus was a Titan known for his keen intelligence. In cleverness he surpassed even Zeus, as he had a forethought, an ability to discern and think ahead. Prometheus gave humanity fire for which Zeus punished him by having him bound to a rock on the top of the Caucasus mountains in Georgia, while a great eagle ate his liver every day only to have it grow back to be eaten again the next day. His myth has been treated by a number of ancient sources, in which Prometheus is credited with (or blamed for but still was credited) playing a pivotal role in the early history of humankind. The myth is symbolic and signifies decline of proto-Georgian culture represented in Prometheus and the rest of the Titans, and expansion of Greek culture in Europe. Symbolism is quite keen as, on one hand, it quite accurately denotes defeat and demise of proto-Georgian kingdoms of Troy, the Amazon, Western Iberia, Cappadocia, Western Mushki and others by the newly migrated Greeks; on the other hand, it shows that the one remaining Titan, Prometheus, was chained to the Caucasus – today's Georgia, ever-dwindling in size and number for the past millennium, which is located in the Caucasus and consists of three proto-Georgian people of Mushkis, Iberians and Colchis.

Protestantism – One of the four major divisions within Christianity. The term is most closely tied to those groups that separated from the Roman Catholic Church in the sixteenth-century Protestant Reformation.

Protocol – a set of guidelines or rules.

Racial Segregation – The practice of keeping one race separate from another in all public places.

Raison d'etat – French term meaning "reason of the state."

Raison d'etre – reason of being of something or of existence.

Ralph Waldo Emerson – an American essayist, philosopher, poet, and leader of the transcendentalist movement in the early 19th century. His teachings directly influenced the growing New Thought movement of the mid 1800s. Emerson was a close friend of Henry David Thoreau.

Rational choice – from rational choice theory of Anthony Downs and other articulating that human as intelligent are always making rational decisions both politically and economically.

Reciprocal Justice – Simple addition and subtraction; commonly known as an eye for eye.

Regimes – Types of government.

Republican Government – Indirect democracy; or rule by the representatives of the people; a government not influenced by hereditary monarchy.

Republicanism – the ideology of governing a nation as a republic, where the head of state is appointed by means other than heredity, often elections.

Res Cognitans – Latin term meaning "thinking being."

Res Publica – belonging in the realm of public affairs common good or public sector as opposed to private business.

Revolutionary – Someone who assists in starting a revolution.

Riba – Arabic term meaning usury and is forbidden in Islamic economic jurisprudence.

Right of First Occupant – A concept developed by Rousseau stating that a person in the state of nature claimed land by settling it first.

Right to Resist – The right of the people to revolt against their government.

Ronald Reagan – the 40th President of the United States (1981–1989) and the 33rd Governor of California (1967–1975). His second term of presidency was primarily marked by foreign matters, namely the ending of the Cold War. He publicly described the USSR as an "evil empire" and supported anti-Communist movements worldwide.

Rosa Parks – An African American civil rights activist who refused to give up her seat on an Alabama bus. Her act led to the desegregation of Alabama buses.

Russification – To cause, usually by the brute force of Russian imperialism, something or somebody to become Russian in character, to impose Russian "culture". It is an idea long existent in Russia to impose Russian values on the world.

Scottish Enlightenment – The period in 18th century Scotland characterised by an outpouring of intellectual and scientific accomplishments.

Secularism – The belief that religion and religious bodies should have no part in political or civic affairs or in running public institutions, especially schools.

Self-love – Human quality which prevents man from being an adequate judge of his own affairs.

Self-interested rational persons – the presumed state of the citizens attempting to establish a just society.

Self-preservation – A person's ability to live well.

Septuagint – A Greek translation of the Hebrew Bible made in the 3rd and 2nd centuries BC to meet the needs of Greek-speaking Jews outside Palestine. The Septuagint contains some books not in the Hebrew canon.

Shariah – The body of Islamic religious law. It is the legal framework within which the public and private aspects of life are regulated for those living in a legal system based on Islamic principles of jurisprudence and for Muslims living outside the domain.

Shota Rustaveli – A Georgian poet philosopher of the 12th century, and the greatest classic of Georgian secular literature. His only surviving work is an epic poem "The knight in the panther's skin".

Social Contract – A broad class of republican theories whose subjects are implied agreements by which people form nations and maintain a social order. Such social contract implies that the people give up some rights to a government and other authority in order to receive or jointly preserve social order.

Social Democracy – A political philosophy broadly based on the equality of all within the context of a democracy.

Social Idealism – The philosophical theory which maintains that the ultimate nature of society is based on mind or ideas.

Social Philosophy – Philosophical theories dealing with the nature of society.

Socratic Dialogues – The writing style of Plato's works whereby a discussion leads to answers.

Sophrosyne – An etymological term meaning moral sanity and from there self control or moderation guided by true self-knowledge.

Southern Christian Leadership Conference (SCLC) – An American civil rights organization. SCLC was closely associated with its first president, Dr. Martin Luther King, Jr.

Sovereign – The absolute authoritative power of a government over a people and a territory.

Stalinism – Stalinism is associated with a regime of terror and totalitarian rule of Joseph Stalin in the former Soviet Union. Grouped with Marxist-Leninism and Chinese Maoism as left-wing totalitarianisms.

State of Nature – The condition of man prior to entering civil society; the social contract equivalent of the original position.

Stoic – Stoicism was a school of Hellenistic philosophy founded in Athens by Zeno of Citium in the early 3rd century BC. The Stoics considered destructive emotions to be the result of errors in judgment, and that a sage, or person of moral and intellectual perfection, would not suffer such emotions.

Sunnah – Muslim way of life.

Tabula Rasa – Latin term meaning "blank slate" used by John Locke to describe the human mind, especially at infancy.

Tafsir – The Arabic word for exegesis or advanced commentary, usually of the Koran.

Talkhis – an intermediary commentary, usually of the Koran.

Talmud – A record of rabbinic discussions pertaining to Jewish law, ethics, customs, and history. It is a central text of mainstream Judaism.

Taoism – A Chinese philosophy that advocates a simple life and a policy of noninterference with the natural course of things. It was founded in the 6th century BC by the mystic and philosopher Lao-tzu.

Tax Resister – A citizen who practices the refusal to willingly pay a tax because of opposition to the institution that is imposing the tax, or to some of that institution's policies.

The golden rule – the universal moral principle stating that you do onto others as you would want them to do to you.

The Montgomery Bus Boycott – A political and social protest campaign started in 1955 in Montgomery, Alabama intended to oppose the city's policy of racial segregation on its public transit system.

Theology – The study of religion.

Theosophist – A scholar of theosophy, which is any religious philosophy based on intuitive insight into the nature of God.

Thomistic School of Philosophy – is the philosophical school that arose as a legacy of the work and thought of Thomas Aquinas. The word comes from the name of its originator, whose Summa Theologica is arguably second only to the Bible in importance to the Roman Catholic Church.

Timocracy – Rule by the honorable.

Titan – was a race of powerful deities that ruled during the legendary Golden Age. Their role as Elder Gods being overthrown by a race of younger gods, the Olympians, is a mythological paradigm, which depicts Greek peoples' overthrowing of proto-Georgian, Caucasian people. Caucasians were indigenous inhabitants of Europe with their own distinct culture and political system, while Greek tribes were migrants from Asia. Battle between the Caucasian aborigines and newly arrived Greek tribes took centuries, which resulted in annihilation of many proto-Georgian kingdoms, such as Troy, ousting of some proto-Georgian kingdoms to the East, namely to the Caucasus and Anatolia, for example, Iberians and Cappadocians and eventually Greek dominion in Europe. In some cases the battles of the two cultures resulted in mixing of the two peoples, for example Rome was founded by the survivors of Troy, but later Romans ethnically mixed with Greek and Italian tribes. Struggle between the Titans and the Olympians represents a true historical struggles of the two cultures – Caucasians and Greeks.

Total Humiliation – Deterrent for bad behavior which includes public scorn and ostracism for an unacceptable act.

Totalitarian Advantage – worldly advantage which a tyrant derives over moral men from breaking the rules of moral conduct. Totalitarian Advantage has nothing in common with Competitive Advantage – the former is achieved by dishonesty and total disregard for morality, as well as legality, the latter – with honesty and adherence to moral principles. The result of Totalitarian Advantage is the economic and political growth of tyrannical individual or the tyrannical special interest groups or the states, while the result of the Competitive Advantage is common good, as a person with such an advantage keeps contributing to common economic welfare of the society or the state.

Totalitarianism (or totalitarian rule) – a political system under total control of the state with no restraints on its authority and efforts to supervise all aspect of public and private life wherever feasible.

Transcendentalist – A follower or a scholar of transcendentalism, which is a philosophy emphasizing reasoning and divine.

Tripartic Soul – Three parts of the human soul according to Socrates –reason, courage and desire or instinct.

Troy – a proto-Iberian (proto-Georgian) city state, which was destroyed by Greeks in the Trojan War. This event is described by Homer in his "Iliad". Survivors of Troy later founded the city of Rome. Descent of proto-Iberian people, the indigenous population of southern European continent, its mixing with Greeks and Italians and the creation of Rome, the ascent of Greco-Roman race and Persian Empire are at length described by St. Augustine in his book "The City of God" and in works of Zviad Gamsakhurdia. They both trace diminution of Caucasian race in Europe and subsequent Asiatic domination brought on by migrating Greeks back to Titans, Prometheus, Jason and Argonauts, Trojan War and the Amazons.

Tyranny – Oppressive government by one who exercises absolute power cruelly and unjustly. Rule of one in self-interest.

Utilitarianism – The ethical doctrine that the greatest happiness of the greatest number should be the criterion of the virtue of action.

Veil of ignorance – requisite lack of awareness which prevent self-serving biases that perpetuate injustice in society.

Vigilante Justice – The idea that if crime goes unpunished, the people will take justice into their own hands thus causing a violent community.

Virtu – Machiavellian term most accurately defined as skill or prowess.

Yankee – somebody who comes from one of the states of New England

Zeno – Founder of stoicism.

Zviad Gamsakhurdia – a dissident, political activist, scientist, philologist, theologian, philosopher, writer and an expert on Georgian and American Literature, who became the first democratically elected President of the Republic of Georgia in the post-Soviet era. He wrote a number of important literary works, monographs and translations of British, French and American literature, including translations of works by T. S. Eliot, William Shakespeare, Charles Baudelaire and Oscar Wilde. He was also an outstanding Rustvelologist. He was ousted on January 6, 1992 by a large band of criminals freed from Russian jails and armed by Russian forces to destabilize newly independent Georgia and ultimately to re-conquer it and bring it under the domination of Russian Empire. On December 31, 1993 Zviad Gamsakhurdia was assassinated by Russian KGB in Samegrelo region of Georgia.

INDEX

BIBLIOGRAPHY

Plato. *"The Collected Dialogues of Plato"*. Princeton University Press. 2005.

Plato. *"Republic".* Barnes and Noble. 2004.

Aristotle. *"The Works of Aristotle the Famous Philosopher"*. Bibliolife. 2007.

Aristotle. *"The Nicomachean Ethics"*. Dover Publications. 1998.

Cicero. *"The Republic and the Laws"*. Oxford University Press, USA. 1998.

Cicero. *"Selected Works"*. Penguin Group (USA) Incorporated. 1960.

St. Augustine of Hippo. *"Confessions"*. Penguin Books. 2006.

St. Augustine of Hippo. *"The City of God"*. Random House. 1999.

St. Augustine of Hippo. *"Teaching Christianity"*. New City Press. 2007.

Benjamin Franklin. *"Poor Richard's Almanack"*. Peter Pauper Press, Inc. 1983.

St. Thomas Aquinas. *"Selected Writings"*. Penguin Group (USA) Inc. 1999.

St. Thomas Aquinas. *"On Law, Morality, and Politics"*. Hackett Publishing Co. 2003.

Niccolo Machiavelli. *"Prince and Other Writings".* Barnes & Noble. 2003.

Niccolo Machiavelli. *"The Essential Writings of Machiavelli"*. Random House Inc. 2007.

St. Thomas More. *"Utopia".* Yale University Press. 2001.

Saint Thomas More. *"Selected Writings".* Knopf Publishing Group. 2003.

G. K. Chesterton. *"The Dumb Ox"*. The Doubleday Religious Publishing Group. 1974.

Thomas Hobbes. *"Leviathan: With Selected Variants from the Latin Edition of 1668"*. Hackett Publishing Company, Incorporated. 1994.

John Locke. *"Second Treatise on Government and a Letter Concerning Toleration"*. Dover Publications. 2002.

Jean Jacques Rousseau. *"Rousseau's Political Writings"*. Norton, W. W. & Company, Inc. 1987.

Jean Jacques Rousseau. *"The Social Contract"*. Penguin Group (USA) Incorporated. 1968.

Montesquieu. *"The Spirit of the Laws".* Cambridge University Press. 1989.

Immanuel Kant. *"The Groundwork of Metaphysics Of Morals"*. HarperCollins. 1965.

Immanuel Kant. *"Prolegomena to Any Future Metaphysics"*. Hackett Publishing Company, Incorporated. 2001.

John Stewart Mill. *"Principles of Political Economy: With Chapters on Socialism"*. Oxford University Press, USA. 2008.

Henry David Thoreau. *"Henry David Thoreau: Essays"*. Create Space. 2010.

Henry David Thoreau. *"WALDEN and Other Writings"*. International Collectors Library, Nelson Doubleday, Inc. 1970.

Henry David Thoreau. *"Walden and Civil Disobedience"*. Barnes & Noble. 2005.

Adam Smith. *"The Wealth of Nations"*. Everyman's Library. 1991.

Adam Smith. *"The Theory of Moral Sentiments"*. Liberty Fund Inc. 1984.

Karl Marx. *"Communist Manifesto and Other Writings"*. Barnes & Noble. 2005.

Karl Marx. *"Capital: A Critique of Political Economy"*. Penguin Group (USA) Incorporated. 1992.

Confucius. *"Essential Confucius"*. HarperCollins Publishers. 1993.

Confucius. *"The Analects"*. Dover Publications. 1995.

Ilia Chavchavadze. *"Complete Works"*. Soviet Georgia. 1984.

Ilia Chavchavadze. *"Verses and Poetry"*. Soviet Georgia. 1989.

Davit Guramishvili. *"Davitiani"*. Sakartvelo. 1992.

Shota Rustaveli, Sulkhan-Saba Orbeliani, Davit Guramishvili. *"Children's Library"*. Nakaduli. 1990.

Zviad Gamsakhurdia. *"Letters and Poems"*. Khelovneba. 1991.

Lao Tzu. *"Tao Te Ching"*. Barnes & Noble. 2005.

Averroes: Ibn Rushd. *"Averroes' Middle Commentaries on Aristotle's Categories and de Interpretatione"*. St. Augustine's Press. 1998.

Averroes: Ibn Rushd. *"Middle Commentary of Aristotle's De Anima"*. St. Augustine's Press. 2001.

Marcus Aurelius. *"The Emperor's Handbook"*. Scribner. 2002.

Marcus Aurelius. *"Meditations"*. Penguin Group (USA) Incorporated. 2006.

Philo. *"The Works of Philo: Complete and Unabridged"*. Hendrickson Publishers. 1993.

Eusebius. *"The Church History"*. Kregel Academic & Professional. 2007.

Origen. *"Origen: An Exhortation to Martyrdom, Prayer and Selected Works"*. Paulist Press. 1979.

Pseudo Dionysius the Areopagite. *"The Complete Works"*. Paulist Press. 1987.

GEORGIAN INTERNATIONAL UNIVERSITY PRESS

AMERICAN HEROES	Zviad Kliment Lazarashvili
HENRY DAVID THOREAU: ESSAYS	Henry David Thoreau, Lazarashvili
MICHAEL TOREY	Janet Mathewson
A MATTER OF PRIDE	Janet Mathewson
POLITICAL THEORY MADE SIMPLE	Lazarashvili, Ihejirika, Steel
PANTHEON OF POLITICAL PHILOSOPHERS FIRST EDITION	Ihejirika, Lazarashvili, Chapidze
CAPITALISM IN THE 21ST CENTURY	Stasen, Lazarashvili, Chapidze, Ihejirika, Ramishvili
FIFTEEN POETS	Lazarashvili, Stasen
NEW ENGLAND POETRY	Janet Mathewson

MORE ABOUT GEORGIAN INTERNATIONAL UNIVERSITY CLASSICS

GIU PRESS CLASSICS

American Literature
New England Literature
English Literature
Philosophy
Hagiography
American History
Political Science
Orthodox Theology
Georgian Literature
Psychology
Law
Education
Pedagogy
Economics
Finance
Management
Marketing

Made in the USA
Coppell, TX
28 December 2019

13835086R00185